MW00477878

RIVER CITY

a nurse's year in Vietnam

memoir

Patricia L. Walsh

TOA PRESS LLC
Boulder, Colorado

 For information, address TOA PRESS LLC, P.O. Box 2262, Boulder, Colorado 80306.

Walsh, Patricia L.
RIVER CITY a nurse's year in Vietnam : memoir / by Patricia L. Walsh
303 p. ; 23 cm.
ISBN 978-0-9822989-0-9 (trade pbk.)
1. Walsh, Patricia L. 2. Vietnam War, 1961-1975–Personal narratives, American. 3. Nurses–United States–Biography. I. Title.

Printed and bound in the United States of America.

10 9 8 7 6 5 4 3 2 1

Author's Note

RIVER CITY describes my 1967-68 Vietnam experience. I could not relate it without involving other people, nor could I include all the individuals who strongly impacted me during my year in Danang. Except for my brother Jack, I have changed names and identifying characteristics to protect people's privacy. I have combined some people and events for efficiency. Keith was a high ranking U.S. government official in Danang, but not at the consulate. I did know a consulate official who went to Hue for Tet and was killed, but he is not part of this story.

Cover photograph – Patricia L. Walsh in 1967 at her Danang hospital with one of her nurse anesthesia students and a patient with an amputated leg from a land mine.

CHAPTER ONE

The press of faces at Tan Son Nhut airfield looked as confused as mine my first day in Saigon. Only one week had passed, but already I had learned to simply walk in a straight line across the chaotic streets filled with military vehicles, private cars, small battered taxis that looked like finalists in a demolition derby, scooters, motorcycles and cyclos, hoping everyone would steer around me. The cyclo three-wheeled contraptions had a small covered seat up front in which the Vietnamese managed to crowd up to five passengers, and a bicycle-like apparatus in the rear that the operator pedaled to propel the vehicle along at a surprisingly brisk pace.

I elbowed my way like a seasoned diplomat through the perspiring throng of Vietnamese and Americans to the plane that would take me to Danang. The small craft with Air America painted on its side sat baking on the steaming tarmac.

An American pilot stood next to it arguing with a Vietnamese dressed in an airport uniform. As he spoke, the pilot pointed towards a cluster of civilians who squatted nearby clutching bundles and baskets of household items and clothing, or holding fretful children who were dressed only in small shirts ending above their bare buttocks. One woman held a crate of ducklings that quacked incessantly in their cramped compartment.

"I can't take all those people, plus the shit they're carrying!" the pilot shouted above the roar of departing planes. "It's too much weight!"

"It good, it good," the official said in a calm voice that was strangely more audible. "We fill tanks only half."

"That means I'll have to land halfway to refuel! I'm not letting Charlie shoot up my ass for a bunch of civilians!"

The airport official signaled the Vietnamese crewman filling the plane's tanks to stop. But when the crewman began descending the ladder, the American pilot angrily motioned him back up. He obediently climbed up the rungs, only to be ordered by the Vietnamese official to come back down. A tug of war began, with the pilot pushing the confused-looking man upward while the official pulled him down by his pants leg, until he looked in danger of losing his trousers. The much larger American eventually won and the tanks were filled to capacity.

"You choose eight people and that's it," the pilot told the official. "If you don't want to do that, I won't take any of them."

Eight passengers were quickly singled out of the group, leaving the others to jabber unhappily as they collected their parcels and children. I watched them depart in their black pajamas and conical hats before joining the pilot, who had taken refuge in the shade of the plane's wing to escape the tropical sun.

"Hi - Pat Walsh," I said as I stooped to speak to him where he squatted beneath the wing. "Do you have room for me?"

"Sure do, Miss." His sour expression changed to a pleasant smile. "Especially a little girl who doesn't look like she weighs a hundred pounds soaking wet." He duck waddled out from under the wing and stood up. "You new here?"

"I've been in Saigon a week," I said, knowing that still made me a newcomer. "Danang will be my permanent assignment."

The pilot removed his white aviator hat with black and gold trim and wiped perspiration from his brow with the back of his hand. His crew cut looked peculiar after the long-haired men I had become accustomed to back home. "Hotter than a deep fryer," he said. "Should be cooler up-country."

I knew that the fighting made land travel impossible and felt guilty when an additional passenger was turned aside to make room for me on the small aircraft. I only wished it had been the woman with the ducks.

"We haul the locals around to promote good will," the pilot told me as we boarded. "But Americans always have priority."

The frightened quacking of the ducks, combined with the chatter of the Vietnamese passengers, produced a deafening din in the hot, crowded cabin. I turned to the window to watch the lush green jungle below, but when a sudden burst of smoke erupted from the trees, the pilot banked the plane steeply and headed out toward the South China Sea where we would not be a target for ground fire.

"Hang on," he called back from the cockpit, separated from the cabin by only a curtain.

The light craft bumped erratically in the air currents over the water, causing the passengers to moan miserably and press dirty rags to their mouths. I reminded myself I was a nurse when they began to vomit on themselves, the floor and one another. The ducks demonstrated a unique form of air sickness by getting diarrhea. The pungent odor, coupled with the stench of regurgitated rice and fish, was threatening to make me unload my own breakfast when the pilot pulled back the curtain and invited me to join him up front.

"I don't have a copilot today," he said. "You might as well take advantage of a comfortable seat."

I accepted, only briefly troubled by the fact that there would be no one to land the plane should the pilot become incapacitated by illness or a well aimed bullet. "Thanks," I said as I fastened myself into the copilot harness. "There's more vomitus back there than I've seen in my whole medical career."

"You're a nurse?" He pulled the curtain back in place so we were alone, except for the groaning in the rear.

"A nurse anesthetist. I put people to sleep for surgery," I added when he looked confused.

"I thought doctors did that."

"They do, but anesthetists do the same thing. Sometimes we work together, sometimes alone." He was nodding as if he understood, but I was accustomed to the confusion my job title caused. "Anesthetists are registered nurses with two additional years of training in anesthesia," I explained. "Anesthesiologists are physicians."

"And here I was thinking you were a doughnut dolly." His smile was charming below dark aviator glasses.

"What's a doughnut dolly?"

"You are new," he said with a laugh. "They're Red Cross girls."

"Are they nurses?"

"No, none I've ever met anyway." We hit an air pocket, and the protest from the rear hit crescendo pitch as the pilot pulled the plane back up at an attitude that left even my stomach at the lower level. "They're called doughnut dollies because of the doughnuts they hand out to G.I.s at USO centers," he said without any indication of distress.

"Is that all?" I asked.

He turned to look at me. "Is that all what?"

"Is that all they do, hand out doughnuts?"

"Oh." He flashed another of his radiant smiles. "They visit hospitals and talk to the guys, or write letters for those who can't. Some are a little friendlier than others," he added with a wink. "If you know what I mean." It was said in the same flirtatious manner as the journalists in Saigon who wouldn't allow an American woman to have a cup of tea alone. Hotel bars were opened at dawn to accommodate them, and it had soon become apparent to me that a significant portion of the rampant drug and alcohol abuse they reported back home took place within their own ranks.

"Is this a government-owned airline?" I asked to change the subject. "Or is it just named Air America?"

"It's government, more or less," the pilot replied. "Tell me how you got lucky enough to become a bush ape."

"A what?"

"A bush ape. That's what we call people who're sent out to the bush."

"I volunteered," I said, laughing at the term. "After one week in Saigon I would have volunteered for anything."

"It's a lot safer in Saigon and a lot more fun."

"You don't like Danang?"

"I spent a lot of time up there when I was in the Air Force. I figured I might as well come back and cash in on some of the big bucks flying these milk runs when I got out."

The passengers in the rear quieted as the plane stabilized at a higher altitude. Even the ducks had become silent, or shit themselves to death.

The sun glared off the windshield just in front of me, and I closed my eyes to soothe the headache it caused. The next moment I heard a voice from the radio speaker. "Air America six-oh-one, straight-in approach, runway three-five."

"How long have I been sleeping?" I asked, surprised that the trip was nearly over.

"About three hours." He looked at me and smiled. "You must have done a lot of partying in Saigon."

"I'm still not used to the time change." I didn't tell him the partying in Saigon was the reason I asked to be transferred. The carnival-like atmosphere was not what I had expected. Hordes of journalists, government contract workers and bureaucrats engaged in the endless pursuit of entertainment as they roamed the hotels, bars and restaurants catering to foreigners. Even the hospital where I was assigned seemed insulated from the war taking place just a short distance from the capital.

Danang was different even from the air. The entire area surrounding the large airfield had been defoliated, leaving the trees stripped bare by strong chemicals used to deny the enemy a hiding place beneath the jungle canopy. Craters the size of baseball diamonds pockmarked the red earth.

Suddenly the radio blared a warning to clear the approach. "Air America six-oh-one, right turn, depart the area; emergency inbound." The voice was calm and clear.

The pilot slammed the plane into a sharp bank, producing a chorus of moans and renewed retching in the rear. I looked back at the airfield in time to see a bullet-riddled military plane making a straight-in landing, its damaged wings dipping unsteadily from side to side.

"Looks like he's been up north," the pilot said. "He's pretty shot up."

We were cleared back to the airfield and landed like a mosquito on a wide runway intended for bombers and transports and taxied through row upon row of aircraft splotched with brown and green camouflage. Men in camouflaged flak jackets and helmets worked on the planes, some of which had significant damage. There were several high walls of sand bags strategically placed on the airfield.

"Welcome to the real war," the pilot said as if reading my thoughts. "This is the land of crispy critters." I turned from the window to look at him. "That's what we call people burned by napalm."

I left the cockpit without comment or thanks. The cold wet air that greeted me was a shock after Saigon's oppressive heat. I waded through red mud to a shack with a weathered Air America sign tacked over the door. A woman with red hair sticking out from under the hood of a rain poncho stood waiting inside next to a young man with a choirboy face.

"You must be the new anesthetist," the man said as he reached for my single suitcase. "I'm Leo and this is Shelly. Welcome to River City."

"Are you both anesthetists?" I asked.

"We were when we came over here," Shelly said. "I'm not sure what you'd call us now." She handed me a sweater. "I thought you might not be prepared for this mud hole so I brought this cute little number from my private collection." It was said in a Mae West voice, and the bust line holding out the front of her poncho lent considerable credibility to the impersonation. The sweater smelled of mildew, but I gratefully pulled it on. "Everything mildews during monsoon," Shelly apologized. "Even the people." She sniffed one of her arms and wrinkled her nose. "Jungle rot."

"It was so hot in Saigon," I said. "I never expected it to be cold up here."

"Headquarters never warns newcomers," Leo said. "We're just ending six months of monsoon rains, then we'll have six months of heat."

"Were there any spooks on Casper International Airlines?" Shelly asked as we left the building. Both she and Leo wore knee-high rubber boots which protected them from the thick mud oozing into my shoes.

"She means Air America," Leo said when I didn't answer. "It's common knowledge that it's run by the CIA to jockey its people around."

"I was the only American," I said.

"Ugh, a planeload of peasants," Shelly said. "Did they have any critters?"

"Ducklings, who shit the whole way."

"Ah! A perfumed flight."

There was no conversation possible as the vintage, dented Travelall station wagon jolted over an unpaved road, swerving to avoid starving dogs that searched for unclaimed morsels of food in heaps of garbage left to rot in the rain. When we reached a freshly blacktopped section, my head stopped shaking enough to take a look at the city where I had volunteered to live and work for eighteen months.

Most of the houses were constructed of scraps of corrugated tin or pieces of wooden packing crates with "U.S. Army" stamped at regular intervals. Some were built entirely of flattened American beer cans, the different brands creating a haphazard design.

The further we drove from the air base the more substantial the buildings became. When we reached the old part of the city, the shanty town was replaced by two-story villas of yellow and white stucco with colorful shutters and ornate balconies. Sand bags climbed up their walls, and American jeeps were parked in their driveways. Unlike the dirt and asphalt road leading from the air base, these streets were cobblestone.

Leo skillfully guided the Travelall through swarms of motorbikes with whole families balanced on them and American troop trucks with grim-looking men huddled under canvas canopies to escape the rain.

One young man pointed to Shelly, who had lowered her rain hood to reveal curly red hair, and yelled, "Look! Round eyes!" The other troops all began shouting and waving.

Shelly leaned out of her front passenger seat, waving. "Hi guys! Nice day for a war!" I waved from the back seat.

Pedestrians mingled with the traffic, pulling crude wooden carts piled high with furniture, firewood or baskets of rice and produce. We passed a covered marketplace where naked chickens hung by their necks in minuscule stalls crowded one upon another. Vendors hawked food, bolts of cloth, sandals made from discarded tires and an array of plastic kitchen items in vivid reds, oranges and blues. An old woman squatted next to a pyramid of Sunkist oranges. The marketplace ran parallel to a wide, mud-brown river winding its way through the town.

"The Danang River," Shelly said with a wave of her hand.

"It's pretty," I said.

"Full of rats and sewage."

"How about a beer?" Leo asked over his shoulder. "We're down to emergency rations at the hospital so there's not much going on."

I nodded my approval, and he pulled the vehicle up to a shack suspended on poles out over the river. "The Bamboo Hut," Shelly said. "Our refuge from the mule-shit pie we work in."

Leo bartered with a flock of small boys clamoring for the job of guarding my suitcase while Shelly led me inside. "It's not a good idea to stand in groups out in the open," she told me. "You're an easy target for a gook with a grenade."

The place was filled with mismatched tables and chairs. We sat at a wooden table overlooking the river, where she ordered three beers from a bent old man. "It's the only safe thing to drink outside the military clubs," she said. "They have locally produced cola too, but it tastes like warm camel piss."

When the Vietnamese beer with 33 on its label was served, my colleagues raised their bottles to toast my arrival. I took a long swallow of the lukewarm brew before I noticed the body of a rotund worm curled at the bottom of the bottle. After resisting the impulse to toss it over the side of the open porch to the river below, I tried inconspicuously to peer through the glass of my companions' bottles to see if they also had a worm. But the amber glass was too dark, and I chose to pretend to sip at my beer while sparring with its inhabitant to keep it at the bottom. I had heard of a South American drink that contained a worm and I didn't want to appear squeamish on my first day, especially when I noticed the dried blood under both Shelly and Leo's fingernails.

"I thought your hospital was supposed to be busier than Saigon's," I said. "I asked Saigon to reassign me to a place where I was needed."

"We can't work if we have nothing to work with," Leo said. His voice took on a weariness that contrasted sharply with his youthful appearance of pink cheeked skin and soft grey eyes. "A lot of our supplies are cumshawed from military hospitals in the area," he said. "And we've had a heavy run on casualties lately that has pretty much depleted us."

"What's 'cumshawed'?" I asked, amazed by the unending assortment of jargon.

"You scratch my back, I'll scratch yours," Leo translated. "The military gives us whatever it can spare because the guys feel sorry for our patients. We try to pay them back with a bottle of booze or something, all on an unofficial basis, of course."

"Lucky for you there's enough of us ladies to charm the supply sergeants," Shelly said. She was rearranging curly red hair that fell to her shoulders. Her eyes were as green as the scrub gown she wore.

"Shelly's boyfriend Tom gets us a lot of things," Leo said as he smiled at her. "He's an orthopedic surgeon out at Navy Hospital."

"Wait until you see the fetching little endotracheal tubes we've fashioned out of discarded enema tubing," Shelly said in her Mae West voice.

I looked at her in disbelief, revolted by the thought of putting used enema tubing down someone's throat. "You don't actually put that in people's tracheas, do you?"

"Only after we soak it in disinfectant," Shelly replied, as if that made it acceptable.

"We use anything they're going to throw away," Leo said. "Or whatever they can spare from their stockpiles." He had a face that was at once believable; skin that had never been marred by acne, and hair as fine and golden as a child's. "We beg a lot from the American military hospitals," he said. "If it wasn't for them, there're weeks we couldn't stay in business."

"I thought USAID was responsible for supplying us," I said. The United States Agency for International Development that employed us was a branch of the Department of State and the major conduit of humanitarian aid for Vietnam.

"They're spending billions over here," Leo said. "But the supply planes are unloaded by Vietnamese and most of it ends up on the black market. Viet Cong come into our hospital with American-made splints on their fractures and our I.V.s running in their veins."

"But why don't you tell the people in Saigon?" During my time in the capital I had visited one entire building filled with people assigned only to supervising the shipment of medical and nutritional supplies.

Shelly and Leo exchanged amused looks. "Saigon could paper its walls with the cables we've sent them," Leo said. "We've even gone down there to tell them personally that we're not getting our shipments. They pull out a stack of vouchers indicating the supplies have been sent and refuse to believe anything we say."

"But can't they see for themselves when they visit your hospital?"

That brought a burst of laughter from Shelly, who signaled the elderly Vietnamese squatted near the door to bring another round of drinks. I pointed to my unfinished bottle and motioned for him to bring only two.

"You'd better learn right up front not to count on anyone in Saigon," Leo said. "I've been here fifteen months and have yet to see one USAID official at our hospital."

"I don't see why you let the Vietnamese unload the planes if they're stealing everything," I said. "Why not do the unloading yourselves?"

"USAID is afraid that might make us look like ugly Americans," Shelly said. "As it is, we just look stupid."

I envied her casual indifference. The hospital I had been assigned to in Saigon was fairly clean and over staffed for the few patients to be cared for. Danang's civilian hospital was the largest casualty handling station in all of South Vietnam. And now I learned it was also the most poorly equipped.

"You might as well take a look at the place while we have the time to show you around," Leo said as he got up from the table.

"Some people catch the next flight home," Shelly said. "I'm only here because of Tom."

CHAPTER TWO

We drove to the northern end of the city, which was much smaller than the sprawl of Saigon, and stopped before two large gates which had USAID written above the handshake logo on both sides with something in Vietnamese below. An old man who squatted in front of the gates scrambled up and swung them open, revealing a large dirt courtyard filled with Vietnamese adults and children in soiled bandages and dirty plaster casts. They moved slowly, many with the help of crudely made crutches in place of amputated legs. Farm animals mingled with the people, fouling the ground, and mixing with the smell of old blood and rotted flesh to produce a pungent, decaying odor that hung densely in the damp April air.

Shelly waved dramatically at the scene as she turned to me. "Vietnam's version of the Mayo Clinic."

The compound consisted of three long stucco buildings arranged in a U shape with covered verandas opening onto the crowded courtyard. The verandas were filled with more people in ragged clothing and bandages. Iron beds with no mattresses lined the verandas, each occupied by two or three patients.

Surrounding the main complex were several low wooden hovels bursting with additional patients in soiled bandages and filthy plaster casts. Scantily clothed children leaned listlessly against the buildings. Gunfire and explosions rumbled in the background.

A small boy watched us from the back of a water buffalo in a rice paddy adjoining the hospital grounds as we drove slowly into the melee and stopped at one of the main buildings. Leo and I got out and Shelly slid behind the wheel of the vehicle to drive to Navy Hospital, where she hoped to procure enough suture, I.V. solutions and needles to get the operating rooms functioning again.

I followed Leo into a compact room crowded with people reading mail and smoking cigarettes. He shoved my suitcase under a chair and introduced me to my coworkers, who looked up from their letters only long enough for a perfunctory hello.

"We might as well start the tour with the O.R.," Leo said when we were back in the main corridor. He led me down a screened-in ramp lined with squatting patients holding dirty scraps of paper. "They're all waiting for surgery," he told me. "I hope Shelly gets back in time to do them while we don't have any fresh casualties."

"What are the papers they're holding?" I asked.

Leo stooped next to an old man and spoke to him in impressive Vietnamese. The patient willingly handed over his scrap of paper, which Leo stood to show me. "These are the only records they have," he said. "All we require is a hematocrit of twenty-five or over."

I knew he was serious, but it was hard to believe they were putting people to sleep with such low red cell counts. I was used to transfusing anybody with a hematocrit under thirty before even considering an anesthetic.

"Be sure you check their mouths for betel nut," Leo cautioned. "We let them chew it because we have no preoperative sedation to give and the stuff seems to mellow them out. But if you don't make them get rid of it before you put them to sleep, you might have a wad of it stuck in a trachea."

"It looks like only the women are chewing it." The women worked their jaws continuously and a thin red line of juice that looked like blood trickled from both sides of their mouths.

"The men smoke opium," Leo explained.

He said something to the patients in Vietnamese, and they bowed their heads toward me and said, "Chao Ba."

"I didn't have language training," I apologized.

"They're saying 'Hello Mrs.'," Leo translated. "They don't address you as Miss unless they know you're unmarried. Then they say Chao Co."

"Chao Ba," I said to an elderly woman, bowing my head the same as she had.

"Be careful how you say Ba," Leo cautioned. "With the wrong inflection you could be calling her a cow."

"USAID told me we would have plenty of interpreters," I said when we moved on.

"We have one, but he's not always easy to find."

We passed through a set of swinging doors leading to the operating area. "I wish I hadn't agreed to forgo my three months of language training," I said. "But Washington told me they had an urgent request for an anesthetist in Saigon."

"Bullshit. Headquarters in Saigon sends those bogus requests so it looks like they're working hard." When I looked surprised he said, "Saigon didn't hesitate to send you up here when you asked for a different assignment, did they?"

"No."

The dark central corridor of the O.R. area we entered contained a double concrete sink, a mop stuck in a bucket of dirty water and a large garbage can overflowing with putrid dressings and casts, crawling with flies. I could make out three operating rooms opening off the corridor, which were deserted except for a lone American woman swatting flies. We went into the one where she worked and Leo introduced her as the American nurse in charge of surgery.

"It looks like Pat and I have a few things in common," Jean said after a quick study of me.

"You could be twins," Leo laughed. We were the same size except for Jean's slight dominance in height, and both had freckles, short dark hair and blue eyes. Like the other women on the team, Jean wore no make-up.

"I didn't think anyone was as thin as me," I said. "I must have sweated off ten pounds in Saigon's heat."

"Being skinny is an advantage over here," Jean said. "Overweight people don't do so well in the hot season."

While we talked, flies landed on our faces and tried to crawl into our mouths and noses. I swatted furiously at the persistent pests, but Leo and Jean seemed not to notice them.

"Why do you have the windows open?" I asked. Surgery suites at home rarely had windows, and surely never open to airborne contamination. I watched in horror as flies crawled over the operating table, feasting on old blood that had dripped into its crevices, and onto the concrete floor.

"I know it isn't very aseptic," Jean said. "But the power is off and we can't get enough light through those damned frosted windows to see anything."

The row of translucent windows had panes of thick milky glass that looked as old as the rest of the building. The windows cranked outward to a spacious courtyard and a vibrant green garden, where I observed several patients leaving the hospital to deposit their body wastes directly on the flourishing vegetables.

"They believe in human fertilizer," Leo said when he saw me watching. "They call it night soil."

"But they're sick." The thought of diseased patients infecting others caused me to shiver within the warmth of Shelly's sweater. "Aren't they infectious?"

"Of course," Jean said. "But the garden keeps them from starving to death."

"And they've already got everything they could get," Leo said, before turning to Jean, "Shelly's out at Navy cumshawing. If you're willing to show Pat around the rest of the hospital, I could get some patients ready so we can get started as soon as she gets back."

"Get Jim's ready first," Jean told him. "I'll be ready to go as soon as my nurses get back from siesta."

"Jim Ramirez is our orthopedic surgeon," Leo explained when Jean left to complete a few tasks before taking over my tour of the hospital. "He doesn't mind working without lights and we do most of his cases under spinal."

"Do you and Shelly do spinals?" Only physicians were allowed to do them where I had trained, although nurse anesthetists were responsible for watching the patient and handling any complications which arose once the drug was injected.

"Jim taught me how to do them after I got here," Leo said. "I showed Shelly when she came later."

"I hope you'll be patient with me," I said. "This is sounding a lot more complicated than Washington led me to believe."

"You already know how to manage spinals once they're in," Leo said. "Putting the needle in is nothing."

Jean came back in the room and climbed up on the operating table to hang a long sticky strip of flypaper over it after first removing one that was covered with carcasses. "If the Vietnamese anesthesia students can learn to do spinals, you can to," she said with the same edge of impatience in her voice as when I questioned the contaminated garden. "And they have none of the medical background you do."

Leo took me back through the central corridor to a second operating room as starkly furnished as the first. There was another antiquated surgery table with an antique, rusted anesthesia machine at its head, a supply cupboard with mostly empty shelves, a single instrument table and a Mayo stand which was pushed over the operating table to hold frequently used instruments. The overhead light was dark because of the power failure.

"Are the Vietnamese anesthesia students being trained here? Neither Saigon or Washington said anything about an anesthesia school."

"I started it about a year ago," Leo said. "When I was here by myself and had too many patients to handle alone. We have a few problems with them, but they're getting better about not going out for tea while they have a patient asleep." He smiled at my reaction. "Shelly's been a big help teaching them. She talks tough about the locals, but she's really very good with them."

A group of giggling Vietnamese nurses came into the O.R. and Jean immediately gave them their afternoon assignments. Leo took me to a third operating room as dismal as the others.

"We do everything below the waist under spinal," he said. "That way we can save our oxygen for the ones who absolutely have to be put to sleep, belly wounds, chest cases and heads. If they're injured on both ends, we try to do the lower half under spinal, then put them under general for the upper part."

"You have to ration even oxygen?"

"We ration everything, including time."

The fourth room he showed me was nothing more than a cubbyhole containing a plaster covered casting table, one wooden examining table and no overhead light. "We do minor procedures in here," he explained. "Like fractures and revision of amputations."

I said nothing as he led me back to the dim central corridor. "I wish the power would come back on," he said as he looked up at the bare light bulb. "Jim is good about operating without light, but the patients lose a lot more blood when he has no suction or cautery to control the bleeding."

"How does he read x-rays with no electricity?" I pointed to an unlighted x-ray view box on the wall of an adjoining operating room.

"We tape the films up to the windows."

Despite the flies, I was beginning to feel grateful for the all-purpose windows.

"Ether is our chief anesthetic," Leo continued as we returned to the screened corridor where surgical patients waited. I took care to avoid the red clumps of discarded betel nut, but it squirted out from beneath Leo's rubber boots as he walked ahead of me. "I know you're probably not familiar with ether," he said. "But you'll learn."

"Why ether?" The antiquated electric suction machines I had seen in the operating rooms would pose a special danger around an outdated, explosive anesthetic.

"It's cheap, it has a wide margin of safety and we can give it open drop when we don't have any oxygen." He stopped to look over a patient's record. "Besides, it's easy to get. The military hospitals keep it on hand, but they never use it because they have plenty of other things. They give us as much as we want."

Jean caught up to us and introduced me to a petite Vietnamese man whose darting black eyes seemed to take in everything at once. "This is my counterpart, Mr. Hai," she said. "The Vietnamese nurse in charge of the operating rooms."

Mr. Hai, dressed in O.R. scrubs, inclined his head slightly. "Chao Co," he said, after first looking at my left hand to see that I was not wearing a wedding ring. "Welcome Vietnam." I returned his bow.

"I'll take over the tour now," Jean said, dismissing Mr. Hai and Leo.

"Does everyone have a Vietnamese counterpart?" I asked. I had to quicken my pace to keep up to her as we left the screened corridor.

"That's how Vietnamization is supposed to work," she said. "We're here to teach the locals how to take care of themselves." She paused a moment then added, "Unfortunately, we usually end up doing most of the work while they stand around and watch."

We entered a large ward across from the employee lounge where Leo had first taken me. Ancient iron beds lined the peeling walls, each containing two or three patients. There were few mattresses, mostly thin straw mats spread across rusted springs. The floor was covered with additional patients on canvas stretchers and others were shoved underneath beds. A tangled network of tubes connected their emaciated bodies to bottles of blood or glucose solution suspended from a wire stretched the length of the room. Drainage bottles were placed randomly amongst the clutter to empty distended stomachs and bladders, or to collect bloody discharge from chest tubes.

"This is the intensive care ward," Jean said. "You bring your patients here for recovery from anesthesia."

As she spoke, a tall, slender blond woman approached. She held a wad of stinking dressings in one hand and rested the other on her hip while she regarded me with a look approaching contempt.

"This is Margaret," Jean said. "The charge nurse."

"Are all of these patients recovering from anesthesia?" I asked.

"These are my ICU patients," Margaret replied in a clipped British accent. "Yours are over there." She pointed to a cramped corner of the room where two patients lay on canvas stretchers resting directly on the dirty floor.

"That's the recovery room?"

"The recovery space," Margaret corrected. She adjusted a starched white cap perched atop her neatly combed hair. It was the first nurse's cap I had seen on the rather shabbily attired staff. "We are just kind enough to look after your patients until they are ready to be transferred to another ward."

She indicated a lone oxygen tank and suction machine. "As you can see, we have all the latest conveniences." She turned abruptly and returned to supervising a group of young Vietnamese girls who were changing dressings.

"Don't be offended by Margaret," Jean said when we were outside her ward. "She'll bust her ass to save patients and teach her nursing students, but she doesn't care much for Americans."

"There's a nursing school too?"

"The instructor's in the States on sick leave. But Margaret likes to show them the ropes herself in the intensive care unit."

A motorcycle sped past, filling the corridor with fumes and noise as we flattened ourselves against a wall. The Vietnamese head nurse of the operating rooms, Mr. Hai, was riding it.

"He likes to keep it inside so it isn't stolen," Jean said. "The Vietnamese steal from one another as much as they do from us."

While we walked to one of the adjoining buildings, she told me there were approximately twenty people on the advisory team; Margaret from England, a few Canadians and the remainder Americans. The various sponsoring agencies, including the U.S. Public Health Service for which she worked, combined their staffs under the auspices of USAID to make administration simpler.

We made our way along a covered veranda, where hordes of patients with surgical dressings pulled themselves back from the eves to avoid the cold monsoon rain that had begun to fall. Many of them were children with missing arms and legs.

"The overflow of patients stays out here or in the shacks," Jean said, indicating wooden hovels adjacent to the main structures. "The hospital was built by the French during their occupation in the fifties. It was originally intended for about three hundred patients, but we estimate our census at over a thousand, besides all the family members that come in with the patients."

"And dogs, pigs and chickens," I added.

"They don't go anywhere without their critters."

Jean stopped next at a makeshift x-ray department where I met the American technician in charge. There was no radiologist, so the surgeons were responsible for reading their own films.

"Gail shoots the films and develops them," Jean said. "She also manages to train a few Vietnamese in her spare time."

The attractive young woman continued sorting through a stack of x-ray films with U.S. Army stamped on them. "In case you're wondering," she said in a Midwestern accent much like my own. "This is all outdated and would be incinerated if I didn't take it off the Army's hands."

"We all have our supply sources," Jean said. "Gail has friends at an Army hospital outside of town."

We continued on to a room designated as a laboratory by a hand-painted sign over the door. When we entered I was immediately struck by the orderliness of the room, where a bespectacled American worked over blood and urine specimens with the assistance of several Vietnamese.

"Hi, Greg Troy," he said, standing to shake my hand.

"Nice lab," I said.

"Thanks. We try to keep it up." He wore glasses so thick it was difficult to see his eyes. The blood bank he showed me was actually an old kitchen refrigerator, which was jammed with bags of blood bearing the stamps of military hospitals.

"It's all outdated," Greg told me. "I worked out a deal with the guys at Navy Hospital to let me have it instead of dumping it when it gets too old to use."

"Is it any good?" I was relieved to hear wounded American soldiers were receiving only fresh blood, but I wondered whether he was doing the Vietnamese a favor by giving them the military's rejects.

"It causes some reactions." Greg spoke as casually as Shelly had when she described using discarded enema tubing. "But it keeps them alive until they can produce red cells on their own." He told me how he tried to educate the people to give blood, at least for their wounded relatives, but the Viet Cong had convinced them Americans were trying to bleed them to death if they donated. "That's not the only problem," he added. "The people are all so anemic from T.B. and worms they don't have any blood to spare."

Rain was falling in grey sheets when we climbed a slippery set of stairs to the hospital's upper level. "The medical wards are up here," Jean said as she led the way. "Most of our patients are surgical, but we also get typhoid, cholera and plague."

She took me to an airless, windowless room that smelled worse than the pigpens on the Minnesota farm where I was raised. A dim overhead light flickered on, indicating the return of electrical power, but I wished the room had stayed dark. Dozens of patients lay on flimsy woven mats or directly on the bare concrete floor. Women who looked near death tried to comfort squalling infants engaged in the futile attempt of extracting nourishment from their withered breasts. There were no sanitary facilities and flies swarmed over the filth on the floor, then crawled over patients or into the draining eyes and noses of the babies. The adults made a feeble attempt to brush the insects away, but the children seemed to accept them as a way of life.

I heard laughter behind me and turned to see a group of Vietnamese girls in spotless white uniforms. They stood in the doorway watching us.

"They like to look over newcomers," Jean said.

"Why don't they try taking care of the patients instead of gawking and giggling?" I did not bother to conceal the irritation I felt.

"They're laughing at the way you're swatting at flies," Jean said, causing my hand to stop in midair.

I brushed past the group of onlookers and retreated down the stairs. Jean followed quickly. "They don't go into the wards because they're afraid of catching a disease," she said. "You can't blame them when they've had none of the immunizations we take for granted."

I turned to face her on the stairs, ignoring the cold rain that fell on us. "Then why don't you give them the damned shots and put them to work?"

Jean's face flushed with anger. "Because we don't have the damned shots," she said just as sharply. "We received all our immunizations before we came over here and can go out to Navy Hospital for boosters whenever we need to. But they can't use our military sources and no local physicians have access to the serum."

"You don't have any public health programs to inoculate the people?" My voice was incredulous. "Washington told me we've had medical advisors here for years."

"Our primary responsibility is to care for casualties of the fighting," Jean said in a more patient voice. "We do what we can for the victims of disease, but there's very little public health work being done." She continued down the stairs, wiping the rain from her hair as she walked. "Newcomers aren't held in very high esteem because it takes precious time to break them in. I suggest you not make it any harder on yourself by criticizing people for what they haven't done, rather than giving credit for what they have."

"I'm sorry," I said when I caught up to her. "But Washington told me I would be working in a modern, well-equipped hospital. This place is disgusting."

Jean was moving quickly along another veranda. "You might as well find out just how disgusting," she said over her shoulder. "This is not an easy job, Pat. We need people who can contribute their share in spite of the conditions."

She stopped at a screen door at the very end of the veranda, where the stench of decaying flesh assailed my nostrils with such force I had to fight to keep from retching. I was about to tell her she was going too far testing my resolve by showing me the morgue, but the place she waved me into was far more gruesome than any morgue I had ever seen.

Patients who looked half decomposed moved about as if in slow motion. Eyes stared out from bloated red and purple faces from which entire layers of skin had been burned away. Ribbons of flesh hung from arms and legs like loose shingles flapping in a storm.

"The burn ward," Jean said quietly.

I felt as if I was about to faint and my stomach churned uncontrollably. I was backing toward the door when a nurse with weathered skin and black hair streaked with silver stopped what she was doing and turned to us. "Be with you in a minute," she called from across the cramped ward where she worked with the aid of a young Vietnamese woman. I began breathing through my mouth so the putrid air would not have to pass through my nose. The nurse finished wrapping the charred stump of a child's arm and came over to where we stood. "Could I help you?" she asked in a voice as regal as her bearing.

"Don't let us interrupt you," Jean told her. "I just wanted you to meet our new anesthetist."

"Thank heaven," the woman said with a smile. "I thought you might be from that Concerned Citizens group that's always pestering me."

I learned that Ruth was a former Navy and missionary nurse with years of experience in developing countries. "We appreciate any help we can get from the anesthesia department," she said to me in a voice so soft I had to strain to hear. "Some of our patients have severe airway burns that need special attention."

Jean insisted Ruth return to her work, and I watched in awe as she supervised the most unique debridement operation I had ever witnessed. Burn patients at home were taken to the operating room and heavily sedated, or given an anesthetic, to remove necrotic tissue. Ruth accomplished the task by using a buddy system of patients placed in a long line. A young girl near me peeled away bits of dead, loose flesh from the patient in front of her, with only an occasional subdued moan when the person behind her pulled loose clumps of burned tissue from her own back.

"Are they medicated?" I whispered to Jean.

"We have nothing to give them," she replied. "They've never had analgesics so they don't really expect to be free of pain."

"Careful of my door," Ruth called as we left the ward.

Jean closed the screen door with exaggerated care. "It took her a long time to get this," she said. "It was awful before with all the flies."

"I'm surprised the government got it to her," I said.

"They didn't. The Seabees built it."

The rain had let up, and we walked out to the area behind the burn ward. "This is Ruth's latest acquisition," Jean said as she stopped next to an old bathtub propped up on blocks. "She brings the bad patients out here to soak off their dressings."

"Who fills it?" I asked, noticing the holes where pipes should have been.

"She does."

We stopped next at a generator that was supposed to provide electricity when the city power failed, which was a frequent occurrence. Jean pointed to a crank sticking out from it. "We hand crank it if we we're doing something really critical when the power goes off," she said. "The gasoline engine on it doesn't work."

"Were those patients burned by napalm?" The question had been pushing all other thoughts from my mind.

"Most of them. Some by cooking fires."

Nausea was quickly replaced by rage as I remembered the Air America pilot referring to them as crispy critters.

"That's why the Concerned Citizens Ruth mentioned are always bugging her," Jean said. "They're against the manufacture and use of napalm and take lots of pictures to make their point back home."

"I hope they do more than take pictures."

"They occasionally take a patient back to the States for skin grafts or reconstructive surgery."

"Why do that?" I argued. "They'd be better off getting Ruth some decent equipment to care for them right here."

"Or giving her the money they spend on their own airfare for morphine and penicillin." Jean's tone made it clear she did not need a newcomer to point out the obvious.

Perhaps to reward me for making it through the burn ward, she took me next to a blessedly clean ward where all the patients had at least a portion of a bed to lie in. There were windows to let in fresh air, and a large overhead fan to circulate it through the room. A Vietnamese nurse worked over the patients with the assistance of an old woman in wide-legged black pajama bottoms and a white blouse.

"She was trained in the States," Jean said of the nurse. "Her husband was sent there for pilot training and she went to nursing school."

"But why is her ward so much cleaner than the others?" I kept my voice low so the nurse wouldn't hear.

"She has a lot fewer patients, for one thing. And I guess she gets some special treatment by the Vietnamese in charge of the few supplies that do get through. She also gets immunizations at the air base where her husband is a pilot."

"Hello," the nurse called without interrupting her work. Her assistant gave us a black toothed smile and I smiled back.

"What's that stuff on the old woman's teeth?" I asked. Most of the peasant women had it, making them appear toothless at first glance.

"Lacquer," Jean replied. "Some say they do it to cover the stains of betel nut, but I've heard others say it's considered a mark of beauty in the peasant class."

"Number one," Jean said to the busy nurse, waving a hand to encompass the well-kept ward. The nurse blushed and inclined her head. "Everything is rated on a scale of one to ten," Jean explained when we were outside. "Number one is the best and ten is very bad."

We were headed back to the main entrance when we encountered a crowd of Vietnamese clustered around a cyclo, chattering excitedly, waving their arms and shouting directions. "What are they doing?" I asked Jean.

She worked her way through the crowd, with me following in her wake. "Christ, look at this."

Two people were trying to bend a cadaver into a sitting position so it would fit in the seat. "Why are they doing that to a corpse?" I asked in disbelief.

"We have no way of transporting the bodies of patients who die."

The stiff body was eventually coaxed into the cyclo and tied in place with several ropes. A woman climbed into the cyclo next to it, and the driver got up on his high seat in the rear to begin the journey home in the unique hearse. Shelly drove into the compound from Navy Hospital just as they began to pull away.

"This isn't a hospital," she said when she saw the corpse. "It's a goddamned freak show."

I returned with Jean to the employee lounge, which she unlocked with a key she wore on a chain around her neck. The chain also held her dog tags, the same as the set I had been issued in Saigon. I wore them around my neck with my name, religion and blood type available for anyone who might pick me up unconscious from injuries. They hung lower on their military issue chain than the small cross on the gold chain my mother had given me before departing.

"I hope you brought your own uniforms," Jean said when we were inside the lounge. "We don't have any to give you." Her operating room scrub dress bore the stamp of an American hospital where she had worked prior to volunteering for Vietnam. "Most of us brought uniforms with us or wrote home for them after we got here."

"I have a couple in my bag." I didn't add that I wasn't so sure I would be staying long enough to use them.

"Oh, oh, I'm glad Shelly's back with supplies." Jean was looking out a window in the lounge, where I could see several American troop trucks entering the hospital compound. "It looks like we're getting a bunch of casualties."

The troop trucks were filled with wounded Vietnamese and the American troops held onto the sides, slogging through red mud that clung to their boots.

CHAPTER THREE

By the time I had changed into a scrub dress, the screened corridor leading to the surgery suite was filled with moaning patients. American Marines carried in more from a troop truck backed up to our receiving area.

Leo opened a triage room off the corridor and instructed the stretcher bearers to carry the additional patients in there while he shooed away the patients waiting for surgery to make room for the more urgent cases. Shelly was already sorting through the new arrivals in the corridor to determine who needed care first.

"Trouble in River City," she said to me.

With the precision of experience, she applied tourniquets to severed limbs, put in I.V.s and pumped blood into hemorrhaging patients.

"This stuff is so damned thick you should serve spoons with it," she told Greg when he brought another armload of bags of blood. She wrapped a blood pressure cuff around one of the plastic units and pumped it up tightly to force the viscous blood into a woman who was obviously in shock. Greg returned to the lab for more without comment.

"Isn't it too old when it won't even drip?" I asked Shelly.

"It causes some jaundice," she replied. "But they're yellow anyway." She moved on to another patient with no lag in her efficient rhythm.

I went into triage where Leo was to see if I could help. Many of the patients he worked on had been on a crowded bus that drove over a land mine, blowing away their legs or feet. Jagged pieces of bone protruded from torn flesh, and blood flowed from wounds faster than it could be forced into their veins. Most of the children had escaped serious injury by being above the level of impact on their mother's laps. But their frail bodies were riddled with bits of metal Leo referred to as shrapnel, and they screamed hysterically for the mothers who had protected them and now lay near death.

The troop trucks had just pulled away when two military field ambulances sped through the gates. Navy corpsmen unloaded victims, who had lain for hours in a rice paddy after being caught in the middle of a firefight. In some cases sufficient mud had oozed into their wounds to stop the hemorrhage, but others had not been so lucky. One canvas stretcher was piled with small children; limp corpses mingled with the wounded, who whimpered pitifully as we eased them from the tangled mess. Mothers clutched dead children to their breasts and wailed inconsolably as they swayed back and forth in their squatting position. Children screamed in terror as they tried to arouse dead parents in a room that now looked and smelled like a slaughterhouse.

When all of the patients had been carried inside, one of the corpsman approached Shelly and me in the screened corridor where we worked. "Sorry we can't stay and help," he said. "We have to get back to the field."

"That's all right," Shelly said kindly. "Thanks for bringing them in."

"Please don't thank us." The corpsman nervously adjusted his blood spattered helmet. "We're sorry about all the kids." He turned abruptly and joined the other corpsman waiting for him down the corridor.

"It's hardest on the medics and corpsmen," Shelly told me when they were gone. "They aren't part of the killing, but they have to witness it and try to patch up the injured."

"But why are American military called to pick up injured civilians?"

"They don't have to be called, Pat. The Marines you saw carrying in the patients were the other half of the firefight they were caught in." When she looked up from where she was starting an I.V., I saw a woman much older than the one with whom I had shared a beer little more than an hour ago.

I went back to work, but I was having difficulty assimilating what Shelly had said. American military were shooting people, who they later picked up and brought to a hospital staffed by American government workers, to be cared for with supplies cumshawed from the military. The bewilderment must have shown in my face.

"It's crazy," Shelly said, pausing from her work. "We all know it's crazy, but we just take care of the patients and don't ask questions. The guys feel bad enough about the people they bring in."

"Then why don't they stop shooting?"

"Look, Pat. Our guys don't have to do a damned thing for these people." Her green eyes were harsh beneath the surgical cap covering her hair. "They choose to stay in the area after a firefight, risking their lives to sniper fire and mines, to pick up civilian casualties. The Viet Cong never do that; they just retreat into the jungle with their casualties and let the civilians die." She returned her attention to the patient she was caring for. "Enough bullshitting; we need to work."

Jean came back from the O.R.s with another American nurse. "Pat, this is Julia. She assists the surgeons and helps train our O.R. nurses."

Julia offered her hand with an inviting smile. "Welcome to River City," she said. She was taller than Jean, with dark hair and olive skin. Her eyes were stunningly crystal blue and her figure was as voluptuous as Shelly's.

Leo poked his head out of triage. "Pat, could you take over in here?" he asked. "I have some of them ready for surgery and can get the O.R.s started if you watch the ones still getting blood and I.V.s." Julia went in and helped him carry a stretcher to the O.R.

Before going to the O.R. to do cases, Shelly showed me how to roll the patients over and look for hidden injuries, then mark their location on the victim's forehead or chest with an indelible marker. "The surgeons don't have time to look for bullet holes and shrapnel wounds," she said. "Write down what you find and any I.V.s, blood or drugs you've given, besides blood pressure and pulse. And be sure to get anything that looks suspicious x-rayed before you bring them to the O.R. We don't have time to waste searching for metal that can be located on film."

"But how do I keep the x-rays straight with no charts?" I asked. Some of the patients had tags on their toes noting treatment given by the corpsmen in the field, but most had no identification whatsoever.

"Lay the x-rays at the head of the stretcher next to the patient as soon as they're taken and let us worry about it in the O.R.," she said. "We can match them to the injuries if there's no name."

She was gone before I could ask how I was supposed to get the people over to radiology and back, since the canvas stretchers required two people to carry them. Shelly anticipated the problem and brought an elderly Vietnamese janitor to help me.

"Take the ones with tourniquets first," she instructed. "They'll lose more tissue if we don't get them to x-ray and into the O.R. right away."

"What about these?" I asked, pointing to several patients Shelly had set in one corner of triage. They were breathing shallowly and stared silently at the ceiling, too weak to moan.

"We'll do them when we finish with the others," she said. "If they make it that long."

"But they need to be done first."

"We don't have the time or blood to waste on people who probably won't survive," she said somewhat wearily. "Even if they made it through surgery, no one is going to look after a double amputee. There's nobody to bring them food and care for them long term."

"But we have to do something." I knew I was wasting precious time arguing, but I couldn't stop myself. "We can't just let them die."

"We would need a blueprint to put them back together," Shelly said impatiently. "While we worked on them, five other people with a good chance of survival could die."

The concept seemed heartless, but that's what triage was intended to do - identify the most salvageable and care for them first. It was the number saved that was important, not the individual.

"You can give them a little of the morphine I brought from Navy Hospital," she said in a more compassionate voice. "Not much though; we don't have any to spare."

I followed her back down the corridor toward the O.R. doors as Leo came out to get another patient. "I can't give morphine to people in shock," I protested. "It could kill them."

"So they'll go happy," Shelly said in the irreverent manner I was beginning to find annoying.

"I fail to see the humor in that," I said.

"Well, you'd better start seeing it," she shot back. "Or you won't last long."

When she was gone, Leo said, "If a minute dose of morphine pushes them over the edge, they were probably going to die anyway. At least you gave them some relief from their pain."

"Please don't leave me alone with all these patients." I could hear the panic in my voice. "I can't decide who's going to live or die."

"That decision was made by someone else," Leo said flatly. "We didn't shoot anyone."

He motioned for me to help him. I picked up one end of a canvas stretcher by the two wooden poles sticking out as handles and helped carry the patient to the O.R. For the next three hours I continued the back breaking work, kneeling on the rough concrete floor next to canvas stretchers, until I thought my knees and cramped legs would collapse. Leo returned from the O.R. and taught me how to look for veins for I.V.s in the female patients' breasts, which were distended from nursing their children well beyond one year of age. Some of the men had good veins in their legs from pedaling cyclos, but others seemed hopeless. Their veins were so collapsed by shock I was about to give up when my determination led me to an unexpected discovery.

"Jesus! She's starting I.V.s a la cock!" Shelly said when she came into triage and saw me inserting a needle in a penis. "Wouldn't you know that would be the last place to give up its blood supply." I was surprised when I heard myself laughing with her.

Leo brought me a young Vietnamese man to interpret while he returned to giving anesthesia in one of the operating rooms. "Lan can explain to the patients what you're doing so they'll cooperate," he told me. Lan did not bow like the other Vietnamese; he leaned sullenly against the wall, waiting for me to summon him for translation.

We were alone only a few minutes when I asked him to help the janitor carry a patient back to the O.R. The interpreter looked defiantly at me, clicking an outrageously long nail on his right little finger. "My job is to translate," he said in flawless English. "I do not carry stretchers."

"But what I need right now is an extra pair of hands," I insisted.

"Call me if you need an interpreter." He swaggered out of the room with his head held so high he looked like he might have to duck to get his five foot frame through the door.

I picked up the stretcher with the janitor and reluctantly left critically injured patients alone in triage. We were struggling to negotiate the stretcher through the swinging doors leading to surgery when I spotted Lan sitting in a small doctors' lounge opening off the O.R. corridor. He made no attempt to help us, burying his head even deeper into what appeared to be a Vietnamese comic book.

"Get out here and help with these patients!" I shouted at him.

Lan offered no response, but an American surgeon scrubbing his hands at the concrete sink offered encouragement. "Give him hell," he called. "It's about time somebody did."

Jean heard the commotion and came running from one of the O.R.s, demanding to know what was going on.

"Leo told that interpreter to help me," I complained. "And he's sitting in there reading a comic book."

"Lan, did Co Pat ask you to help her?" Jean asked.

"She asked me to carry stretchers," he replied without moving from his chair.

"Is that right?" Jean asked me.

"That's what I needed."

"Lan is an interpreter."

"But I'm not interested in talking to patients," I said. "I'm too busy trying to save their lives."

"He's paid to interpret." I found her calm professionalism as frustrating as Lan's refusal to help.

"Who pays him?" I demanded.

"USAID," Jean replied.

"If Uncle Sam is paying him, why can't we require him to do whatever needs to be done?"

"The Vietnamese staff members have all been given job descriptions," Jean continued in her diplomatic tone. "And they stick to them."

"What about my job description? I'm an anesthetist, not a stretcher bearer." I was having difficulty holding the occupied stretcher I was still helping to support.

"Please lower your voice." Jean put a hand to her forehead as if she had a headache. "I don't have the time right now to referee an argument."

"I'm sorry."

"It's all right," she said with the smallest hint of a smile. "New people tend to yell a lot."

I helped the janitor deposit the stretcher in an O.R. and started back toward triage, but the surgeon at the sink called me over to him. He looked to be in his mid thirties, despite a receding hairline and bifocals. A gold Star of David hung around his neck.

"You'd better take it easy," he said. "You're liable to get a reprimand from headquarters for telling that little bastard off."

"Me get a reprimand?" I asked incredulously. "How about him?"

"You made him lose face in front of his peers." The surgeon nodded toward a group of Vietnamese workers watching silently from the other end of the corridor. "That's a capitol offense with Asians."

"Shit," I said in a defeated tone. "I'll never fit in over here."

"If you do, start worrying. That mean's you're losing your sanity."

The surgeon shook the water from his hands and went into one of the O.R.s. Jean later told me his name was Ron Shaffer, the only general surgeon assigned to the hospital on a full-time basis. He had joined the U.S. Public Health Service in the hope of avoiding the draft, but Public Health had sent him to Vietnam for a two-year tour, leaving behind a wife and two children he missed desperately.

"The rest of us are all volunteers," Jean said. "We made the choice to come over here and make the best of it by going to the beach when the weather is good, or partying when we're not too tired. But Ron's a family man who doesn't believe in messing around."

Jim Ramirez, on the other hand, was a single orthopedic surgeon who seemed as happy to be in Vietnam as Ron was miserable. Almost all the afternoon's casualties had at least one fracture, and he went through them at a pace that would have kept three orthopedists busy at home. Amputations took no more than thirty minutes, and casts were applied and the patients moved out of the O.R. before the plaster had a chance to dry.

"Keep 'em rolling," he said every time I helped carry a new patient into his room.

"There's plenty more where these came from," I said.

Jim was a physically fit man who wore a scrub suit that had been modified for tropical humidity by cutting out both sleeves and chopping the pants off above the knees. His muscled arms stuck out of the ragged armholes like sturdy branches and he looked a bit like Lil' Abner with his short pants and combat boots.

We were finishing the last of the casualties when darkness began to fall. The surgeons were having difficulty reading x-rays taped to the windows, due to another power failure, and the supplies Shelly had collected were almost gone.

"Time to head out," Ron Shaffer said when gunfire sounded in one of the rice paddies bordering the hospital. "Do what you have to, close them up and leave the rest 'til morning."

"It's not secure here after dark," Leo told me as we carried his last patient to recovery. "We try not to work after sunset."

"Don't we have any protection?" It was the first I had taken time to notice there were none of the armed guards present on almost every street corner in Saigon.

"This is a civilian hospital," Leo told me. "The military has no responsibility for our safety."

"But what about USAID? We do work for the American government."

"USAID is as concerned for our safety as they are our supply problems. They don't even provide us a bunker." The heavily sandbagged fortresses were outside every building that housed Americans in Saigon. "You can carry a weapon if you want," Leo said as we returned to triage to check on the few remaining patients. "Some people do, but most of us depend on the decency of the people not to hurt medical personnel. The Viet Cong we treat have never given us a problem."

I turned to look at him. "We treat Viet Cong?"

"And some North Vietnamese. You can tell them by the calloused strap marks on their shoulders from carrying supplies down the Ho Chi Minh trail."

"Leo, how can you be so casual about all this?"

He looked surprised. "I don't know," he said after some thought. "I guess you get that way when you've been here as long as I have." Leo had only three months left of his eighteen month tour with USAID.

The patients we had set aside had not made it to the end of the day. Leo instructed the janitors to take them to the morgue, then to carry patients who could wait until morning for surgery to one of the wards.

Someone had managed to leave the hospital long enough to get sandwiches and cold drinks from a military officers' club and they sat waiting for us in the lounge. There was no water to wash with, so I stuffed a sandwich into my pocket to eat later. The others held their sandwiches by the wrappers and ate with bloody hands.

Lan was standing by the emergency room door when we left, almost as if he had been waiting to give me a murderous look. "I guess he thinks I'm the original Ugly American," I whispered to Shelly.

"Oh, screw him," she said when we were out of earshot. "The lazy little gook deserves to be kicked in the ass."

When I tried to step up into our vehicle my legs refused to cooperate. I had crawled from stretcher to stretcher on the concrete floor so long my muscles were frozen into a cramped position.

"You have to learn to squat the way the peasants do," Shelly said as she helped me into the Travelall.

Leo remembered to bring my suitcase from the lounge and shoved it into the third seat in the rear. I looked at it in disbelief when I realized I had been in Danang only one day.

CHAPTER FOUR

Leo dropped Shelly and Julia at a large villa in the center of the old section of the city, after which he drove Jean and me to a cinder-block building located at the end of an alley lined with tin and cardboard shacks. "This is temporary housing," Jean told me. "You stay here until someone leaves and frees up permanent quarters."

Leo carried my bag into a deserted lobby and up a set of crumbling stairs. A balcony overlooking the alley had several doors leading from it. "How long have you been waiting for permanent quarters?" I asked Jean while Leo fumbled with the lock on the door to my room.

"Six months," she replied. "By the time Leo leaves it'll be eight or nine."

"She's taking over my quarters," Leo said as he coaxed open the warped door.

The room was like a nun's cell, with a narrow bed, one dresser and a wooden wardrobe that reeked of mildew. An adjoining bathroom had a cement floor carpeted with green slime.

"I'm right next door," Jean said. "I'll wake you for work in the morning." She departed without further comment.

Leo carried my bag inside and showed me how to lower the heavy wooden shutter over my lone window. "Be sure to keep this down at night so you don't have glass flying around the room," he cautioned. "Danang always gets some action around midnight. We call it the bewitching hour." I tried not to look alarmed. "If the noise starts out loud and gets quieter, that's outgoing fire by our troops," he instructed. "If it starts out quiet and gets louder, that's incoming and you need to take cover."

"Where?" I had seen no bunker anywhere near the building.

"You don't go anywhere," he replied. "If you went running around outside you could be mistaken for the enemy, especially since you're so small. Just get under your mattress and stay put until things settle down."

The sky suddenly lit up with a burst of strange orange light followed by a volley of gunfire. "What's that?" I asked, ready to dive under my bed.

"Just a flare," Leo said. "They shoot them up over suspected enemy positions and they illuminate the area as they float back to ground by parachute. It's nothing to worry about."

The sound of gunfire rumbled in the distance as the light from the flare slowly faded, like a candle drowning in its own wax. I paid close attention while Leo showed me how to crawl beneath my mattress if the fighting intensified.

"But how will I know if I need to take cover?" I asked when he was finished. The gunfire and explosions currently taking place were already alarming to my unaccustomed ears.

"You'll know," he said with a smile. "If the building starts to shake, the mattress will protect you from falling objects."

The fatigue was beginning to show in his face as he gave the last of his instructions. "Don't drink any water that hasn't been boiled," he said. "The old woman who cleans the place will bring you some in the morning." I looked at the dresser where an empty pitcher and glass sat. "You'll have to get by with Coke for tonight," he said, nodding toward the soft drink I had crammed into the opposite pocket of where I stowed my sandwich.

"I'll be fine," I said. "I took a drink before we left the hospital."

His eyes widened. "You drank water at the hospital?"

"It was in a bottle in the locked lounge."

"I'm afraid you're in for a long night. That was probably tap water someone brought in to wash hands."

"Oh shit."

"That's exactly what you're going to be doing," he said with a laugh. "If it gets too bad, knock on Jean's door. She's used to newcomers with Ho Chi Minh's revenge."

He said good night, and I watched from the balcony as he backed out of the alley with the headlights on the Travelall off so he wouldn't attract attention in the darkened city. Back in my room, I went to the small bathroom and turned on the shower jutting from the wall with no protective enclosure. A burst of mossy smelling water spattered to the floor, followed by the hissing of empty pipes. After trying the faucets on the sink, I gave up and used a tissue moistened with warm Coke to wash as much dried blood as possible from my hands. I drank what remained of the beverage and took a few bites of sandwich, which sank heavily to the depths of my stomach.

I hung my few dresses in the wardrobe and got ready for bed. My sheets were damp and cold, and although my body cried for sleep, my window panes rattled with each explosion in the distance. And my mind could not forget the patients we had set aside in triage. I wanted to talk to someone about whether we should have left them until the end of the day; what turned out to be their last day. But Jean was exhausted and I did not want to bother her with newcomer morality.

A cigarette kept me company while I recalled the events that had brought me to a place with such alien problems. The ad in the Los Angeles Times asked for volunteers willing to join a medical team already in Vietnam. I was twenty-four, single and feeling dissatisfied with the routine of getting through the week by waiting for the weekend. And like other Americans, I was disturbed by the war I tuned in on the six o'clock news each night. Being one of fifteen children from a poor farm family, I felt especially sorry for the children.

With the impulsiveness of youth, I made an appointment to be interviewed in downtown L.A. and managed to talk the USAID recruitment official into waving the twenty-five year age requirement. Before my family knew of my plans, I was on my way to Washington for orientation and language training.

A week passed in Department of State briefing rooms, where we were introduced to Vietnamese culture and given our goals as advisors. There were optimistic reports about the progress of the war and our success at teaching the Vietnamese our way of life. Occasionally we were locked in a vault-like room to hear classified information, which varied little from what was being discussed in beauty parlors and bars across the country. Each evening I went to my hotel with an armload of papers and booklets containing organizational charts and government policies, understandable only to those who had composed them. I worried over the backlog of reading until a more seasoned recruit told me to set the reams of papers outside my room each night to be carried away with the trash.

There were immunizations for everything; plague, cholera, typhoid, typhus and yellow fever, all of which left my arms stiff and aching. Language training was just beginning when I was summoned into the medical director's office and asked if I would leave immediately to fulfill an urgent request for an anesthetist.

My family did not try to dissuade me when I stopped in Minnesota for a brief farewell. But I could see the sadness in their eyes and wondered if it was fair for me to have volunteered for Vietnam when I already had a brother stationed on a destroyer off the coast. When it came time to board the plane my father said simply, "Pat, come back to us."

As I huddled in my room in Danang listening to the sounds of war all around, I remembered how frightened I was during my childhood years of nuclear paranoia. Sunday sermons were filled with ominous warnings of mushroom-shaped clouds and newspapers contained elaborate plans for fallout shelters, complete with detailed lists of the food necessary to outlast the deadly fallout. With all my brothers and sisters, there was barely enough food for the table, let alone months of existence in a shelter. Prayer was the only thing we had in abundance and each night we faithfully recited the family rosary for peace.

A series of sudden explosions rattled the building and bits of plaster rained down on me. The shuffling of anxious feet could be heard in the alley outside and fingers of light filtered through the cracks in the wooden shutter covering my window. I peered cautiously through its slats at a deserted landscape illuminated by the pumpkin glow of overhead flares.

Another series of explosions filled the sky with red and yellow light that caused me to retreat from the window. I was crawling beneath my mattress when the cramps hit.

For nearly an hour I sat in the bathroom, racked by the spasms of dysentery and terrified by the gunfire that continued to grow in intensity. I cursed my stupidity for drinking unboiled water, and for signing up to come to such an awful place. Every time I pulled the chain dangling from the ceiling, I cussed the American government for not even providing me with a toilet that flushed.

The noise was subsiding when I was able to return to bed, but it resumed again in earnest after only a brief respite. I peeked through the wooden shutter again, feeling weak and frightened. People were dying out there, or receiving the terrible injuries I had seen at our hospital.

It did not surprise me when I realized I was worrying about all the people, including the enemy. I thought back to the nuns in my childhood catechism class who had taught us to pray each night for our side to win the Korean war. They were shocked into sending a note home to my parents when I asked what God intended to do for all the Korean children asking the same thing in their nightly prayers.

Another wave of spasms sent me running for the bathroom, where intense pain kept me doubled over for more than an hour, too sick to care about the escalating fighting. A gecko on the wall watched me before skittering away.

When I was able to crawl back to my bed, I lay their crying. The noise of battle was loud enough to keep my weeping from anyone on the other side of the wall, and to mask my laughter when I realized what a joke I had played on myself. All those rosaries to keep me safe from war and I had volunteered to put myself right in the middle of one.

I pulled the blankets up over my ears to muffle the low rolling rumbles and the sharp sudden bursts. There would be casualties in the morning and I needed rest.

CHAPTER FIVE

The anesthesia supply room, which looked more like a closet, was tucked away on one side of the O.R. corridor. Shelly and Leo were already there when I arrived at seven the next morning.

"What's this?" I asked, picking up a heavy brass instrument from an otherwise bare shelf. The apparatus was crudely designed and held together with yards of yellowed adhesive tape.

"That little beauty is left over from the French," Shelly said. "It wasn't much good when they were kicked out in '54, so you can imagine how efficient it is now in '67."

"But what is it?"

"A laryngoscope," Shelly said with mock surprise. "What else?"

The instrument was intended to be passed down the throat of an anesthetized patient to directly identify the vocal cords before inserting an endotracheal tube between them, through which oxygen and inhalation anesthetics could be pumped directly into the lungs. But the laryngoscopes I was accustomed to were made of sleek stainless steel and had a small, brilliant light built into the end of them to make visualization of the trachea easy. This one looked big enough to intubate water buffalo in the nearby rice paddies, and the small light in it was as dim as the one overhead.

"Don't worry," Leo said. "We have a couple of good laryngoscopes we keep in the locked lounge when we aren't using them."

I tried to open a large cupboard but found it locked. "That's off limits," Leo said. "It belongs to Mr. Hai."

"Jean's Vietnamese counterpart?"

Leo nodded.

"It's his private stash," Shelly said. "The sneaky little V.C."

Shelly had made an early morning run to Navy Hospital so we would be able to do cases. The civilian casualties had not yet been picked up from the previous night's fighting, but several patients had been brought from the shacks surrounding the hospital to have secondary procedures on their orthopedic injuries. Leo took me with him to the O.R. where he would be giving anesthesia to teach me how to do spinals.

"Becky is my most senior student," he said when he introduced a young Vietnamese setting up the first case. "I gave her the nickname because I can't pronounce her real one." Becky smiled and bowed to me. "She's getting married soon to a man from Hue," Leo continued. "That's the old imperial city about fifty miles north of here."

"You come see Hue?" Becky said to me. "Very beautiful." Her dark almond eyes were friendly above her white surgical mask.

"Thank you, maybe I will sometime."

"They've preserved a lot of the ancient architecture," Leo said. "I've been there twice."

Jean and one of the janitors came into the room carrying a stretcher. The patient lying on it had a gangrenous-looking leg that Jean had just cut out of a plaster cast.

"We get behind with some of these patients and their casts are left on too long," Leo said in an apologetic tone. "But Jim can save almost anything."

Becky was to do the first spinal while I observed, then I would do the second. The patient was placed in a sitting position on the operating table. Leo swabbed the man's back with an antiseptic while Becky opened the spinal tray and pulled on sterile gloves.

"Leo," I said when Becky was about to start. I pointed to several dead ants among the assortment of outdated glass syringes and needles.

"It's O.K." He motioned for the Vietnamese student to go ahead with the long spinal needle she was about to insert in the patient's back. My eyes registered the disapproval I felt. "Sometimes we open packs where they're still alive because the autoclave cools down during lags in power," Leo said. "If the bugs are dead, at least we know the heat was high enough to sterilize things."

"We can't keep them out of the packs," Julia said from the sideline. "The hospital's full of bugs and rats." The American nurse was drying her scrubbed hands and forearms before donning a sterile gown and gloves.

Becky deftly inserted the needle and clear spinal fluid dripped from its open end. She reached for the syringe containing the drug, attached it to the needle and injected with one swift movement.

"Number one," Leo said.

"Thank you." Becky's eyes reflected pride.

"She's learning English from the fellow she's going to marry," Leo told me. "He works as an interpreter at the American consulate here in Danang." Becky's face flushed when her fiance was mentioned.

A Vietnamese nurse was scrubbing the patient's leg when I noticed he was still clothed in the traditional black pajamas of the peasant class. She had merely rolled up the pant leg on the affected leg and taped it in place.

"Don't you put them in a hospital gown for surgery?" I asked.

"We don't have any gowns," Julia said as she arranged instruments. "And if we took his clothes off they would probably be stolen."

"Most of the patients we treat have only one set of clothes," Leo explained. "We don't want to be responsible for losing them, and it takes too much time to undress them when we're busy."

Jim Ramirez bustled into the room with soapy water dripping from his arms and hands. "Ready to go?" he asked while drying his hands and pulling a sterile gown over his sleeveless shirt and short pants. Without waiting for a reply, he snapped on sterile gloves and sliced into the man's leg, which Julia was holding. "I did what I could to save this thing when he came in," he said to no one in particular. "But there's no saving it now."

He rapidly encircled the infected leg with a deep incision and picked up a small hand saw. The room was filled with grating and grinding as he worked the rusted instrument back and forth through the bone, cursing its dullness. I winced when the bones cracked apart, but the patient seemed oblivious to what was happening.

"Do you always do amputations with the patient awake?" I said quietly to Leo.

"Anything below the waist is done under spinal," he repeated. "We could give him some sedation, but he looks pretty spaced out on opium." Leo laughed and the old man looked up and laughed with him, thinking it was the thing to do.

I helped carry the patient to the recovery room, where we shoved the lower half of his stretcher under a bed to protect his stump from being jostled. When we returned to the O.R., Dr. Ramirez was already at work on a patient Shelly had anesthetized in the next room.

The patient I was to put a spinal in was left over from the previous day and had several fractures from pieces of metal imbedded in his leg, a typical shrapnel wound. Leo was patient while I made two attempts to insert the long needle between vertebrae in the patient's stooped back. When I finally did get spinal fluid back, my hands were shaking so badly I had trouble attaching the syringe containing the drug.

"Good job," Julia said from where she counted sponges. Her eyes were even bluer above her white surgical mask.

Jim took only minutes to remove the shrapnel and set the fractures, after which he applied a cast. Then he pulled an indelible marker from his shirt pocket and drew a picture of the fractures on the cast over their approximate location and wrote the date of surgery.

"He does that so any surgeon coming after him will know what he's dealing with," Julia told me. "Jim completes his tour in three months."

"The same time I finish mine," Leo added.

"We're getting to be regular short-timers," Jim said as he left the room.

When twelve o'clock arrived, Shelly and Julia invited me to lunch at their house. New casualties were beginning to trickle in, but Leo assured us it would take at least an hour to get them transfused and x-rayed for surgery. "You have lunch and come back and relieve me," he said. "I'll take siesta off."

If the casualty load was light the American team took noon to three off for siesta, the same as the Vietnamese. Only a skeleton crew remained on duty to handle any emergencies. "We used to work twelve hours straight through," Shelly told me as we left the O.R. "Until we realized the Vietnamese were right to take time off to rest, especially during the hot season. We come back at three ready to work at full steam until seven in the evening, when we have to get out of here because of security." The Vietnamese staff manned the hospital at night by directive of USAID headquarters, which did not want to be responsible for American medical personnel being kidnapped by enemy soldiers looking for someone to treat their wounded in the jungle.

Julia had lit a cigarette the moment she left the O.R. I lit up in our truck-like car, but Shelly didn't smoke.

Shelly drove to the old section of the city and down a narrow alley to the rear of a yellow stucco villa. Shacks like the ones bordering temporary housing filled what used to be a back courtyard. The American military occupied many of the neighboring villas, and rows of sandbags were stacked around their foundations and covered their graceful French doors. Shelly and Julia's had retained its elegance because of the lack of protection for civilians.

"I hope your toilet flushes," I said as we got out of the jeep. "My dysentery might start up again when I eat."

"Our maid hauls water from the well to fill the toilet tank if the water's off," Shelly said, pointing to an open well behind the villa. "I sometimes wash out here when there's no water for a shower."

"I'll bet your neighbors like that." Several pair of eyes watched us from the shadows of nearby shacks.

"You should hear them jabber when we whip out our razors and shave our legs and pits," Julia said.

We ascended a curving staircase to the second-floor quarters. A smiling Vietnamese woman met us at the door, and Shelly spoke to her in halting Vietnamese before showing me into a spacious living area furnished with a sofa and chairs. There was a dining area at the far end of the room and wide French doors opened from it onto a balcony, where a small monkey presently cavorted.

"I'm afraid your cook isn't prepared for company," I said.

"No worry, Co," Shelly said. "She always cooks enough for unexpected guests."

I was surprised when Margaret came up the stairs. "She ought to be used to unannounced guests by now," she said. "It's like a bloody hotel around here."

Shelly gave her a bored look. "Tom sneaks into town to see me whenever he can get away from Navy Hospital," she said to me. "Margaret tends to get jealous."

Margaret tossed her starched nurse's cap into a chair and removed the pins holding her blond hair in place on top of her head. She was older than Shelly, but with her hair hanging loosely down her back she did not look so severe.

"Sneaking off to the bedroom in the middle of the day is a vile American habit," she said "Civilized people can control themselves until evening."

"The British prefer to grope in the dark," Shelly said.

The housekeeper, Tien, was tiny, like all Vietnamese, and wore the traditional peasant woman's attire of wide-legged black pants and white shirt. Lacquer had been removed from her teeth, but the black remnants remained in the crevices.

"Does she speak English?" I asked.

"She can read recipes on American cake mixes my mother sends me," Julia said. "But she doesn't speak it."

Julia spoke to Tien in fluent Vietnamese.

"Duc, duc," Tien said going to the kitchen for another plate.

The chicken Tien served was tender and moist, and the vegetables cooked just enough to enhance their flavor. "This is wonderful," I said, eating from a mound of fluffy rice. "Who taught her to cook?"

"She used to work for a wealthy French family during their occupation," Julia replied. "We were lucky to find her."

"Tien and their bread are the only good things the Frogs left behind," Margaret said. I found it comforting to know Americans were not the only people she disliked.

Margaret said nothing during the meal and got up from the table as soon as she finished. The chattering monkey on the balcony lunged excitedly against the glass doors when he saw her, jarring them open enough to admit a gust of cold air that set the overhead fan turning.

"Goddamned flea-bitten monkey," Margaret grumbled.

"His name is Bac Si," Shelly corrected. It was the Vietnamese name for doctor.

"Is he yours?" I asked.

"Tom's corpsman picked him up somewhere in town, but the C.O. out at Navy Hospital wouldn't let him keep him."

"Thank god for one sane American." Margaret rewound her hair into a tight bun on top of her head, pinned her cap in place and departed for the hospital on the bicycle she preferred to ride instead of sharing a vehicle.

"Does she ever stop?" I asked.

"What? Bitching or working?" Julia asked as she lit a cigarette.

"Either."

"Not often. Margaret's a real loner, but she does date a guy from the American consulate."

"She dates an American?"

"She claims it's because she has no one else to choose from," Shelly said. "But she's pretty thick with Keith."

Tien removed our plates and replaced them with small cups of hot tea, which was cheering in the drafty, unheated house. She spoke briefly to Shelly and disappeared quietly down the back stairs.

"She has to check on her little girl," Shelly said. "Her husband was killed in the war, so she lives with her child and a sister in one of the shacks out back."

Tien was as ageless as the rest of the Vietnamese, who either looked youthful or ancient. There seemed to be nothing in between.

"I wish I had completed language training so I could understand what people are saying," I said. "Leo said Saigon was pulling a fast one when they asked to have me sent over ahead of schedule."

"Typical Saigon tactics," Julia said as she exhaled smoke. "But don't worry about not having language training. Washington spent three months teaching me how to ask directions to the train station, and there's not a fucking train in the whole country."

I must have looked surprised. I had the impression Julia was somewhat shy.

"Excuse my language," she said. "But the F word is as common in war as bullets. We use it for everything. God stop this fucking hemorrhage on a patient, or I'm so fucking tired I'm going to pass out right in the O.R."

I smiled at her and looked around the high-ceilinged room. "I hope I can get a place like this," I said. "My room at temporary housing makes me claustrophobic."

"It's not bad when the power's on and we can use our electric blankets to keep warm at night," Shelly said.

"I wish I'd had the sense to bring one. I almost froze last night."

"I'll loan you my Sears catalog so you can order one. They send anything over here, except bathtubs. We've tried." Shelly finished her tea and got up from the table. "If you order a blanket and a pair of rubber boots now you might have them by next monsoon season."

"I need to order some dresses too," I said as I got up. "I brought so few I'll have to wash them as I use them, which should be fun with our unreliable water supply."

Julia was going down the stairs. "War is hell," she said over her shoulder. "How would you like to be wading through the muck out in the jungle with the guys, and dodging bullets to boot?"

"I'm sorry." And I truly was.

"Forget it, you might get to dodge a few bullets yourself."

Leo had several patients ready for surgery when we returned and more casualties were being carried in by American military. "How about breaking Pat into ether?" he said to Shelly. "I'll stay here in triage and keep you supplied with patients." I felt guilty we had taken so much time for lunch, especially since Leo would now have to work straight through siesta because of the casualties.

Ron Shaffer displayed extraordinary patience while I struggled with my first ether anesthetic. I could not keep the patient at a consistent level of unconsciousness and each time he lightened up he coughed and choked. Ron was trying to repair multiple bullet holes in the intestines, which flew wildly around the surgical field each time the patient strained. Not only was I making an intricate surgical procedure more difficult, the straining caused huge roundworms in the intestines to be forced through the bullet holes into the abdominal cavity. Julia was kept busy trying to hand instruments and catch the slippery parasites so she could hand them to the Vietnamese instrument nurse, who threw them into the trash bucket at her feet.

"They all have T.B. and worms," Shelly told me when she saw I was trying to give anesthesia with my eyes closed. "That's why they're so anemic."

When something started squirming in the patient's mouth, Shelly calmly inserted a suction catheter. "Turn off the suction machine," she said as she withdrew the catheter and held it over the trash. I did as she instructed and a large worm dangling from the catheter's end dropped into the trash bucket. "They don't like ether," she said as I fought to retain my lunch. "A few of them always try to escape through the mouth or nose."

"Is there anything else that doesn't like ether?" I asked when I could speak.

"Lice. That's why I wrap the patients' heads in a towel so they don't jump on me."

"You'll get used to it," Ron said over the anesthesia screen separating us from the surgical field.

"I don't know," I said skeptically. "I'm having a hard enough time getting used to giving ether, especially right next to an electric suction." The machine was running constantly to help Ron control bleeding in the abdomen.

"Hell, the humidity is too high here to have an explosion," Shelly said.

Despite my incompetence, the patient awoke with no complications. "I'm sorry it was so hectic," I apologized to Ron.

"That's all right," the surgeon said. "The important thing is to keep trying." When he pulled off his gown I saw that his clothes were soaked with perspiration from the case I had made more difficult.

The next anesthetic was a spinal and I got it in on the first try. "Beginner's luck," I said when Shelly congratulated me.

"Beginner's luck nothing. You'll be so good by the time you go home you can show those smug anesthesiologists a few things."

"Hey, don't we have an anesthesiologist?" It was the first time it had occurred to me that I had met no physician on our anesthesia staff.

Shelly laughed. "They prefer a nicer climate. With no bullets in the air."

I had been out of anesthesia training only two years, but long enough to know that anesthesiologists preferred positions in places like Denver and San Francisco.

"We give almost all the anesthesia over here," Shelly told me. "Just as we have in all wars." She didn't bother to lower her voice in the presence of Doctor Ramirez, who was busy sawing off the patient's leg. "Battle trauma is the toughest anesthesia you'll ever encounter, but not one anesthesiologist has come here with the two-month volunteer program the A.M.A. sponsors."

"You girls are a couple of cynics," Jim said. Julia laughed.

We were interrupted by the Vietnamese head nurse, Mr. Hai, who marched into the room and up to the head of the table. "Oxygen het roi," he said to Shelly. "You go Navy, get more."

"You go warehouse get more," she said in the same accent.

"Het roi warehouse." His dark eyes flashed above his mask.

"Het roi Navy." Mr. Hai came only to Shelly's shoulders, but he was intimidating with the long claw he clicked on his little finger, the same as our interpreter. Leo had told me the overgrown fingernail was a sign of status, distinguishing the intellectuals from the working class. But Shelly insisted the claw was to open the hundred day old eggs that were considered a delicacy.

"I go Bac Si Chen," Mr. Hai said in a challenging voice.

"O.K., O.K.," Shelly said. "I'll see if I can get more oxygen."

He marched back out of the room and the Vietnamese nurses assisting with the case giggled. Julia gave them a chilling look which quieted them.

"The little creep orders me to get oxygen when he knows perfectly well where ours is being diverted," Shelly said.

"Who's Doctor Chen?" I asked.

"The Vietnamese physician in charge of this dung heap," Shelly replied. "USAID pays him to take care of our patients, but he spends most of his time treating the wealthier citizens of Danang at a private clinic he runs on the other side of town." She glanced toward the Vietnamese nurses in the room and lowered her voice. "He's made enough money off us to send his children to Paris so they'll be safe from the war while they get an education in private schools."

"Don't we have an American doctor in charge?"

"Doctor Fitch? He's just filling in until USAID can find someone with a brain."

She told me the American medical director had resigned, in part, because of the black marketing of our supplies and the unwillingness of USAID officials to stop it. Dr. Fitch had offered to cover the director's position until USAID could recruit a replacement.

"There aren't exactly a lot of doctors clamoring to come over here," Julia said.

Jim had completed the amputation and Shelly and I moved the patient to recovery, carrying the heavy canvas stretcher between us. "Chen and Hai are into the black market up to their shifty eyeballs," Shelly told me over her shoulder. "A lot of our supplies go to Chen for his private clinic. He gives Hai a cut so he can sell them to the Viet Cong."

"But why don't you go to USAID if you know what's happening?"

"It's gossip I've overheard from the Vietnamese," she said. "And reporting it would only get me in trouble."

When we finished the last of the casualties, Leo asked me to join him for dinner at an officers' club in town. Our transportation was a motor scooter he had purchased on his own because so many people were assigned to the hospital vehicles.

I sat sidesaddle on the back, imitating the Vietnamese women on motorcycles and scooters that whisked past us in the busy street. But the locals had several passengers balanced on the vehicles, some sitting in front of the driver and others stacked on the rear.

"What's that awful smell?" I called to Leo above the rush of air as we sped along the river.

"That's the unique smell of the orient tourists are always talking about," he called back. "They might be disappointed if they knew it was just plain old shit." He pointed to an open sewer, which ran parallel to the cobblestoned street before emptying into the river.

The Navy club was located down a dirt road on the outskirts of the city. Armed sentries guarded the sandbagged entrance and they carefully scrutinized our government I.D. cards before admitting us.

The exterior was drab grey stone, but the interior was a surprise. A large dining room held dozens of tables with starched white cloths covering them, and Vietnamese waiters carried food to a few diners. Leo escorted me to a dimly lit lounge adjoining the dining area, where we sat at a long bar lined with padded leather stools. There were tables in the bar as well, with upholstered chairs of dark red leather.

"The place doesn't start filling up until after seven," Leo told me. "Except with reporters." He nodded toward two men dressed in safari suits sitting down the bar from us.

"I don't buy these numbers," one of them said between sips of a drink. "They're doctoring the north's body count." He handed the yellow pad he had been consulting to his companion.

"They get all worked up over body counts," Leo said quietly. "It seems to be the critical issue of the war."

"I hope it isn't all bar stool journalism," I said. "I thought it would be different outside of Saigon."

"There're good guys out in the boonies trying to get the real stories," Leo said. "But ones like these are involved in a whole new brand of journalism. They don't report what they see, or even what they think they see. They write their stories according to the way they would like to have seen them happen, then add a few names and hometowns to go with them." He paused to take a swallow from his drink and glance again at the journalists. "I think it started when the press corps got pissed off about the military briefings in Saigon they call the 'five o'clock follies'. When the press found out it was being lied to by the brass, reporters retaliated by creating stories to make the military look bad. They got so used to creative journalism, now they don't want to ruin a good story with the facts."

Leo was my senior by only a few years, but his experience created a noticeable gap. "How long did it take before you felt like you knew your way around over here?" I asked. "I mean understanding what the war is about and learning how to deal with the Vietnamese and the supply problems?"

He looked at me and laughed. "Don't be too impressed." He ordered another round of drinks even though my glass was still half full. "Throw back enough of this stuff and you become a real expert," he said, picking up his fresh Scotch. "It's only when you're trying to save a room full of innocent people blown apart for nothing that none of it makes sense."

CHAPTER SIX

Sunday was our day off. Even the enemy seemed to regard it as a day of rest. My colleagues were tired from long hours over a period of months, or more than a year in Leo's case, but I was fresh and eager with nothing to do. The boredom turned to homesickness when I thought of my family gathered together for the traditional Sunday dinner of fried chicken, mashed potatoes and lemon meringue pie.

Anxious to get back to work, I walked to the hospital the next morning and was already busy in triage when Shelly arrived. She brought with her an envelope that bore the letterhead of Commander Miles, USAID's regional director.

"Doctor Fitch just gave this to me," she said. "It's for you."

I read the letter twice before I spoke. "He's ordering me to apologize to Lan," I said in disbelief. The interpreter had lodged an official complaint with USAID because I yelled at him when he refused to carry stretchers.

"It's just politics," Shelly said with a wave of her hand. "Go mumble something to the little creep and forget it."

"But why should I apologize to him for trying to take care of his own people while he sat on his ass?"

"Why should I have to beg supplies when my tax dollars are paying for the ones going to the Viet Cong?" Shelly abandoned the conversation to start an I.V. on a woman.

I started toward the O.R. to find our interpreter, but was nearly run down by a band of ragged patients scrambling through the swinging doors. Jean was right behind them, wielding a mop and yelling, "Di! Di!".

"One of these days I'm going to start hitting instead of just threatening," she said to me when the people, who took nightly refuge in her O.R. suite, had escaped down the corridor. “They clutter the damned place up and leave the operating tables covered with lice.”

Each morning Jean chased the intruders out and then Julia and the Vietnamese technicians wiped down the O.R. tables, lights and cupboards with alcohol, just as nurses did in the U.S. If there was no alcohol, she made them use water. If there was no water, at least the dust was redistributed. When the casualty load slackened, Jean gave the janitors buckets and brushes and made them scrub the bloodstained walls and floors. With no soap or antiseptic solution available, it was doubtful they were accomplishing much in the way of asepsis. But the American nurses operated on the premise that the Vietnamese should learn to do things right in the event that they might one day have the proper things with which to work.

“Are the squatters gone?” Ron called down the corridor to me. “I try not to arrive before Jean’s morning cattle drive.”

“All clear,” I called back to him. “I was almost trampled.”

Ron went to the surgery scrub sink and turned on the faucets. Several bursts of air were followed by a thin trickle of cold water he quickly shoved his hands under. “You never know when it’s going to quit,” he said as he scrubbed in the scant stream. “Another day in the plastic horror show.”

“I got the reprimand you predicted.” I held the letter up for him to see. “Commander Miles says I have to apologize to Lan.”

Ron shook his head slowly from side to side, causing his bifocals to slip down to his white surgical mask. He wore a scrub suit with the sleeves cut out and the pants trimmed almost to the knees, the same as Dr. Ramirez. But Ron’s excess pounds made him look like an overweight little boy in short pants. “You might as well go grovel and make him happy.”

“Maybe I should quit instead.”

“That would make him even happier.”

I went to the small doctor’s lounge where Lan waited with an expectant look on his face. When he saw the stiff white letter in my bloodied hands, he began clicking the claw on his right hand in orgasmic delight.

“I’ve been asked to apologize for yelling at you,” I said.

“Duc, duc, yes, yes,” he translated for himself.

“I apologize.”

“Duc, duc,” His head bobbed in cadence with his clicking as he waited for me to continue. A cluster of his coworkers congregated in the doorway behind me.

“That’s all I have to say.”

"That all?" He got up from his chair to face me.

"That's all I was ordered to do." I made my way through the crowd, feeling a sense of satisfaction from the disappointment in their faces.

The oxygen Shelly had managed to cumshaw from Navy Hospital was gone by noon, leaving several casualties who could not be done under spinal.

"We'll have to do them under open drop ether," Leo said. "I used to do it all the time before Shelly started getting oxygen for our gas machines."

"And half the patients choked to death on their worms," Shelly reminded. It was impossible to put an endotracheal tube in a patient anesthetized by the open drop method, which meant their tracheas were not protected from meandering parasites. In addition, their lungs were easy prey to regurgitated food they had ingested before being injured.

"Can you get some more oxygen?" I asked Shelly.

"Tom's C.O. is wise to my raids," she said. "I can't risk getting him in trouble."

"There's a possibility we could get it at the air base," Leo said. "I talked to an Air Force guy the other day who says the pilots use O_2 for high altitude flights up North."

"The only high altitude flying I know about is when Tom sneaks into town for siesta," Shelly said in her Mae West voice. Leo laughed at the impersonation. "But I'll tell you what," she added in a serious tone. "You find us a new source of oxygen and I'll see if I can start getting us some nitrous oxide. It'll take the C.O. awhile to figure out I'm cumshawing a new item."

It would indeed be a luxury to have the anesthetic I had always taken for granted at home. Nitrous oxide, commonly known as laughing gas, was not in itself potent enough for deep surgical anesthesia. But in combination with other agents it produced a smooth anesthetic that reduced the dosage of all other drugs.

We decided it would be best for a female to approach the men at the air base, and since Shelly was already cumshawing her share, I volunteered. Leo told me Jean dated a pilot stationed at the base. "I'll introduce you to a flight surgeon I know," she said when I went to her for help. "But from there on you're on your own."

Her suture and scalpel supplies were depleted, and she was going with me to the base to see if she could replenish them. Shelly met us in the parking lot with two empty oxygen tanks.

"You'd better take these," she said. "They can probably fill them from their bulk supply." We loaded the tanks with Navy Hospital insignias into the back of our Travelall. "Be sure you know what you're promising when you make a deal with the supply sergeant," Shelly called to me as we drove away.

"What does she mean by that?" I asked Jean.

"The guys don't do favors for nothing."

I was still worrying about what I might be asked in trade for oxygen when we pulled up to the sandbagged gates of the air base. While armed sentries checked our identification, I looked over a hangar-like building that housed the Post Exchange.

"There's Layfield's jeep in its usual parking spot," Jean said. She pointed to a hospital jeep parked in front of the PX.

"Who's Layfield?" I asked.

"Our chief nurse. She only drops by the hospital when we have visiting dignitaries."

Not far from the main gate was a somber, wooden building set back several yards from the road. A sign over the door read: UNCOVER IN RESPECT FOR THE DEAD.

"A lot of bodies are shipped home from here," Jean said when she saw me looking at the military morgue.

"They're adding on to it," I said. A construction crew worked almost soundlessly as they added to the already sizable structure.

"The Seabees really hate that job."

We drove in silence. "Do you know any Seabees?" I asked finally. I knew from my Navy brother that the construction battalion was a good outfit to know.

"We're occasionally invited to parties at their place," Jean said. "They built a house for themselves in town."

"Maybe we could get them to build us some sawhorses to set the stretchers on in triage," I suggested. "It would save us a lot of scraped knees and backaches."

Jean gave me one of her infrequent smiles. "I think you're beginning to get the hang of this place."

We were skirting the end of the runways, where a sign cautioned motorists to beware of low flying aircraft. Jean ignored the warning until a screaming jet passed so low over us that I crouched down and jammed my fingers into my ears. "Damn, I always forget to look," she said when I crawled back onto the seat.

She drove to the far side of the base and stopped in front of a building designated as a medical clinic by bright red crosses on a white background. A hand lettered sign above the door read: GYN EXAMINING ROOM, KNOCK BEFORE ENTERING.

"A little aviator humor," Jean said as she led the way inside.

A Navy doctor leaned over a Marine pilot lying on an examining table. An oxygen mask covered the pilot's mouth and nose and a bottle of glucose solution with vitamin C ran into his arm.

Jean's face paled with concern when she saw it was her boyfriend. "What happened?" she asked the flight surgeon.

"Nothing to worry about," he said. "His iron nerves turned to mush last night when he got back from visiting Uncle Ho, and he decided to calm them by getting blasted."

The pilot reached for Jean's hand. "He's using me for research," he groaned beneath the oxygen mask.

"It's the perfect cure for a hangover," the flight surgeon insisted. "Oxygen and one liter of glucose laced with vitamin C."

Jean introduced the ailing pilot as Rick and the flight surgeon as Jerry. Rick could manage only a faint smile beneath his green plastic mask, but Jerry shook my hand and offered me a tour of his clinic. He wore a tan, zip-up flight suit, the same as Rick, but did not have a military crew cut. Both men were square jawed handsome and physically fit.

"I wish they would stop opening the damned club out here when the men come back from their night runs," the flight surgeon said as we returned to his patient. "They're going to kill the pilots with booze before Uncle Ho has a chance."

"Well we can't just come home and go beddie-bye after dropping a load of bombs," Rick mumbled inside his mask. "If they didn't open the bar and serve watered-down drinks, we'd probably be chugging it straight from the bottle in our hootches."

"Are you ladies just here to visit the sick?" Jerry asked. "Or is this one of your look-pathetic-and-beg missions?"

"I need scalpels and suture," Jean said in a hesitant voice unlike her usual brusk manner. "And whatever else you might find lying around," she added with a flirtatious smile.

"I'll see what I can find if you'll stay here and watch your quivering hero," Jerry told her.

I followed the flight surgeon outside so Jean would have time alone with her friend. While I waited next to our vehicle, I spotted a hangar posted with warning signs indicating the presence of oxygen. Jerry emerged from the supply hut with a large plastic bag that he carried over his shoulder like Santa Claus. Jean came out of the clinic and climbed behind the wheel.

"Do you think I might be able to talk to the people who handle the oxygen?" I asked Jerry.

He looked toward Jean and rolled his eyes heavenward. "You've been giving this girl lessons," he said. "She doesn't want to leave without a full load."

"We're completely out of oxygen," I said. "Could you just introduce me to whomever is in charge of it?"

"You're always out of oxygen," Jerry said. He leaned casually against my side of the jeep. "You're out of everything at that dung heap where you work."

"You've seen our hospital?"

"Seen it?" Rick yelled from inside the clinic. "You can smell it from here."

"Maybe we could have dinner sometime," I said, glancing first at Jerry's bare ring finger.

"Now I know you've been giving her lessons," he said to Jean. "You can go over to the hangar and ask if they'll give you some O_2, but don't tell them I sent you."

"Thanks," I said.

"How about Wednesday night for dinner? It's steak night at the Navy Club."

"Steaks in the middle of a war?"

"There's no war on Wednesday nights. We've declared it our official night off." Jerry was tall and slim, with a mustache that was as rakish as his smile. I accepted the invitation for steak night and Jean started the Travelall.

"Don't stay in that pan of worms after dark," Rick called out to us when he heard the engine start. "The place is crawling with Cong."

"And you stay out of the club," Jean shouted back. "It's crawling with drunks."

"They don't seem to think much of our hospital," I said when we drove away.

"I've talked them into helping us a few times when I've had a date with Rick and had to work late," Jean said. "Jerry's set some fractures for us, but he refuses to do surgery with our lousy instruments."

"Military doctors are allowed to practice in civilian hospitals?"

"In their free time. Shelly's Tom does cases whenever he can, but that isn't often since he's so busy at Navy Hospital."

Jean stopped near the rear doors of the hangar that had oxygen signs posted at regular intervals. "Don't be long," she said. "We have patients waiting."

It was lunch time and the hangar area was deserted. I wandered inside and was looking over a streamlined aircraft in the cavernous enclosure when a young airman appeared and asked who I was looking for.

"It's gotta be an officer," he said before I could answer. "There ain't no roundeye woman lookin' for no enlisted man."

"I'd like to see the person in charge of oxygen," I said, remembering to smile.

"That's me." He leaned back against the plane I had been admiring while he studied me.

"What kind of plane is that?" I asked, suddenly nervous about bartering with a pimply-faced boy who was more interested in my legs than what I had to say.

"Phantom," he said, continuing to look at my bare legs beneath my white scrub dress.

"I work at a civilian hospital in town," I began. "We're having trouble getting our shipments from Saigon and need a place to get our oxygen tanks filled."

"I never heard of a hospital in town," he said suspiciously. "Who you taking care of?"

"Vietnamese, mostly women and kids."

His face softened, but only momentarily. "You one of them movie stars coming over here causing trouble?"

I laughed at the suggestion. "I'm a nurse," I said. "And I'm paid by Uncle Sam, the same as you."

"It'd still be illegal givin' you military issue," he said.

"How about a fifth of your favorite booze in return?"

He licked his lower lip. "Bring your tanks out tomorrow after sundown. But keep it quiet." He looked around the hangar to make sure there was no one to overhear.

"I brought a couple of empties just in case," I said quietly. "They're out in my vehicle."

He sighed deeply and looked around again. "O.K., back her up here and I'll fill 'em." But when the airman saw the tanks he refused to put oxygen in them. "I ain't fillin' no fuckin' Navy tanks," he whispered. "I'd be double screwed if I got caught."

"But we can't do cases until we get oxygen," I pleaded. "And we have patients who are waiting for surgery."

"All right, but not those." He loaded two large Air Force cylinders into the back of our car and covered them with a heavy tarpaulin. "If you get stopped, you don't know where them things came from."

"I'll bring them back as soon as they're empty," I said. "What kind of liquor would you like?"

"Whiskey, just plain old whiskey." He seemed anxious for me to be on my way.

"Will Jack Daniels do?"

"Are you shitting me?"

"I can get it for three dollars a bottle at the government dispensary in town."

"Jack Daniels will do just fine," he said and retreated back into the hangar.

We drove back into town beneath a leaden grey sky ready to dump its deluge. When we pulled into the hospital compound we found several ambulances and trucks in the parking lot. Margaret and Shelly were helping Navy corpsmen unload moaning casualties and Leo was running triage.

"I hope you got oxygen," Shelly said above the bedlam.

"Two big tanks," I said. "They wouldn't fill the Navy ones."

"I got nitrous oxide and a shitload of other stuff," she said. "Tom's C.O. is in Saigon for a meeting."

Some of the patients had been hit with White Phosphorus, which not only produced severe burns but continued to smolder wherever it touched. Smoke spiraled from the fierce wounds, creating a nauseating stench of cooked flesh.

I was starting I.V.s in triage when Jim Ramirez came in to inspect the burn patients. "Get them back to us as fast as you can," he told me. "That crap will keep burning until we cut out the affected tissue."

The treatment sounded reasonable for those with burned fingers and toes that could be easily amputated, but the phosphorous was not confined to limbs. "What about the ones with burns on their abdomens and chests?" I asked.

"We'll debride what we can," Jim said. "Then they become Ruth's problem."

Shelly carried in a laundry bag filled with the supplies she had cumshawed. "I've got just the thing for Ruth," she said, digging down into the bag. "Navy gave me a bunch of burn dressings."

They were a new kind, with an antibiotic soaked into the gauze. There was also a lubricated coating to prevent the dressings from sticking to the wound.

"How did you ever talk them out of these?" I asked as I inspected one.

"Frying people is an American tactic," she replied. "The military hospitals don't get as many burn patients as we do."

Shelly left the bag of supplies for me to use in triage and asked a loitering janitor to help her with the stretcher of a patient who was ready for surgery. "You'd better take this one first," I said of a newly arrived child. "She's about to bleed out."

Shelly instructed the janitor to set down the stretcher they had started to pick up, but she could not make him understand she wanted help with the one containing the hemorrhaging child. After several futile attempts, she gathered the child up in her arms.

"The old piss-ant is so spaced out on opium he doesn't know what he's doing," she said as she stomped out of the room.

An hour or more had passed when I carried a stretcher past the O.R. where she worked. Her voice could be heard above the chattering of Vietnamese nurses hurrying in and out of the room.

"The kid's heart just stopped," Jean told me as she rushed by.

Julia was giving closed-chest massage while Ron hurriedly closed the abdominal incision. Shelly was administering drugs, pumping blood and coaching a male anesthesia student working with her how to force air into the child's lungs between chest compressions.

"This blood is so thick it has lumps," she said when I went to offer my assistance. "Run over to the lab and see if Greg has anything fresher. His students sometimes stash good units in the back of the refrigerator in case one of their family members comes in."

I didn't relay Shelly's remark to Greg, but I couldn't help noticing when he reached to the back of the refrigerator and came up with a unit of blood that was barely out of date. "This is more like it," I said when he handed it to me. "It's almost usable."

"I can't change things overnight," he said. "As long as they do their work

I let them hoard a few bags of the good stuff." His eyes were patient behind his thick glasses.

By the time I returned to the O.R., Shelly was getting a faint heartbeat and the child's color was improving. Now the patient's blood must be returned to its normal pH after being altered by lack of oxygen.

"Do we have any bicarb to reverse the acidosis?" I asked.

"Only these beauties." Shelly held up two enormous glass ampules of drug left over from the previous regime.

"Do you understand French?"

"Hell no, but there's enough Latin in the labeling to make an intelligent guess." She drew up a small amount of drug. "A little of this, a little of that," she said as she injected it into the patient's I.V. tubing. "These people are tough to kill."

"You're doing something right," Julia said. The child's heartbeat had strengthened and she started breathing on her own.

Ron was putting in the last of the skin sutures when the child began moving her arms and legs. When she opened her eyes, Mr. Shat, the anesthesia student helping Shelly, backed away from the table and ran out of the room.

"Take over," Shelly said to me and went after him.

The Vietnamese nurses watched solemnly as the child woke from her anesthetic and began to cry. Even Lan, who watched from the doorway, lost his usual expression of arrogance and looked almost frightened. Julia spoke to them calmly in Vietnamese, but one by one, they slipped out of the room.

"Ignorant peasants," Shelly said when she returned a short time later to where I waited with the patient. Her anesthesia student had not only left the O.R., Shelly could not find Mr. Shat anywhere on the hospital compound.

"They think we confused the spirits by bringing the child back to life," Julia said as she gathered bloody instruments to be washed and sterilized.

"Serves you right for messing with the spirits," Margaret told Shelly and me when we took the child to recovery. "Word has gone through the whole hospital that you're a couple of witches."

"I've been called worse," Shelly said.

The haunted O.R. had to be staffed by Americans the remainder of the day. When the cases were completed, Jean assembled the entire Vietnamese staff and asked Lan to translate Shelly's explanation of what had transpired. Shelly told them resuscitations were commonplace in the United States and that the Vietnamese staff would soon be taught how to do them. Lan translated to the apprehensive group, which did not look at all reassured.

"Why did Ong Leo not do these things before you came?" Lan demanded of Shelly.

"Because Mr. Leo was too busy to spend so much time on one patient," she replied.

"They do not like this bringing back from the dead," Lan said of the Vietnamese staff. "The spirits do not know where to go."

Leo came in to try to convince them that what we did was common practice in modern hospitals, but a curtain of mistrust hung heavily between the two teams. Even Becky seemed to have abandoned her friendly acceptance so familiar to us.

"Tell them I'll give a class on resuscitation this Saturday," Shelly said to Lan. "Everyone is invited."

"I will tell them but they will not come." He clicked his claw while he spoke.

"I'll bring lunch."

"That will not work this time."

Lan was right. Even though Shelly had her maid prepare special cakes and meat pastries, not one Vietnamese showed up for the lecture. We gave the food to the patients occupying the hospital's verandas.

"Stupid gooks," Shelly said as she wheeled the Travelall out of the hospital compound. "They won't trust us until one of their precious relatives needs resuscitation. Then they'll expect us to perform miracles."

CHAPTER SEVEN

The monsoon season gave way to warmer weather, lending some improvement to the mood of both teams. We worked in unison to unload ambulances, grateful that we no longer had to carry stretchers through thick mud. But the dry season had its disadvantages.

There was red dust everywhere. And even though we wore barefoot sandals and cut the sleeves out of our uniforms, the oppressive heat made our bodies weep perspiration, which ran down our extremities like small muddy rivers. The women with short hair, like Jean, Julia and myself, had it cut shorter. And those with long hair began wearing it knotted on top of their heads like Margaret's. Siesta became as precious to us as it was to the Vietnamese, and our pace slowed to match theirs. The only cool spot in the hospital was the air-conditioned office of our acting medical chief, where we picked up mail from a rack nailed to a wall.

Dr. Fitch was a general surgeon, like Ron, but rarely spent time with patients. When he did, his shoulder length hair and full beard prompted unkind remarks from both Americans and Vietnamese. Only when we wished to linger in the cool of his office to read our mail did we engage him in polite conversation.

I had been in Danang a full month and had yet to meet our nursing supervisor, Mrs. Layfield, whose office adjoined Dr. Fitch's but remained shuttered and dark. Leo told me she was more interested in the unique social opportunity created by being an American woman in a country awash with lonely G.I.s. It wasn't surprising, then, that my first encounter with her was at a social function.

Ever since the weather had warmed, Shelly talked about going to the beach. We made plans to go on a Saturday afternoon after she delivered her weekly anesthesia lecture to the Vietnamese students, who were once more attending classes. We had done no resuscitations recently and would liked to have believed the incident was forgotten, but attendance had only picked up when we began providing soft drinks and snacks purchased at the PX.

We did a few emergency cases on Saturday morning, and Ruth and Jim Ramirez offered to stay behind in case others came in. Even Margaret put in only a half day, but she rode to the beach with Leo on his motor scooter. Shelly brought Bac Si in our vehicle, and she and I wrestled with the unruly monkey in the rear seat while Jean drove.

My exposure to the area had been primarily the city of Danang and the slum that spread out from it to the air base. But today we headed out of town in the opposite direction, passing through green and yellow countryside where elders stooped over their rice crops as children ran along the raised dikes separating one water-filled paddy from the next. Small boys rode lazily on the wide backs of water buffalo, guarding them from thieves or from straying too far in the open fields.

"It's pretty out here," I said. "I wish Ruth and Jim could have come."

"They don't socialize much," Jean said. "They actually enjoy spending most of their time at the hospital."

Jean was driving and Julia sat in the passenger seat lighting one cigarette with the butt of another. Her movie star figure included long, shapely legs. We all wore bikinis.

We drove parallel to the Danang River for some distance, then the road turned sharply toward a wooden bridge spanning the water. The structure looked newly built and was guarded by armed sentries who inspected our car before allowing us to proceed. One of them took an inordinate amount of time checking the back seat, where Shelly sat in a particularly skimpy bikini with her monkey. "There ain't no place to hide a grenade back here, soldier," she told him.

"Yes, ma'am," he said, nearly stumbling backward into the water.

Jean drove quickly across the bridge while sentries posted along its length fired loud volleys toward the water. "Are they shooting at someone down there?" I asked, trying to see over the railing.

"They're aiming at debris floating down the river," Julia explained. "If the enemy has hidden an explosive in a bunch of branches or whatever, they'll detonate it before it reaches the bridge." The wooden structure was the only link between the town and the deep water piers where ships docked, but I was the only one to breathe a sigh of relief when we reached the other side intact.

We passed a huge helicopter installation on the ocean side of the road, and just across from it a shanty town with dozens of dirty children playing in the red dust. Women in short skirts leaned lethargically against the shacks watching the road. When they saw our car they sprinted down the sandy hill toward us.

"Boom-boom! Boom-boom!" they chanted as they flapped their skirts to reveal bare bottoms.

"Jesus!" Jean jammed on the brakes as two of the women laid down in the road right in front of us.

The others swarmed around our vehicle, but their greedy expressions changed to scorn when they saw we were of the same sex. "Numbah ten!" they shouted angrily. "G.I.! G.I.!"

"Cabbage Patch," Shelly told me when Jean set the car back in motion. "The local red light district."

The prostitutes returned to their shacks, except one toothless old woman who stood at the edge of the road flapping her dress over her waist to expose a pitifully sagging anatomy. "Boom-boom, boom-boom," she chanted in a disinterested monotone.

"God, who'd be desperate enough to screw that old crone?" I asked.

"That's Sophie," Shelly said. "The Vietnamese talking billboard."

"General Walt, the commanding general of I Corps, has tried to shut the place down but the guys keep sneaking back," Jean said. "Several of them have been killed by V.C. grenades while they were in there screwing."

"Talk about the earth moving," Shelly said.

I laughed heartily with the others. "Who do all those children belong to?" I asked as I looked back at Cabbage Patch. Most looked under five years of age and were either naked or wore only a ragged shirt.

"They're the by-product of the boom-boom business," Julia said. "Their mothers don't want them and they're ostracized from the rest of society because they're half American." Cabbage Patch and Sophie weren't so funny anymore.

"That's where Tom is," Shelly said. She pointed to a cluster of metal Quonset huts with red crosses painted on all sides. Several men in blue pajamas sat dozing on sandbags in the warm sun, but sprang into action when a medevac chopper set down on the landing pad in front of the complex. The stretcher bearers worked quickly, ignoring the dust that pelted them as they unloaded the casualties with the medevac's blades still rotating.

"I hope they get another orthopedic surgeon soon," Shelly said as she watched them. "I'm getting tired of carrying on a romance in the O.R. storeroom."

"I wish they would get another one so Tom could come in and help us when Jim leaves next month," Jean said.

The first helicopter had barely cleared the landing pad when a second one whirred into place. "Uh-oh, bad omen," Shelly said. "I guess I know where I'll be spending the evening."

Jean made a left turn before reaching a dark jagged prominence which jutted majestically up from the sandy terrain. "Marble Mountain," Julia told me. "You can climb around there during the day, but the V.C. crawl out of its caves at night and start shooting."

I was surprised Navy Hospital was located so near a Viet Cong stronghold; further evidence that the war had no front lines. Even as we approached the startlingly white beach bordering clear turquoise water, gunfire rumbled ominously in the background.

"My god, who's fighting the war?" I asked as I looked over hundreds of G.I.s swimming, playing volleyball, grilling hamburgers and drinking beer.

"The guys get to come to China Beach for short R&Rs," Jean said. "They also get one rest and recuperation out of country."

"The married ones go to Hawaii to meet their families," Shelly said as she gathered up Bac Si and got out of the car. "The single ones go wherever the boom-boom is best."

Her red hair and figure, followed by Julia, attracted stares and whistles as we made our way through the press of men. By the time we reached the spot where Leo and Margaret sat, an entire division was following us and entreating us to join their cookouts.

"Oh, good Christ!" Margaret said when she saw Bac Si. "I take one bloody day off to relax and she brings that obnoxious beast."

I had to agree with her when Shelly turned Bac Si loose and he immediately attacked everything on the blanket Margaret had spread on the sand. The men laughed and took pictures of him throwing magazines, lotion and sandals. When he finished, the small monkey sat down in the middle of the blanket and began to masturbate. The more the men laughed, the faster Bac Si indulged his pleasure.

"Get that wretched pervert out of here!" Margaret screamed at Shelly. "I'm not about to sit here while he gets his jollies in front of a bunch of horny G.I.s!"

I looked at Leo, whose face was as scarlet as the bodies of the sunburned men. "Why don't we join the rest of the team on the Vietnamese side of the beach?" he suggested.

"Damned monkey must be queer," Shelly said. "He's never done that in front of us girls."

The Vietnamese beach was separated from the military's by coils of barbed wire running up from the water to the dune line. Bikini-clad Vietnamese girls hung near the fence, inviting the men to cross over. Despite signs warning them not to, several G.I.s were following the prostitutes up the hill to a grove of trees just beyond the sand.

Ron Shaffer, Gail from x-ray and several other members of our team were already settled among an array of vendors selling peanuts and bananas, children hawking Coca-Colas and fishermen pulling nets in from the surf. The cool breeze off the ocean blew our hair and swept away the heat and humidity.

"There's Mrs. Layfield," Leo said. He indicated a woman standing with Dr. Fitch at the water's edge. "You can pick her out by her old bloodshot legs."

The matronly nursing supervisor had a maze of red spider varicosities running up and down her legs. Her more than ample frame had been squeezed into a splash-print bathing suit, and her raven hair was teased into a mountainous tangle atop her head.

Dr. Fitch looked more apostolic than ever standing by the water in barefoot sandals and baggy cotton pants. His long hair and beard blew freely in the breeze and his hands were spread in Christ-like fashion as he conversed with our nursing supervisor.

"You might as well meet Layfield and get it over with," Leo said. "Come on, I'll introduce you."

Mrs. Layfield acknowledged my introduction in a voice that had filtered years of cigarette smoke. "It's about time I met you," she said, as if the delay were my fault. "You do realize you're under the jurisdiction of the nursing department?"

"They told me in Saigon," I said. "I understand it's only to facilitate paper work."

"Oh, don't worry that you might have to take a few orders," she cackled. "I'm well aware of the independent nature of nurse anesthetists."

"Are you enjoying your time in Danang?" Dr. Fitch asked.

"Yes," I replied. "Although I'm not sure enjoying is the word I would use."

"Yes, of course," he said quickly. "How could anyone enjoy such a terrible time in our history." He looked genuinely distressed as he tugged nervously at his graying beard.

Leo interrupted to tell them it was my first time at the beach. "Pat would like to watch the fishermen awhile."

"Yes, please go enjoy," Dr. Fitch said. "I mean, please go and watch the fishermen." He tugged so hard at his beard his face elongated.

"And don't make yourself such a stranger to my office," Mrs. Layfield added.

"Not anymore than she does," Leo said as we walked away. Leo's blond head looked out of place among the black hair of Vietnamese, and his pale skin almost anemic.

We walked along the beach toward fishermen who jabbered excitedly as they clubbed at fishing nets spread on the sand. When we got close enough, I saw that the nets were filled with fish and long, flat-tailed serpents that slithered wildly to escape the blows of their captors.

Julia was squatted on the sand watching. "Sea snakes," she said. "They're always getting caught in the nets." I shuddered and turned my head away. "A lot of guys have been found dead in the water with fang marks on them," Julia continued. "The Navy's trying to develop an antivenin, but so far they haven't found one."

"Why would anyone go swimming where he could get killed?" I asked when the three of us started back toward our group. Leo looked at me and laughed. Only then did I realize the gunfire and occasional puffs of smoke erupting from the jungle just south of us.

"The snakes usually stay further out to sea," Julia explained. "Planes have spotted masses of them tangled together and mistook them for the raft of a downed pilot."

"I think I'll stay out of the water," I said. But my resolve lasted less than half an hour. There had been no water for a shower the past two days and, as the sun grew hotter, I could not resist a giant bathtub that didn't smell of moss.

When I was sufficiently refreshed from the cool water, Shelly asked if I would like to take a walk. She paid a small boy to look after Bac Si and we set off in the opposite direction of the military beach. We passed a walled-off compound she told me was the headquarters of General Walt, the Marine in charge of I Corps. "We're under his command," she said, "because we're so far north."

Just down from his quarters were several concrete buildings and a row of low, grass-thatched huts. Dozens of children played in the sand surrounding the buildings, and nuns in sparkling white habits hurried about.

"That's the Catholic orphanage," Shelly said. "Sister Nicole comes into town once a week to round up strays at our hospital, mostly kids whose parents have died there."

I fingered the gold cross I wore around my neck and remembered I hadn't been to Mass since my arrival in Vietnam. I asked Shelly if she would mind waiting while I went up to say hello to the nuns. "I'll go with and introduce you to Sister Nicole," she offered.

We were climbing the embankment separating the complex from the beach when we heard Jean calling us back. "Shit, it must mean we're getting a load of peasants," Shelly said.

Dr. Fitch and Mrs. Layfield were the only ones not pulling uniforms over their bathing suits when we rejoined our team. Ruth had sent word with two USAID secretaries heading for the beach that we were receiving heavy casualties and were needed immediately.

"So much for fun in the sun," Shelly said as we sped back toward town.

We found our hospital crowded with dark-skinned people wearing only loincloths. Their features were coarser than the Vietnamese I was accustomed to, and they chattered in an unfamiliar dialect.

"Can you understand what they're saying?" I asked Julia.

"No, they're Montagnards."

"They're not Vietnamese?"

"They are, but they live up in the hills and are kind of primitive. The other Vietnamese don't accept them very well."

When our Vietnamese staff arrived, they took one look at the hill people and shifted into slow gear. Lan stood in the screened corridor laughing with Mr. Hai until Jean ordered them to get to work.

"I do not understand them," Lan said. "They do not speak my language."

"You understand them well enough to joke about what they're saying," Jean said to both him and Mr. Hai. "Now get busy."

They refused, and other staff members gathered around and joined in their laughter. The hill people crouched to the floor with their hands held protectively over their heads.

"I'm giving all of you one minute to get to work," Jean warned. "If you don't, I'll see to it that none of you get overtime pay."

Lan translated the message and they began to move, but at a frustratingly slow pace. Even the janitors deliberately jiggled the stretchers they carried to let the strangers know they were not welcome.

"Damn them," Shelly said from where we worked in triage. "We don't get a dime for working overtime and they have to be coaxed to help us."

"I don't understand," I said. "They don't seem to care about anyone but their own relatives."

"It's a matter of survival," Leo said from where he worked on a patient. "They've gone through generations of war and have made it only by looking out for their own family unit."

"But how do we teach them medicine?" I asked. "You can't just care about your family members, you have to care about every patient."

"Medicine isn't all you can't teach them," Shelly said. "They brag about their five thousand years of culture, but they're still eating with two sticks and shitting on their vegetables."

She left for the surgery suite and I glanced out the window to the courtyard, where a woman was presently depositing her share of fertilizer on the garden. A wave of depression made me shiver despite the heat in the crowded room.

"Co Pat?" someone said behind me. I turned to see Becky smiling anxiously. "I help you?"

I forced a smile. "Maybe you could tell the patients in the corridor we'll be out to take care of them as soon as we can." She nodded and left.

"I think we would all be a lot better off if Lan and Mr. Hai would find another job," Leo said from where he pumped blood into a hemorrhaging patient. "They didn't used to be this bad, but lately they seem to cause a lot of trouble between the teams."

"Shelly says they're V.C.," I said.

"Shelly thinks everyone's a V.C. She came over here to be near Tom, not to win the hearts and minds of the people."

It was difficult to make the hill people cooperate while we put I.V.s in them and examined their wounds. Becky tried to talk to them, but they seemed afraid even of her. She told us the people had never been inside anything but a grass hut before today, and they had never seen white men until their village had been overrun by Viet Cong, followed by a platoon of Marines pursuing them. The ensuing battle had left them with the injuries we treated.

Leo somehow managed to get them to put out their opium pipes, which he tied securely to their wrists so they wouldn't be lost. The ones having spinal anesthetics were allowed to smoke during surgery so they would be quiet on the operating table.

"Let's rotate spinals with general anesthetics," Ron suggested when the sweet-smelling smoke filled the O.R. where he was working. "I'm getting high from that crap."

I helped a janitor carry a newly operated patient to recovery, where he was rudely shoved under a bed by the Vietnamese nurses. On my way back to triage I came upon Mr. Hai trying to move an old man who squatted stubbornly in the screened corridor, staring straight ahead while he puffed on his opium pipe. The Vietnamese O.R. chief was having no luck.

"Maybe he's afraid you'll steal his belongings." I pointed to a blood stained bundle the patient clutched closely to him. "What does he have in there?"

Mr. Hai told the old man to show me what he held and he willingly opened the bloody cloth, unleashing a tangle of intestines that slithered to the dirty floor.

"God, he's been disemboweled," I gasped. I had heard of the Viet Cong torture tactic, but I had not believed it until now.

I sent Mr. Hai for help and tried to ease the old man onto a stretcher, but he obstinately refused. Instead, he methodically collected his entrails and wrapped them back in the dirty cloth he had held them in. Mr. Hai did not return but sent Becky to help me.

"Tell him we must take him to the operating room," I told her. "We have to fix his belly."

She spoke gently to the old man, who still refused to lie down on the stretcher. "He does not wish to go with you." Becky kept her head lowered as she spoke, avoiding my eyes. "He say people like you hurt him."

"The Viet Cong hurt him," I said indignantly.

"He say Americans."

"O.K., then it was Americans. What we need to do now is put his belly back together."

Becky talked some more, then listened while her elder spoke in an animated monologue. I stood silently in the background, nervously waiting for his guts to fly free every time he gestured with one of his gnarled hands. When he finished his story, he returned to staring straight ahead, smoking his pipe.

"He say he working in rice paddy like father before him when Viet Cong come to village," Becky translated. "They kill many peoples and hide in houses. White men come burn down houses and shoot guns. Many people hurt and Viet Cong run away. White men make people get in noisy machines that float through air to place where you want to fix belly." She looked directly at me. "He want to know why you make hole in first place?"

It was the first time I had heard Becky speak English other than a few isolated phrases. I wanted to tell her she was learning well and that I was proud of her. I wanted to tell her anything but the truth about what she had just asked. I looked into her youthful face, then to the ancient brown one that waited for an answer.

"Tell him I don't know," I said finally.

Becky spoke to the old man again and he looked up at me with his cataract-clouded eyes and laughed. Stung by guilt for something I did not do nor understand, I became aggravated by his simple logic. "Tell him to get on that stretcher right now or he won't get any rice," I ordered.

I turned my back while Becky translated so I wouldn't have to look at the scorn so clear in his wrinkled face. The old man picked up his bundle and stepped stubbornly over the stretcher I had placed in front of him. As I watched him shuffle down the corridor behind Becky, I felt as ancient as he looked. He had been introduced to Americans, modern weapons and medicine all in one day. And all of it had been repugnant.

CHAPTER EIGHT

Even though it was Sunday, I dropped by the hospital the next morning to make sure the Montagnards received their share of the meager daily food ration. Leo had the same idea and was already standing guard on the veranda, where the hill people's stretchers had been carried during the night. When they were all chomping happily, Leo and I went to the O.R. to help Dr. Ramirez with some orthopedic cases he wanted to do from the shacks.

"I finished off the last of the I.V. solutions," Leo said when the cases were done. We sat in the locked lounge having a cigarette before returning to our respective quarters. "We're out of needles too."

"Shelly can't get any," I told him. "I stopped by to see her this morning and she has a bad case of dysentery."

Leo exhaled wearily and ground his cigarette out in a can cover used for an ashtray. "I guess I could drive out to Navy and see if they would give me anything."

"I'll go with you," I said. "To smile at the supply guy."

We crossed the bridge spanning the Danang River in our Travelall and drove the short distance to the turnoff leading to Navy Hospital and the beach. But a dilapidated truck was stalled, blocking the road and a backlog of American troop trucks and civilian vehicles waited while the Vietnamese driver tried to get it started.

"Get that piece of shit off the road!" a Marine in the back of a troop carrier shouted.

"Why don't they just drive around it?" I asked Leo. "Their truck could easily make it through the ditch on either side."

"You never drive off the road, Pat. The Viet Cong set up roadblocks that look like a stalled car or an accident, hoping it will lure Americans into the ditches. If you're dumb enough to fall for it you'd be blown to bits by land mines they've planted."

The old truck finally sputtered to life with a burst of scraping metal and exhaust. The Marines cheered, and the waiting vehicles began to edge slowly forward.

Leo parked clear of the helicopter landing pad at Navy Hospital and we entered a Quonset hut marked RECEIVING ONE. It was a simply built room, but lined from floor to ceiling with shelves that contained anything one could possibly need to handle mass trauma. Several wounded Americans were presently being treated by doctors and corpsmen.

At one end of the room a young Marine lay silently staring at the ceiling while blood was pumped into both arms. Two surgeons clamped severed blood vessels on the mutilated stumps where his legs had been. One of the surgeons was Shelly's boyfriend Tom.

"Land mine," the corpsman said quietly when I walked over to where they worked.

"Hello, Pat," Tom said when he looked up briefly. He went back to clamping torn vessels that oozed in spite of tourniquets. "What can we do for you?"

His manner seemed irreverent even though I knew he was doing everything possible for the patient. I had seen injuries like this - and worse - in our own triage, but my feelings were different. The frustration I felt caring for Vietnamese in an ill-equipped, civilian hospital was worlds apart from the revulsion that filled me as I looked down at the Marine's sunken blue eyes in a pallid, bloodstained face.

"Are you visiting or cumshawing?" Tom asked. The freckles spattered across his face gave him a youthful appearance to match the energy he exuded as his hands worked briskly on the patient. His khaki uniform looked rumpled, as if he had caught a few minutes sleep in it, but it was not saturated with perspiration like my dress. Each building in the complex had a generator to provide air-conditioning. I was happy they had it, but it provided little consolation to the wounded or the staff.

"We can come back later," I told Tom.

"Is that an American girl?" the Marine asked weakly.

"Sure is." The corpsman motioned for me to come closer and I moved to the side of the stretcher which, unlike ours, had wheels on it and was elevated to a level that made it easier to work on the patient. The Marine's eyes fastened on my face as steadily as they had the ceiling, imploring me to keep them from the monstrous sight at the end of his stretcher.

"What's your name?" he asked through parched lips. He had to spurt out the words between gasps of air, as if he was drowning. I looked at his chest, which appeared uninjured, and assumed he was weak from pain and blood loss.

"Pat," I said. My voice sounded too loud in the quiet room.

"Hi, I'm Ray." He tried to shake hands but couldn't lift his arm because of needles and tubing. I put my hand over his and felt the cold clamminess of shock.

"What're you doin' in Nam?"

"I'm a nurse at a hospital in town."

"I didn't know there were female … nurses in Danang. You should work … out here so we wouldn't … have to look … at these ugly corpsmen." The corpsman smiled at the patient and continued to pump blood.

"Someone has to look out for the people who get caught in the middle," I said. "We take care of wounded Vietnamese civilians." The young man's brow furrowed and I immediately regretted my words. "They're mainly women and children," I said quickly. "Not people actually involved in the fighting."

"It's good someone's … takin' care of them," the Marine said between gulps of air. "There're lots of people … gettin' blown away … for nothin'." His voice trailed off and I looked toward Tom, who turned a thumb downward below the level of the stretcher. When I looked puzzled he lifted a sheet covering the Marine's midsection to reveal a wad of bloody packs stuffed into a gaping hole in his pelvis.

The patient suddenly rallied, jerking his eyes open and trying to sit up. "Hey, take it easy, buddy," the corpsman said. He gently pushed him back to the rubber mattress covering the stretcher. "We'll be taking you to the operating room as soon as we get this blood in."

"No big deal," the Marine said. "Where you from?" he asked me.

"Minnesota."

"No shit? I'm from Iowa." He looked up at the blood running into his veins. "Guess I'll be headin' … back to the world … soon as the docs … get me fixed up." It was his first admission that he was injured and I wondered if he knew how badly. My hand tightened on his involuntarily and he smiled up at me. It was the sweet smile of a little boy kept home from school with a fever.

"Sure is great … havin' a nice … American nurse … to hold my hand."

His voice was weaker and he blinked repeatedly to clear his vision.

"I'll come hold your hand whenever you want." As I spoke, his hand went limp and his mouth dropped open to release its last breath.

The heat outside was a shock after the air-conditioned coolness. Leo lit a cigarette and handed it to me. "It was nice of you to talk to that guy," he said.

"All that sophisticated equipment, Leo, and they still couldn't save him." I felt too light-headed to smoke the cigarette smoldering between my fingers.

"Not many like that even make it to the hospital. He was just lucky enough to be injured close-by and picked up right away."

"Lucky?"

"Sorry, poor choice of words." He lit himself a cigarette and inhaled deeply. "I've seen guys like that before. I'm not sure they comprehend how badly they're hurt, or whether they just choose to block it from their minds."

"I was hoping he had enough morphine on board to dull his senses." I dropped my cigarette to the red dirt and ground it out with my sandal. "Maybe we're better off in our primitive hole where we're too busy worrying about supplies to pay attention to emotions," I said.

We watched as helicopters took off and landed at the nearby Mag 16. "I care about our patients," I said. "But they're all strangers to me in a strange country. Coming out here where they look like my kid brother makes it my war, too."

"The military medical teams have a tougher psychological burden," Leo said. "We have it a little harder physically."

"I wish I could go to church." I wanted to do something for the young man I had just seen die.

"I've already gone to Mass in town," Leo said, glancing at his watch. "But there's a chapel out here that might have a twelve o'clock service."

"I didn't know you were Catholic."

"I figured you were when you told me you had fourteen brothers and sisters." He winked and took hold of my arm. "I'll walk you to the chapel before I go see what I can do about supplies."

We started up a sandy path that led to a row of buildings on a hill overlooking the metal grated landing pad. "Leo, do you think we should be taking things from here?" I asked. "They might need it for our own boys."

"They don't give us anything they can't spare," he said. "Most of it would just be thrown away because it's being replaced by newer designs." The Navy had recently given us all of their O.R. linen when they changed to disposable paper items to cut down on laundry.

A chopper whirred into position on the landing pad below and I turned to watch stretcher bearers run to unload it. They were patients dressed in blue pajamas who were well enough to work but not strong enough to return to their units. The men they unloaded were dressed in battle attire, with bandoleers of ammunition still hanging across their bloodied bodies. I turned away and continued up the hill.

The chapel was a modest plywood structure with a plain cross above the door. I was comforted to find the room crowded with patients who had managed to survive their injuries.

The congregation sat quietly until a harried looking chaplain hurried in, still pulling vestments over a uniform stained with blood from the latest arrivals. He said Mass quickly, pausing to listen each time a chopper passed overhead. None landed during the service, but when a loud burst of gunfire erupted in the direction of Marble Mountain he turned and gave the entire gathering general absolution.

"He's a bit gun shy," Leo said when I told him later. "He hasn't been here long and wants to make sure everyone is prepared to meet his Maker if he hasn't had a chance to go to confession."

Leo had the back of our Travelall piled with more of the cloth surgeon's gowns that had been replaced by paper ones. The linen hid the cumshawed I.V. solutions and other supplies stacked on the floor beneath them. "We'd better head out," Leo said as he started the engine. "Before the C.O. happens along on a Sunday stroll."

We hauled the supplies into our locked lounge and retired to the Navy club for air-conditioning and food. After several cold beers, we decided to skip lunch.

"Thanks for taking me to the chapel," I said. "It felt good to go to church again."

"I'll pick you up on Sundays if you want me to." Leo's smooth face and light weight clothes looked peculiar in the macho world of combat boots and mustaches.

"I think you must be the only person on the team who attends church regularly," I said.

"It's a habit," Leo said. "I was in the seminary a couple of years and I'm still afraid I'll be punished if I don't show up."

"Same here," I said. "I spent a year in a convent."

Leo looked surprised. "Why did you leave?"

"I was only fifteen and joined out a sense of obligation to my mother. You know how every big family needs a priest or a nun." He nodded knowingly and ordered us another round. "I got tired of peeling potatoes and hemming nun's habits because I was always late to chapel, or in some other kind of trouble. They weren't unhappy when I left."

"Me neither." Leo pushed a strand of loose hair back from his brow. "But I miss it sometimes."

We had one last beer before returning to the heat outside, which made me feel as light-headed as I had after talking to the boy from Iowa. "I'd better back off on the booze," I said. "I've consumed more in two months than I did the whole time before I came here."

"It's a hazard of the job," Leo said as he helped me into the car. "But it does make it easier to sleep when you have a sufficient amount of alcohol pumping through your vessels."

I was hungover the next morning and paused to have a final cigarette before entering the hospital. A group of female patients sat on the steps to the emergency entrance, each combing the hair of the woman on the step in front of her.

"What're they doing?" I asked when Shelly joined me. The women paused occasionally to pick something out of the hair they combed and pop it between their teeth.

"Search and destroy," Shelly answered. "They're hunting for lice then biting them to death."

"Jesus."

Margaret had come up behind us. "Only Americans would find nit-picking entertaining," she said and swished up the stairs ahead of us.

"I still can't believe she's dating an American," I said.

Leo stayed with me in triage the entire morning, teaching me how to conserve even more on supplies. He showed me how to ration one liter of glucose among three patients, using the same I.V. tubing for all. And how the expensive plastic needles we cumshawed from the military to administer blood could be used on more than one patient by carefully extracting them from a vein and rinsing them in an antiseptic solution before reinserting the metal needle that guided the plastic into the vein.

"Shouldn't we give them penicillin to prevent cross-infections?"

"There's barely enough for patients with compound fractures," Leo said. "And they have first priority." I knew he was trying to show me how to manage after he left the following month, but I was frustrated by the marginal care we were continually forced to give.

"Leo, we have to do something about this supply situation," I said. "We can't go on begging from the military indefinitely."

Shelly came into the room to collect a patient and joined in the conversation. "Why don't you ask Mr. Hai about that locked cupboard that takes up half our anesthesia office?" she asked. "My hunch is that a lot of our missing supplies are in it."

The tall wooden cabinet had been a source of curiosity to me ever since my arrival. "That's Mr. Hai's property," Leo said firmly. "Doctor Chen gave him permission to keep it in our office."

"Too bad I'm not better at picking locks," Shelly said.

"What's in it?" I asked when she left with a patient.

"I've never seen Hai open it," Leo said. "I don't think anyone has."

"Well, I'm going to get some penicillin for these patients," I said. "And it's not going to be done by picking locks."

"Good luck," Leo called after me as I left triage.

Dr. Fitch was in his office composing another of the endless memos he sent to Saigon. He looked up briefly before returning to his typewriter.

"Doctor Fitch, I need to talk to you." I stood squarely in front of his desk. He raised his eyes, his fingers still poised over the keys.

"Yes, Miss Walsh. What is it?" He stroked his graying beard.

"We're out of penicillin," I said. "And I don't want to ask the military for it."

"I understand." His face took on a look of exaggerated concern. "You don't have to say another word, I can take care of it."

"You can?"

"Of course. I'll get the penicillin from one of the military doctors I know and give it to you myself."

"What?"

"I'm just trying to protect your privacy," he said in his missionary voice. "I understand how these things happen so far away from home."

"Doctor, the patients need the penicillin, not me." I wasn't sure if I should be amused or insulted. "I'm not coming to you with a case of the clap."

The chief's face reddened and he apologized. I accepted without further discussion so we could get on with the problem of supplies.

"I've just sent a cable to Saigon," Dr. Fitch said when I had given him an update on the situation in the O.R.s. "We should be getting a shipment any day now."

"I've been hearing that for months and we haven't gotten a damned thing. Shelly claims Mr. Hai is hoarding things in that big locked cupboard of his."

"Surely you're not accusing him of keeping things from his own people?" His manner was genuinely shocked.

"Why don't you ask him to open it so we can see for ourselves?"

Although he was reluctant, the chief asked Mr. Hai to come to his office. I was impressed with the articulate Vietnamese he used to ask whether the Vietnamese O.R. supervisor was keeping American supplies from us.

"Het roi! Het roi!" Mr. Hai shouted. "Supplies all gone!"

"You can see that he's telling the truth," Dr. Fitch said to me. I could see nothing but an angry little man whose burning black eyes warned that pursuing the issue would earn me another reprimand.

"All right," I said. "I guess I'll have to go to Commander Miles at headquarters about the supply problem."

Mr. Hai left and Dr. Fitch sighed deeply. "Medical problems are under my domain as long as I remain acting chief," he told me. "There is no need for Commander Miles to be involved."

"I think I'll let the commander decide that."

When I asked Shelly for the keys to the vehicle she offered to go with me. "I'll just lend moral support," she said. "The one time I tried to talk to Miles about supplies he spent the whole time trying to look up my dress."

Vietnamese guards checked our vehicle at the sandbagged entrance to our Danang headquarters using a garden hoe sort of device to which a mirror had been attached. It was intended to reveal any explosives planted underneath the carriage of vehicles entering the compound, but all while they walked around our car the guards kept up an animated conversation, never bothering to glance down at the mirrors.

The Danang USAID building was spacious and air-conditioned to a temperature I found chilling. Shelly took a seat in the reception area and an American secretary showed me into Commander Miles' office after first impressing on me that it was customary to make an appointment.

"Well, hello there," the Commander said, standing to greet me. He was a short balding man in his middle fifties, with eyes that wandered over my body with practiced experience. His complexion was ruddy, no doubt from the alcohol he was rumored to consume on a regular basis. He wore a light blue shirt with an open collar and custom-tailored slacks which accommodated a protruding paunch.

"I'm sorry I didn't make an appointment," I said.

"No bother, no bother." He waved me to a chair back some distance from the front of his desk. I sat down and his red-rimmed eyes focused immediately on my knees, which I clapped firmly together. "What's a little girl like you looking so worried about?" He sat with his hands folded in front of him, elbows resting on his desk.

"We have a critical shortage of supplies at our hospital," I began. "Unless you can get us a shipment, we're not going to be able to take care of casualties."

"Medical logistics are the problem of your chief physician, honey. I can't concern myself with the intricate workings of a hospital when I have hundreds of people to look after." He smiled and his eyes wandered back to the hem of my scrub dress.

"But our supplies are being stolen and rerouted through the black market to the Viet Cong."

"Can you prove that?"

"We get V.C. and North Vietnamese soldiers into our hospital with American-made splints on their fractures and American I.V. solutions running in their veins."

"That doesn't prove a thing. They could have stolen the things from the military as well as from us."

"The military doesn't have the trouble we do because their supply planes aren't unloaded by Vietnamese," I said. "We have to beg things from them in order to operate at all."

"I find that hard to believe. The prima donna military would never concern itself with a bunch of lowly civil servants." I was surprised by the remark, until I remembered Shelly telling me that Commander Miles had been passed over for promotion by the Navy and retired early to civilian government service.

"We get along fine with the military," I said.

"I'll bet you do," he said with a lopsided grin. "Especially you nurses." I wondered if he was going to offer me penicillin.

"We still haven't solved our supply problem," I said.

"Miss Walsh, I have other things to do." He began to shuffle papers around his desk. "If your medical director can't help you, I'm sure I can't."

"Then I guess the only people left to go to are reporters," I said as I got up to leave. "They should be interested in a story about millions of American tax dollars being diverted to the enemy."

I was opening the door when I heard his chair hiss from the release of his weight. "Don't you threaten me, young lady." When I turned, he was coming across the room toward me. "I'll send a cable to Saigon and follow it up when I go there next week," he said, stopping only inches from me. "But I will do it because I choose to, not because of your impudent threat."

"Thank you, sir. We'll keep things running as best we can in the meantime."

I had the door open when he yelled, "Not by fraternizing with the goddamned military! You don't go to them with matters that are under my command!"

Shelly was on her feet and shoving me ahead of her out the door. "Wait until I tell the others about the mouse that roared," she said as we scrambled for our car. Word of my meeting with Commander Miles circulated quickly, and by evening everyone on our team but Dr. Fitch was calling me Mouse.

CHAPTER NINE

We received a shipment from Saigon within weeks, and the operating room staff lengthened its hours to catch up on the backlog created by the previous shortages. Each of us took turns locating overlooked surgical patients in the crowded wards, or in the shacks containing the overflow from the main hospital.

"Start with the shacks today," Jean told me the morning I volunteered to round up patients. "The people out there have been waiting longer."

"How do I know which ones to choose?"

"The ones with the most flies."

She had Lan explain my mission to our two janitors and they picked up a stretcher and followed me outside. But when we reached the door of the first shack they refused to enter, gesturing instead for me to bring the patients out to them. When I stepped into the low-ceilinged hovel, I understood their reluctance.

Dozens of patients and members of their families were crammed into the ramshackle structure, which relied on a row of unscreened windows and holes in the roof for light and ventilation. Ragged bodies lay everywhere in the stinking inferno, either directly on the dirt floor or on thin woven mats that were crawling with flies. Women held up naked infants, imploring me to take them. From their size, it was apparent they had been born in the shacks to mothers too sick to care for them.

I used my inadequate Vietnamese to tell them I was sorry I could not take the babies, and quickly chose a few orthopedic patients who could hobble on homemade crutches. Two healthier looking inhabitants were persuaded to carry an invalid woman to the door, where the janitors loaded her onto their stretcher while being careful not to touch her.

When the ragged caravan was on its way to the hospital, I decided to make a quick inspection of the other two shacks. In each I was greeted with the stench of rotted flesh, old blood and human excrement. Everywhere there were whimpering, naked babies whose mothers all tried to give them to me. I felt like the overseer of a concentration camp as I surveyed the misery in my freshly laundered clothes, concealing a belly full of food I had consumed at the Navy club for breakfast. It appalled me to realize that I had been going past these shacks for months without ever stopping to look inside.

Just as I was about to leave the last of them, the hospital food wagon arrived. Pandemonium reigned as people ran towards the large pots of rice being rationed by a trio of shouting men. There were vegetables from the garden, but not nearly enough to go around, rice and a few fish heads swimming in a thin broth. Patients who were unable to walk bribed their neighbors to collect their share by promising them half the meager portion in payment. In the midst of all the shouting and clanging of metal bowls, the children kept up a pitiful wail, afraid they would be left out.

I fought my way through the swarm and hurried back to our lounge, where I fell into a chair and lit a cigarette. Leo poked his head in to see what cases needed to be done.

"Jesus, Leo," I said as I exhaled a cloud of smoke heavenward. "We have more work to do here than could be done in a lifetime."

"What's put you in such a somber mood?" He came in and took a chair across from me.

"I've just come from the shacks."

"Say no more," he said as he held up a hand. "Whenever I'm insane enough to think I've accomplished something over here I just have to look inside one of those places to know I haven't."

"Those children, Leo. We have to find some clothes for them and provide a decent diet. People can't survive on rice and a few contaminated vegetables."

"There'll never be enough clothes or food as long as the war continues and people are displaced from their homes," he said in a defeated tone. "Believe it or not, I've tried."

"But we can't just ignore the situation."

"I don't know," he said sharply. "You've done a pretty good job of ignoring it until today." His words hit me in the middle of my already unsettled stomach and I snuffed out my cigarette with a trembling hand. "Sorry," he said with obvious regret. "I don't like what's happening out there any more than you do, but I've been too damned busy trying to organize an anesthesia department, train students and keep the O.R.s running to do anything about it."

"I know you have," I said. "And it's me who needs to apologize."

He pulled a surgical cap roughly over his hair. The grey fabric matched his eyes exactly. "What I've accomplished here is a drop in the bucket," he said as he prepared to leave. "We've just been patching people back together and teaching the students to do the same. They don't know the first damned thing about preventive medicine or routine surgery."

"They know how to save people who are half dead," I said. "After that, appendectomies and gallbags should be relatively easy."

"Maybe," he said with an attempt at a smile. "At least I've given them eighteen months of my sweat."

While I worked, I thought of places I could write to get clothing for the children. The Seabees had invited us to a party on the weekend, where I hoped to make a deal for sawhorses for triage. Perhaps I could also talk them into repairing the holes in the roofs of the shacks and putting screens on the windows to keep out the flies.

When Shelly came into triage I asked her opinion. "Don't go turning into a missionary nut trying to save everyone," she said. "One Fitch is enough."

"I'm not the type."

"Good. You find yourself a nice little lieutenant to occupy your free time and you'll work twice as hard when you're on duty."

"Jerry and I have a standing date for steak night," I said. The flight surgeon had driven into town with Jean's pilot friend every Wednesday evening since we met. "But I have a feeling he might be married," I added. "He avoids any conversation about his life back home."

"There're worse things," Shelly said. "Enjoy the relationship for what it's worth."

The Seabees' ability to procure any kind of goods was legend, but I was still impressed when we drove up to their house for the party. It was built entirely of materials for which they had bartered and traded, including a bar of gleaming teak wood from Thailand. A brass rail running its length was to have gone into an officers' club in Saigon, but had somehow found its way to Danang. The bevy of local women the men employed to care for them were serving the party guests trays of meat pastries, shrimp and egg rolls. Liquor was abundant, as well as ice, and music played on an elaborate reel-to-reel tape system wired into every room in the house.

Julia was dancing with a Seabee, her long legs attracting attention from bystanders. "Hi, Mouse!" she called, waving at me. I waved back.

"I thought you didn't like to dance," I said to Leo when he asked me. He never danced at the Navy club in town, where it was difficult for American women to refuse the constant stream of G.I.s feeding the jukebox with dimes. The club occasionally had Taiwanese female singing groups who imitated American singers with sometimes comic results like "Prease Rerease Me, Ret Me Go."

"I think the military should have eminent domain in their clubs," Leo said as we danced to the soft music. "It's different at a private party."

"You're very good," I said as he guided me effortlessly across the room.

Leo laughed at the compliment. "You're just used to dancing with guys in combat boots." He drew me closer to him. "You're a great girl," he said next to my cheek. "I'm glad I met you."

"I'm glad too. I was beginning to think there was something wrong with me, other than the fact that I'm usually covered with blood and flies."

When the song ended he walked out to the deck the Seabees had built across the rear of their house. I followed, and we watched in silence the sporadic bursts of fire lighting up the sky. A firefight was taking place out near Marble Mountain, and flares hung over its sharp black peaks like Japanese lanterns suspended from the heavens. Leo's hair was golden in their amber glow. He sighed and leaned heavily against a rail bordering the deck.

"Is something wrong?"

"I'm just tired and preoccupied about going home next week."

"I wish you weren't leaving."

He straightened up from the railing and turned to me. "I've given a lot of thought to signing up for another tour," he said. "But I've had enough war." He went back to watching the firefight.

"What are you going to do?" I leaned against the railing next to him, our faces illuminated by the orange light.

"I'm not sure. Maybe get a job in a small hospital."

"With no trauma."

He smiled at me. "I need to slow it all down. No more rushing to save lives."

"But you're so good at it. You're a great action junky."

"I've learned a lot over here. All of the medical teams have."

"I read somewhere that the biggest medical advances are made in war, because the military has so many otherwise healthy casualties."

"It makes sense. You get a lot of practice." He kissed me on the cheek and went inside.

"How's the war?" said a Seabee who replaced Leo the moment he left. I was still watching the activity near Marble Mountain.

"It might be pretty if people weren't being killed," I said.

"War is hell." The Seabee sat down in one of the deck chairs and I did the same. "I know I have it damned nice compared to the guys in the field," he said. "A great place to live, someone to cook and wash for me and all the beer I can drink."

"Don't forget the women," I reminded.

The young man laughed and propped his feet on an overturned crate. "The hootch mice?" he said. "They're just some old Bas who're glad to make a few bucks."

"It looks like they have some nice daughters." A young woman brought a fresh tray of pastries to us, bowed and left.

"They like to make a few bucks too," the Seabee said with a smile.

I asked him about the origin of the Seabees and he told me the unique military unit he belonged to had been organized just after Pearl Harbor to construct air fields, housing, hospitals and whatever else was needed to fight the war in the Pacific. Their services were found to be so invaluable, they had become a permanent part of the Navy and presently had over twenty thousand members in Vietnam. Unlike civilian contractors, the Seabee Construction Battalion was protected by the Geneva Convention because its members did not bear arms. If they were attacked by the enemy they were to surrender, with the hope that they would be taken prisoner without injury.

"Civilian contractors are considered guerilla combatants if they carry weapons for protection," he explained. "That means the enemy can shoot them on sight, with no repercussions from the Geneva Convention." He took a long drink of his beer. "They come here because the money's good."

When the conversation lagged, I asked the young man about doing some work at our hospital. He sipped thoughtfully at his drink while I talked, as if he was accustomed to being asked favors.

"We could build you some sawhorses," he said when I finished. "But there's no sense patching holes in a roof during the dry season; they need them for air."

"Could you at least cover them with screens to keep out the flies?" I asked. "And maybe the windows too?"

"I could, but it won't keep 'em out. Where you got filth, you got flies."

Flares were illuminating the entire perimeter when we left the party just before midnight. Everyone made it a point to be in his own quarters before the bewitching hour, when the enemy crawled out of its holes and started fighting in earnest.

It seemed as if I had just fallen asleep when I heard someone tapping lightly at my door. "Mouse, you awake?" I looked at my clock and saw that it was 7:00 A.M.

"What's wrong?" I asked through the closed door.

"We have casualties to do," Shelly replied.

It was Sunday and I had been looking forward to a day off. "How many?" I asked when I opened the door to let her in.

"Enough." The air was already hot and Shelly's dress saturated with perspiration. "Becky came over to my house on her bicycle to tell us to come in."

Military field ambulances were backed up to the emergency entrance when we arrived and Julia was helping Army medics unload them. When I offered to help she handed me a bloodied child.

"Plenty to go around," she said.

I took the child to triage, where Shelly asked me to help her with a young man who had an injury to his chest. "Hold your hand over the hole and I'll go see if I can find someone to put in a chest tube," she instructed.

A piece of shrapnel had entered the patient's chest, leaving a hole through which air was able to enter and collapse his right lung. If we didn't soon get a tube in him to drain off the offending air, it could push his heart to the right side and kill him.

Shelly returned with Dr. Fitch and three men I had never seen before. They were physicians from the A.M.A. Project Vietnam program that sent volunteer physicians to Vietnam for two months of duty.

"Finger in the dike, huh?" the eldest of the three newcomers said. He motioned for me to step aside while he inspected the wound. "Do you have some chest tubes and suction?" he asked.

While Shelly left to get the necessary equipment, Dr. Fitch introduced him as Dr. Gregory, a thoracic surgeon. The younger man with him was his chief resident from their teaching hospital back home. A third physician was a general surgeon named Dr. Jordan.

"Boy, do we need a thoracic surgeon," I said to Dr. Gregory. "Ron's been doing all the chest cases along with the general surgery."

"Of course, he's had a little help from me," Dr. Fitch added.

Precious little, I thought. Thoracic surgery was a complicated specialty general surgeons like Ron did not like to tackle. Our mortality rate and operating time would be significantly improved by the addition of Dr. Gregory and his resident.

"I've had some experience with orthopedics," Dr. Jordan said. "I expect you get a lot of fractures here."

"Do we ever," Shelly said as she returned with the chest tubes and suction. "And our orthopedic surgeon is leaving this week."

"Well, I might need a little more than a week to get acclimated," Dr. Jordan said quickly. He looked to be in his mid-forties, the same as Dr. Fitch, and had the same nervous habit of stroking a beard that grew sparsely across his receding jaw.

Dr. Gregory inserted the chest tubes with the efficacy of experience, never once complaining about the crudeness of the instruments or the primitive suction machine. The resident appeared anxious to please his grey haired professor and said nothing either. But Dr. Jordan watched the procedure with obvious disapproval.

When Ron came into the room and was introduced, he pumped each of the physicians' hands with the enthusiasm of a battle weary soldier meeting his replacement. He invited the surgeons to join him in his O.R. and both Dr. Gregory and his resident accepted. Dr. Jordan went with Dr. Fitch to his house for a cool drink.

"It'll take me time to get used to this heat," Dr. Jordan said as the two departed triage. "I have a lot of trouble with my sweat glands."

"Well, two out of three isn't bad," Shelly said.

We were still doing cases when Rick, Jerry and another pilot showed up at two and asked if we would accompany them to the beach. "I kind of promised the guys in my squadron I could get a bunch of nurses for a party," Rick said. "They're organizing a barbecue in your honor."

"You might have checked with us first," Jean said. "We have a couple hours of work left here."

"It was another of his middle-of-the-night ideas," Jerry said. "They were in the bar and Romeo let his bragging get out of hand."

"Do you think you could make it?" Rick asked. "I hate to disappoint the guys." He wore a flight suit and the ever present dark aviator glasses that made pilots so disarming.

"If you help us," Jean said.

"I'm ready." Jerry rolled up his sleeves. "Where do I scrub in?"

"We don't need doctors today," Jean said. "For once we have enough." Doctor Gregory and his resident were busy operating with Julia as scrub nurse, but Dr. Jordan had still not returned from Dr. Fitch's house. "You can transport stretchers for Mouse," Jean told the flight surgeon. "That will help her get patients ready for the O.R. faster."

"Better yet, why not let Jerry run triage and I'll open another operating room for Dr. Ramirez?" I suggested. "That is, if Rick will carry stretchers."

Rick stood at one side of triage, trying not to look at the patients. "No work, no beach," Jerry told him.

"Do you provide clothespins?" Rick asked.

The extra help made the cases go so quickly we were on our way to the beach in little over an hour. The new surgeons, with the exception of Dr. Jordan, accepted our invitation to join us and plunged immediately into the cool water with us to wash away the blood and sweat of their first day. We then joined the pilots for hamburgers and lukewarm beer.

"God, this is nice." I sat down beside Julia, who was seated next to a young man at a picnic table built by the Seabees for the China Beach R&R center.

"Yeah, a regular fucking paradise." He looked too young to be a pilot and didn't wear the customary aviator sunglasses. I asked if he was with Rick's Marine fighter squadron.

"He's Army," Julia said when the young man remained silent. "He knows one of the guys in the squadron."

"My name's Pat," I said, offering my hand.

"Lieutenant Bob Tamasi, married and not looking for company." He ignored my hand and guzzled his beer.

"C'mon Julia," I said and got up from the table.

"We're not exactly over here to entertain the troops," Julia said as she got up.

"Listen, I'm sorry," he said. "Please sit down." I remained standing. "My wife just had a baby and I'm upset about not being there. I didn't mean to take it out on you."

"Boy or girl?" Julia asked as she lit a cigarette.

"Girl, six pounds and lots of hair." His smile was the same I had seen hundreds of times outside the windows of newborn nurseries.

"Maybe you can take an R&R to Hawaii so you can see her," I suggested as I sat back down.

"If I live that long." His face was no longer that of a proud new father; he looked like the corpsmen and medics who carried patients into our hospital.

"I'm going for a walk," I said. "Would you like to go along?"

"That would be nice," he said. "I think I've had about enough beer."

"I'm ready for a swim," Julia said.

The beach we strolled along could have been California, except for the barbed wire coiled along its length. Artillery thudded in the background and helicopters whirred overhead bringing more wounded to Navy Hospital just across the road.

"So what are you doing here?" the lieutenant asked.

"We're assigned to a civilian hospital in town," I replied. "We take care of Vietnamese casualties."

He stopped to look into my face. "You shitting me?"

"No."

"You mean we shoot 'em and you fix 'em up?"

"I guess you could put it that way."

"Crazy fucking war," he said, walking slowly onward. "You're over here risking your lives to save the people I'm risking my life to shoot."

"It's not so risky for us if we don't go outside the perimeter," I said. "USAID restricts us to a ten mile radius around Danang."

"I'll be going out on patrol in a couple of days," he said after a few quiet minutes. "It's like facing a death sentence."

"Going on patrol doesn't mean you're going to be killed."

"Lady, I'm what's known as a second lieutenant. They start looking for your replacement an hour after you take your platoon out."

The crowd around the barbecue was thinning by the time we returned. The pilots had to get back to the base to sleep before their night flights up north.

"Have a nice afternoon?" Jerry asked when I introduced him to Lieutenant Tamasi. His expression made it clear he did not approve of our lengthy walk.

"He's been telling me about his new baby daughter," I said.

"Congratulations." Jerry's tone was stiff.

"I guess I'll go for a swim," the lieutenant said, and quickly departed.

"Keep thinking of Hawaii," I called after him.

Julia met a pilot who seemed completely taken by her. When it was time to go, she got into his jeep.

Jerry said nothing on the trip back to town and I made no effort to break the silence. When we arrived at temporary housing Rick went with Jean to her room. I took a seat on the balcony overlooking the alley, and Jerry sat next to me.

"If we stay out here we're going to be cannibalized," he said after several minutes of brushing away clouds of mosquitoes. "I'm sorry I hurt the little lieutenant's feelings, but let's not ruin a whole evening over it."

"I want to ask you something, Jerry."

"O.K., shoot. Whoops, never say shoot in a war." He spoke in a Groucho Marx voice. "Say the secret word and you win a hundred bullets."

Impersonations were common. Officers showed up at their clubs in costumes intended to amuse their colleagues. But I wondered if their disguises and impersonations were actually attempts to deny the reality of being here.

"What is it you want to know?"

"Are you married?"

"What brought that on?" He wore his aviator glasses, even though the sun had set, and I couldn't see his eyes.

"I just want to know."

"O.K.," he said quietly. "Yes, I'm married."

"Thank you for telling me."

"I didn't do it voluntarily." He smiled and removed his dark glasses. His hand brushed my thigh.

I got up from where we sat. "Jerry, I don't want to get involved."

"That's all right with me," he said. "I'm a little involved already."

"I mean I don't want to get involved with a married man."

"What's wrong with a little romance to pass the lonely hours?"

"I'm not lonely."

"No, I guess you're not," he said after a pause. "But look at it this way, I could be killed."

"So could I."

"O.K., I give up," he said throwing his hands into the air. "But couldn't we go into your room until Rick is ready to leave?" He brushed at a swarm of mosquitoes feasting on his arms. "Otherwise I'll feel compelled to brush them off you."

Jean knocked discreetly at my door when it was time to leave and the men departed for the air base. I told her about Jerry over a Scotch in my room.

"I think you're wise," she said. "If you don't break it off now, you'll have to do it later."

"We agreed to keep our date for steak night," I said. "Jerry's still fun to be with."

We were about to have a second Scotch when a tremendous blast ripped through the air. Shards of broken glass tinkled down behind the wooden shutter covering my window.

"Get down!" Jean yelled above the roar of a second explosion that was even louder.

More followed while we pulled the mattress from my bed and huddled beneath it. Not until it had been quiet for several minutes did we venture a look outside.

"My god, they hit the air base," Jean said. Orange flames leapt like a giant bonfire into the black sky.

Another series of explosions made the building shake as if it was about to collapse. "Let's go to Shelly's," Jean said in a voice that betrayed her concern. "Her place is sturdier."

We hurried down the stairs and drove through the streets with our headlights off. Sirens could be heard in the direction of the air base and M.P.s rushed through the streets in darkened jeeps.

Tom was at Shelly's, hastily pulling on his uniform as he tried to reach Navy Hospital on her unreliable telephone. "I should never have sneaked into town," he said while he jiggled the apparatus trying to summon an operator. "They'll have my ass if I'm not out there to receive casualties."

Keith was there too, and Margaret was helping him into his clothes while clad only in a thin nightgown. Broken glass from the French doors leading to the balcony covered the floor, and Bac Si chattered excitedly from where he had taken refuge on the rotating ceiling fan.

"Trouble in River City," Julia said when another series of explosions rocked the house and caused the air base to light up as if it were daylight. She was smoking a cigarette.

Tom glanced outside. "They hit the ammo dump," he said. "I've got to get back to the hospital." He slammed down the telephone and started for the stairs.

"I'm going with you," Shelly said. "We don't even have a bunker to get into." A secondary explosion from the ammo dump left our ears ringing. The electricity flickered and went off, but it didn't matter. The fires at the air base lit up the entire area.

"I've got to get back to the consulate," Keith told Margaret. "You go with the others." Margaret was in her thirties and Keith looked to be her age. Both seemed exceedingly calm.

When Keith was gone, Margaret went to get slacks and a shirt, which she pulled over her nightgown as she came down the stairs behind us.

The streets were crowded with tanks, troop trucks and jeeps, all with their headlights off. Unlike us, all of the occupants wore helmets and flak jackets. We had gone only a few blocks when a young man came running towards us, madly waving his arms. "Hey! It's Fast Eddie," Tom said. "I forgot he was in town."

He slammed on the brakes and a young corpsman scrambled into the Travelall. "Thanks," he said breathlessly. Shelly had told me about the corpsman's illegal Vietnamese wife, the reason for his nickname, and I felt sorry for him having to leave her alone during an attack. "How's Bac Si?" Fast Eddie asked Shelly, next to him in the front seat. She assured him the pet that had originally been his was fine.

"Good Christ, half of us will probably be killed and he's asking about a bloody monkey," Margaret said from the third row seat. "I hope he gets his balls fried."

"I hope the bridge is open or he won't be the only one to get his balls fried," Tom said. Not far from the heavily guarded structure the shadowy outline of a tank swung in behind us. "It's O.K., it's one of ours," Tom said as he continued driving full speed.

Shelly looked back toward the South Vietnamese-manned tank. "I don't trust the ARVN even if they are on our side," she said.

As Tom approached the bridge the tank picked up its pace. "I think Shelly may be right," Julia said. "You had better stop and be identified."

When Tom stopped we turned in unison to look down the huge barrel of the tank's cannon, aimed directly at us. "Tell him to get the hell off our ass!" Tom shouted at a nearby sentry. "I'm a Navy doc on my way back to the hospital!"

"Yes sir." The sentry ordered the tank to halt and we sped across the wooden bridge.

This time I was not the only one who breathed a sigh of relief when we reached the other side without the bridge disintegrating into a pile of splinters beneath us. It was only a few miles to the hospital now, but we still had to pass MAG 16, the mammoth American helicopter installation that would also be a prime target for enemy rockets. No one spoke as we turned down the road running past it, but several of us visibly jumped when we heard Vietnamese voices coming toward us. In the light of a sudden flare, we saw the entire population of Cabbage Patch running down the embankment calling, "Hurry up boom-boom! One dollah!" Even old Sophie was there, her eyes illuminated by the fires of the air base as she shrieked out her message and flapped her dress. "Boom boom. Numbah one virgin!"

"Jesus! They're having a fire sale," Shelly shouted.

The tension in the car lightened as we broke into laughter. By the time we reached Navy Hospital, choppers were already bringing in the wounded. The compound was secured, with all lights blacked out and the gates closed and locked. "You'll have to go back to town," Tom told us when he stopped the vehicle short of the gates. "It'll be hard enough for the two of us to get in."

"Be careful," Shelly told him as he got out of the van with his corpsman.

"Don't drive off the road," Tom cautioned. "If the whores run in front of you, drive over them."

He disappeared into the darkness with Fast Eddie, but Shelly did not move into the driver's seat he had vacated. "I don't want to go back there," she said, looking toward the raging fires that appeared as if they were engulfing all of Danang.

Margaret crawled over two rows of seats and set the van in motion. She drove fast, staying in the center of the road with the headlights off.

"Who has a match?" Julia asked with a cigarette already between her lips. "I forgot my lighter."

"Just hold it up and Ho Chi Minh will light it for you," Shelly said.

We hadn't gone far when a deafening roar caused the earth beneath us to tremble and sent our car careening crazily. We looked toward the city but were unsure whether it or the air base had taken the latest hit. It was then that I realized the real terror of war, having no safe place in which to hide. The very shelter you might choose could be the target of the next rocket, or the unintended site of one that fell short of its destination. Never in my life had I been so frightened, and I prayed silently that I would live long enough to write a letter home. There were so many things I had not said to my family.

"They hit another ammo dump," Margaret said as we got closer to the city. I fingered the gold cross around my neck my mother had given me.

"We might as well go to the hospital and get ready for casualties," Jean said when we reached Danang. "It's probably as safe as anyplace else."

"Why not?" Shelly said. "If the whores aren't afraid, why should I be?"

"Nice comparison," Margaret said.
"Fuck you."
It was good to hear them bickering again.

CHAPTER TEN

Leo was at the hospital preparing for casualties and other members of the team were trickling in. There would be no casualties brought in while the attack continued, so we used the time to carry what supplies we had to triage. The power was off and huge rats scurried through the darkened corridors and over our sandaled feet.

Just when we thought the fighting was beginning to subside, an ear-piercing blast sent the patients who could ambulate scurrying in fright. Dr. Gregory stood in the intensive care unit watching people he had recently operated on for chest injuries clamp their drainage tubes, unhook themselves from suction bottles and hobble off toward the surrounding rice paddies..

"How do they know enough to clamp off their chest tubes so they don't collapse their lungs?" Dr. Gregory asked in amazement.

"I taught them," Margaret said as she continued to prepare her ward for new arrivals. "Surely you didn't think I would let them lie around just because they have chest tubes? They have to go to the garden when they need to relieve themselves like everyone else."

The thoracic surgeon looked at her in disbelief. "It's going to be an interesting two months," he told the resident who was always at his side.

"We're Americans! I demand that we be evacuated immediately!" The visiting Dr. Jordan was running down the hall in his pajamas, with our chief running behind trying to reassure him.

"I'm going to make arrangements to get us out right now," Dr. Fitch told him. "Just as soon as I can get through to Saigon." He grabbed a candle from the lounge and disappeared into his office.

"He's probably going to write them a memo," Shelly said.

"This is outrageous!" Dr. Jordan continued. I could see his knees trembling beneath his pajamas pants. "Why don't they just put us on a plane and get us out of here!"

"See that?" Julia said, pointing out a broken window in the lounge toward the fires. "That's the air base."

Dr. Jordan sank into a chair and Ron poured him a shot from a bottle of whiskey someone had brought. There was writing paper too, and Shelly and I both took a few sheets and left to find a quiet place in which to write letters home. "You'll probably hear about an attack here, but I'm O.K. …"

The power remained off, but it was light outside because of the fires and flares. We climbed the scaffolding to the roof of a pediatric hospital under construction next to ours, where the light was best and we had a bird's eye view of the air base.

"I hope our guys kill every one of the bastards," Shelly said as we stood watching the spectacle.

Never before had I wished for the death of another human being, but I did now. "I hope so too," I said.

"Jean is pretty worried about her pilot friend," Shelly said when we sat down on some loose cinder blocks.

"I know." I said nothing about Jerry, or how terrible I was feeling about the flippant way I had reacted to him when he said he could be killed. The whole conversation seemed so trivial now; it didn't matter if he was married, it only mattered that he survive.

We worked at our letters, pausing occasionally when a new explosion rumbled through the smoke-laden air. When the attack began to lessen, the light did also. I felt a shocked sense of guilt when I found myself hoping for another explosion and fire so I could see better. I put the letter aside and sat staring at the horrifying scene two miles away. Leo climbed the rickety scaffolding and sat beside me.

The rockets had stopped landing, but everything billowed acrid smoke that stung our nostrils and burned our eyes. There were no sirens, only muffled secondary explosions and the crackling of flames. It was incredible to watch such devastation befall a modern facility with all the latest in American technology.

"I guess our guys must have found their launching site," Leo said.

"Either that or the gooks ran out of rockets," Shelly said. She climbed down the scaffolding and returned to the hospital.

"The civilian casualties will be the last ones to be picked up," Leo told me. "They're low priority."

“Do you think there will be many Americans?”

“They hit just when the fighters were out on the flight line for their missions up north. I’m sure they caught some of them before they could get airborne.”

We watched the sun come up, then disappear in the boiling cloud of smoke that hung over the city. When no casualties had arrived by six, Leo suggested we drive out to the air base and see if we could lend a hand. Jean came along to look for Rick.

Portions of the shantytown between the city and the base had been destroyed by rockets falling short of their target. Ruth would have a lot of burn patients admitted to her ward.

The closer we got to the base, the more total the destruction. The PX was reduced to rubble, with looters already sifting through its scattered remains. Multi-million-dollar planes sat smoldering on taxiways as others roared into the sky to avenge their attackers. Several barracks had been destroyed, killing or maiming their occupants as they lay in their bunks. Occupied body bags lay in neat rows waiting to be transported to the morgue, which stood defiantly unscathed in the orange light.

After being told the wounded were already en route to hospitals, we drove around the base looking for Rick and Jerry. Leo stopped near the trailer where pilots suited up for flights, and Jean’s face paled when she saw it was riddled with bullets and shrapnel.

“Hey, there’s Jerry!” I shouted. He was hurrying across a damaged runway with a medical bag.

“Rick’s all right!” he called when he saw us waving to him. “He’s on his way up north to give Uncle Ho some of his own medicine!”

Jerry’s face was streaked with soot and his hands were scratched and burned. “I have to go!” he shouted above the roar of a departing plane. “The fire fighters need first aid!”

Jean looked again at the damaged ready room. “I wonder if all the pilots made it out of there,” she said.

“The ones who were able to pull parachute packs down around them did,” a young airman standing nearby said. “I guess it depended on how close you were to the packs whether you took a hit.”

I marveled at how Rick could get into a plane and fly a bombing mission after seeing his comrades die. But pilots were a special breed. They didn’t grieve for their lost friends but simply said the departed had “bought a farm,” and went on a wild drinking binge to celebrate their “retirement.”

Body bags were being carried into the morgue when we returned to the other side of the base. Leo drove slowly because of scattered debris, and we could see the stricken faces of the men assigned the grizzly detail. I wondered how this latest body count would be reported back home; whether our government would come up with a higher number of enemy killed, as it usually did, even though each of the body bags we looked at contained a dead American.

Mrs. Layfield was on the front steps of the hospital when we returned. "There must be reporters around," Leo said. "I haven't seen her in uniform since the last big push."

She stood smoking a cigarette, watching us as we approached. "Would someone please explain why you people are an hour late for work?" she demanded in her gravelly voice.

"Late?" Jean said. "We've been here all night."

"We didn't have any casualties so we drove out to the base to see if we could help," Leo told her.

She tossed her cigarette to the ground and pointed a finger toward the door behind her. "Your responsibility is to this hospital," she said. "You should be in there working instead of fraternizing with the military."

"Oh, for god's sake," I said. "Why does everyone keep harping about the military?"

Mrs. Layfield gave me a chilling look. "You, Miss Walsh, appear to need constant reminding that this is a civilian medical team. I thought Commander Miles made that clear when he straightened out our supply problem and ordered you to cease all unprofessional liaisons."

I was surprised she knew about my meeting with our USAID chief. "Commander Miles got two lousy shipments through," I said. "And we're about to run out of that."

Dr. Fitch joined her on the porch but seemed reluctant to enter the discussion. "Please tell these people they are to stop running to the military," Mrs. Layfield implored in an exasperated voice.

"I've told all of you that our supply situation is under control," Dr. Fitch said obediently. "There's another shipment due here any day."

"I hope you're right," Jean said. A convoy of troop trucks and ambulances was coming through the hospital gates.

The burn patients were the worst. Ruth had stayed with her frightened patients all night, preparing her ward as best she could for new arrivals, but she had little with which to work.

"The burn dressings you got me were wonderful," she told Shelly when she came into triage to see how many patients to expect. "But I'm afraid I won't have enough to take care of all these new ones." She wore her customary long sleeved white uniform, a holdover from the earlier days of nursing when she was trained.

"I'll try to get you some more," Shelly said. "But I can't go to Navy Hospital while they're busy with our own guys."

"No, of course not," Ruth said quickly. "I'll make do until you can."

"What about Layfield's ban on cumshawing?" I asked Shelly when Ruth was out of triage.

"Piss on Layfield. Ruth needs help."

By the time we finished the day's cases, we had depleted the last of Commander Miles' shipments. Jean worried that we would waste the precious gift of thoracic surgeons because she could not keep the operating rooms running the remainder of their two month tour.

"How's Doctor Fitch going to get a shipment through with half the runways out of commission?" Julia said as she smoked a cigarette in the lounge. "They won't let anything but military flights in and out until they're repaired."

Through the broken window in the lounge we could see Mrs. Layfield driving out of the hospital compound in the direction of the PX. "I wonder if anyone's told her the PX is scattered over two square miles?" I said.

"I guess I could go out to the Green Beret camp I used to beg from before Shelly got us Navy Hospital," Leo said. "They'll be too busy trying to hunt down Cong to do any MEDCAP missions for awhile." The Medical Civic Action Programs, known as MEDCAPs, were conducted by specialized Green Beret outfits to make friends with the people they depended upon to conduct their missions. The men had only cursory training in medicine, but they dispensed malaria pills and penicillin to people in outlying areas and did simple things like treating jungle sores.

"Miles will have your balls if you go out there," Shelly told Leo. "And speaking of balls, I have to get home and see if my monkey's all right."

"Maybe we should start writing letters to newspapers," I said. "Or to Congressmen who oppose the war. That might solve our supply shortages."

"The press isn't interested in our problems," Julia told me. "They only come to our hospital when they're hard up for a story and looking for something pathetic, like a kid missing both arms and legs."

"As for Congressmen," Leo told me when we were alone in the lounge, "I already have a plan."

I was surprised to learn he had merely been biding his time, waiting until his tour was up to blow the whistle on USAID. "I've been keeping a daily journal for months, documenting everything Layfield and Fitch have done - or should I say not done? When I leave here I plan to go directly to Washington and lay it in front of the people in charge.

"Do you think they'll listen?"

"You'll know if Fitch is suddenly replaced as chief."

We worked until late, after which Leo offered to buy me dinner at the Navy Club. I thought it might be closed because of the attack, but the bar was filled to capacity. Rick was there with a group of pilots who talked boisterously about their retaliatory strike against the North.

"Do you know what Vietnamese pilots call close formation?!" a pilot shouted.

"Any two planes over Vietnam at the same time!" another shouted back.

"It sure was nice not having to sit over a target getting our asses shot at while the American brass cleared it with the Vietnamese brass before we could drop our load," another said. "Today was real war, dump them mothers and head on out." The others cheered and raised their glasses in salute.

"They must have lost a lot of guys in the attack," Leo said. "They're really putting away the booze."

Leo's departure was delayed a week because of the attack on the air base. It was still not fully operational when he and Jim Ramirez were notified they could catch a ride on a military transport headed for Saigon, where they could connect with a commercial flight. Everyone was surprised when Mrs. Layfield announced she was hosting a farewell party for our departing colleagues the night before their departure.

The party was held at the house she occupied alone, and was on its way to becoming a disastrous flop when somebody suggested making room for dancing. Without first asking our nursing supervisor's permission, we moved her double bed over and inadvertently uncovered a pair of Marine combat boots concealed discreetly beneath it.

"So that's where she was the night of the air base attack," Leo said. "I guess somebody likes her old bloodshot legs."

When the party ended just before midnight, a group of us decided to risk staying out just one time beyond the bewitching hour. "They got their licks in last week," Julia said. "They'll leave us alone for awhile."

Our bravado might have had something to do with the potent punch we had consumed at the party, which was concocted by mixing several quarts of liquor with Kool Aid. After considering moving the party to the beach, and rejecting it when someone remembered it was secured at sunset, we adjourned to the Bamboo Hut. The elderly proprietor did not appear to be unhappy when we pounded on the door until we woke him. American dollars were welcome at any hour.

"I don't want any of his wormy beer," I said when Leo set a bottle of local brew in front of me. The others were already drinking at the same rate they had at the party.

"What do you mean, wormy?" I told Leo about the incident on my first day in Danang, and how I didn't want him or Shelly to think I was squeamish. "You swallowed a worm so you wouldn't appear squeamish?" He howled with laughter. "It probably just got trapped in the bottle at the brewery."

"I didn't swallow the worm," I said with drunken affront. "I kept it at the bottom of the bottle." After considering a moment I added, "I just hope I didn't swallow any eggs it might have laid in there."

"Don't worry," Leo said, draping an arm across my shoulders. "The alcohol would have killed any eggs." I smiled at his reassurance. "The most you could have swallowed was all the shit it expelled when it saw that beer pouring in on it."

His laughter blended with the rest of the rowdy drunkenness in the small open-air bar. Even Dr. Ramirez was there, sitting next to Gail, our x-ray tech. It was the first time I had seen him outside the hospital and he was wholly inebriated.

"Hey, where are we supposed to dance in here?" he called to the proprietor. "This is my last chance to raise hell." The sleepy-eyed proprietor pointed to nonexistent floor space among the crowded tables.

"If we can't dance the only thing left is swimming," the orthopedic surgeon said. He removed his shoes and climbed up onto the railing overlooking the river. "Who dares me to dive into that shit?" People pulled money from their pockets and shouted their bets. "Here goes." Dr. Ramirez executed a perfect swan dive and everyone leaned over the rail to make sure he surfaced in the polluted water. "Who's next?" he called the moment he bobbed to the surface.

"I am." Julia did a backward flip to loud cheers from the appreciative onlookers. Leo and Jean followed.

"Your turn, Mouse!" Julia shouted up to me as she treaded water below. "Don't be chicken!"

"I don't know how to dive!" I called down to her.

"Then jump!"

"Jump! Jump!" the partiers shouted.

I felt as if I was suspended in the air like a flare, floating slowly downward to a place I could not see. The cold water was a shock, and I held my breath as I sank deeper and deeper into its murky depths.

"Are you O.K.?" Julia asked when I struggled back to the surface.

A rat brushed past one arm, and another pushed its nose against the back of my neck. The river smelled like the open sewers draining into it.

"I've had enough," I said, and began swimming for shore. "The rats sobered me up."

The diving contest continued until we heard sirens. "M.P.s," the military yelled and ran for the door. Two jeeps of military police arrived to tell us to disband immediately and return to our quarters. "I'm Doctor Ramirez," Jim told them. "We're just having a little fun."

"Sir, the sentries on the bridge called us because they could hear you all the way down there," one of the M.P.s said. "You're lucky you weren't blown up by a charge hidden in something floating down the river."

We agreed to leave, but only after we made plans to meet at the air base to see Jim and Leo off the next morning. The M.P.s waited patiently, making sure all of us left before they did. They shook their heads when we picked up our shoes and put them on over feet covered with mud and slime from climbing up the river bank. "Medical people," one of them said. "You love 'em, you hate 'em."

CHAPTER ELEVEN

The few of us who showed up at the air base the next morning still reeked of the river. Leo looked peculiar with a coarse stubble of beard across his usually smooth skin.

"I'm so hungover I'll be sick all the way to Saigon," he said as he sat with his head lowered to his knees. "And this stench!" He sniffed at his arms and held them away from him. "I've taken three showers and still stink like a sewer."

"Complain to Jim," I said. "He started it." I held my own aching head.

Jim Ramirez looked as bad as Leo. "Now I know why I stayed away from parties," he groaned. He wiped constantly at his brow, which glistened with perspiration.

Jean, Julia and others looked as hung over as he did. Both men paled when they saw a large C-130 taxi toward the hangar where we waited. The dependable military transport was notorious for not being air-conditioned, as well as riding like a roller coaster.

The plane shut down its droning engines and a wide ramp under its tail section was lowered to the steaming asphalt. Military passengers immediately deplaned and formed up ranks. As they marched off, we saw two airmen struggling down the ramp with an elderly woman who looked near death.

"I'll bet she's my replacement," Leo said.

"Oh great," Shelly said. "Whistler's Mother."

"Good luck," Leo said. He kissed Shelly goodbye, then took me in his arms.

"I don't want you to leave," I said as I struggled to suppress tears. "We'll never manage without you."

"You'll be fine," he said with a weak smile. "We're the ones who have to get on that plane." He and Jim walked slowly across the tarmac. "Don't forget to write," Leo called before they disappeared into the bowels of the transport. I was watching the plane taxi laboriously away when Shelly suggested we claim our new anesthetist.

The two airmen were happy to transfer the limp weight of the woman draped between them to our shoulders. "She vomited the whole trip," one of them said.

"You'll be all right as soon as we get you to a bed so you can lie down," Shelly told her.

While we practically dragged our grey-haired anesthetist to our car, she managed to tell us her name was Gertie. "Be careful where you step," I cautioned when a piece of charred metal crunched beneath one of her feet. "They haven't cleared away all the rubble from the last attack."

Gertie suddenly seemed to realize she was somewhere different and stood up straight to take in her surroundings. "What happened to all those planes?" she asked, indicating several burned-out skeletons of aircraft pushed to one side of a nearby taxiway.

"I guess Saigon didn't tell you what happened up here," Shelly said. "The air base was hit last week."

Gertie looked confused. "But, dear girl, why did our boys do such a thing?"

Shelly looked at me, then back to Gertie. "Our guys didn't do it," she said hesitantly. "The enemy did."

Gertie let out a high-pitched laugh. "God, girl, I'm glad to hear that. You hear such strange things about this war back home you don't know what to believe."

When we put Gertie up front with Julia, she sank back into the seat with a deep sigh. "I can't wait to get to my suite so I can have a cool bath and lie down in the air-conditioning." Julia turned to give an "Oh, oh" look before starting the engine.

Shelly and Jean sitting on either side of me poked me in the ribs as they struggled not to laugh.

Because she still looked so pale, we took Gertie directly to temporary housing so she could lie down. "There must be some mistake," she said when Shelly opened the door to the room she would occupy. "I'm certainly not expected to stay in this drab little closet." She made no move to enter the room identical to mine.

"Everyone stays here until they get permanent quarters," Shelly told her.

"I was here four months before I got a house."

"Four months!" The overweight Gertie staggered into the room and dropped to the bed whose springs groaned as she sunk into it. "I should never have listened to that man from Washington," she wailed. "He promised me a beautiful suite of rooms when he told me I had to come over here."

"What do you mean had to?" Shelly asked.

"When he came to our hospital in Two Oaks, Montana, and said he needed an anesthetist for Vietnam," Gertie said without taking a breath. "The other anesthetist was pregnant so I had no choice but to come."

"But you didn't have to," I said. "You could have refused."

"You mean I didn't have to leave Two Oaks!" Her face turned so red I was glad she was lying down.

"Look, we can take you over to headquarters and you can explain what happened." I looked to Shelly for help, but she had turned her back to conceal her laughter. "When they realize you didn't understand this was a volunteer thing, I'm sure they'll let you return home."

"God girl, I don't know if I can make that trip again." Gertie wore a heavy polyester pantsuit, which I suggested she remove. "I don't want anything out of my suitcase," she said when I started to open her bag to find something cooler. "I'm not staying long enough to unpack."

Shelly went to the bathroom and wet a towel to put across Gertie's brow. "You just lie here and rest," she said. "We'll take care of everything." We assured her we would be back to take her to headquarters as soon as we completed our morning cases.

"How the hell could they promise someone a suite of rooms in this mule-shit pie?" Shelly asked back in the car.

"How could they tell us we would be working in a modern, well-equipped hospital?" Julia replied.

It was well after noon when we managed to get free of the hospital and went to pick up our ailing colleague. Gertie was waiting with a picture of a plush hotel suite gripped tightly in one hand, her suitcase in the other.

"This is what my room was supposed to look like," she said as she shoved the photograph toward us. "That man from Washington gave me his word."

"Did he give you this picture?" I asked. It looked as if it had been clipped from a magazine.

"No, but that's what he described," Gertie said defensively.

Shelly looked at the photograph and returned it to Gertie. "Not even generals live like that," she said. "The guy you talked to has probably never been over here."

Gertie held a handkerchief over her nose as we drove her through town to USAID headquarters. We guided her inside, supported between us, and told Commander Miles' secretary it was urgent that we see him. "I'm sorry, the commander isn't in," the secretary replied. She was no older than Shelly or me, and I wondered if her boss treated her the same way he did most women.

"That's all right, we'll wait," I said.

"For two weeks?" the secretary said. "He's in Hawaii."

"Oh god!" Gertie shrieked. "Oh sweet Jesus!" Perspiration rolled from beneath her grey hair and down her plump face.

"You have to calm down," I said as we lowered her to a chair. Shelly grabbed a newspaper from a nearby table to fan her. "Mouse, get her something cold to drink."

A Vietnamese worker brought a glass of water, as well as several of her coworkers who were attracted from adjoining offices by Gertie's cries. They picked up the magazine picture that had fallen to the floor and congratulated Gertie on her number-one house in America.

Commander Miles' secretary was becoming concerned. "She looks awful," she said. "Maybe you should take her over to your hospital."

"Can you imagine how she would look when she realized that's where she's supposed to work?" Shelly asked.

"Well, she can't just get on a plane and go home without clearing it with Washington." The secretary wore perfume, which was a pleasant relief from the stench of our hospital.

"It has to be cleared with Washington?" I asked. "We would be sending memos for months."

Gertie's eyes flickered open. "I have to stay here four months?" she asked weakly.

"Don't worry," I said. "We'll have you out of here long before that." Shelly helped me get her to her feet, and we half carried her to the door. "We're going to take you back to your room now so you can rest," I told her.

"My room?" she said weakly. "You mean my tomb."

"I think we may be dealing with a terminal case of culture shock," Shelly whispered to me over Gertie's head.

We got our ailing anesthetist to bed, and paid the old Ba who looked after our building to watch her until we returned from work. We were almost out the door when I recalled how frightened I was my first night in Danang. "Don't worry if you hear a little gunfire," I said. "It's nothing to worry about during the daytime."

"Gunfire!" Gertie sat up so abruptly I thought she would fall off her narrow bed. "God girl, nobody told me I would be near the front lines!"

"Nice going, Mouse," Shelly said.

"I was just trying to reassure her."

"Into a coronary?"

It took us several minutes to calm her. "We'll come get you for dinner," Shelly told her when we started to leave the second time.

"I don't want anything," Gertie said in a feeble voice. "Just home."

"She's probably dehydrated from all the vomiting she did on the plane," Shelly said. "We really should get some food and fluids into her."

"It's steak night at the club," I said. "Jean and I could haul her over there with our dates." Shelly was going to Navy Hospital to see Tom.

It looked as if we would not be able to get Gertie out of her room, until Jean told her she would probably be too sick to travel the next day if she didn't eat. Darkness had fallen and Gertie was frightened by the flares being shot over the city, despite assurances by both Rick and Jerry that they were only for illumination. I was glad we had the two men to get Gertie from their jeep to the club.

"Let's get her a drink," Jerry suggested when we reached the bar. "She looks like she could use one."

Gertie had downed two Manhattans when an inebriated young lieutenant put money in the jute box and asked her to dance. We didn't see her the remainder of the evening.

"We have to find her," I said when it came time to leave and she still could not be located. "It's her first night here; she'll panic when the fighting starts up at midnight."

"I don't think the old girl will mind a few mortars tonight," Rick said with a smile. "She's apparently found someone she feels can protect her."

I went to check Gertie's room when we got to temporary housing, but no one answered. When I woke the next morning, I dressed and went immediately to check again.

"God girl, I overslept," Gertie said when she came to the door after several knocks. Her grey hair was tousled and she tried to smooth it while holding the door open only a crack. "I'll get dressed and be right with you. I'm so anxious to see the hospital and start my new job." Her voice was so strong and cheerful, I could not believe it was the same person we had spent the previous day cajoling.

She started to close the door and the sheet draped around her body accidentally slid to the floor, revealing a stretch-mark ravaged body as pitiful as Sophie's. When she dove for the sheet, the door was inadvertently knocked open. There, in her bed, lay a stark naked young man sleeping blissfully.

"God, girl, I'll be right with you," Gertie said as she slammed the door in my face.

I fled down the stairs to where the others waited in the car. "What's that young guy going to do when he wakes up and realizes he's been screwing an old grey-haired lady?" I said between whoops of laughter.

"He won't care," Shelly said. "She has round eyes and no grenades."

CHAPTER TWELVE

A month passed in relative calm, giving Ron an opportunity to make an impressive dent in our unending backlog of patients waiting for surgery. The chest surgeons were doing a series of cases on children with empyema, a complication of tuberculosis which left their lungs scarred and unable to expand properly. The thoracic professor and his resident were excited about the opportunity to conduct such a study, and it provided an excellent learning experience for a group of medical students we had recently inherited.

The students had been attending classes in Hue, the old imperial city north of Danang, at a small medical school staffed by German physicians. The North Vietnamese overran the school, killing most of the staff and many of the students, then burned it down. The few students who managed to escape made their way to Danang, where they hoped to continue their education at our hospital.

Although we could offer them no formal program, each of us wrote to medical contacts back home to collect text books, and the surgeons invited them into the operating rooms to assist on cases. Our Vietnamese staff was so proud of their sophisticated countrymen they competed for the opportunity to work in a room where they assisted. Their eagerness, combined with an ample number of surgeons, produced an efficiency we had only dreamed of.

The only person who seemed unhappy was Dr. Jordan. After taking two weeks to acclimate his sweat glands, he soon found another reason to avoid the operating rooms.

“Let’s get to work,” he said with forced bravado on his first day in surgery. “I’m ready to tackle anything.” He went to the scrub sink, reached for the spigot and let out a horrified scream.

Ron came running from the doctor’s lounge, pulling on his scrub shirt.

"What happened?"

Dr. Jordan stood back from the sink, pointing an accusing finger. "That sink is full of shit!"

Ron looked in and grabbed his nose. "It must have been the squatters," he said through pinched nostrils. "Somebody get Jean."

"I'm already here." Jean came through the swinging doors, having just completing her morning cattle drive.

"Someone shit in the scrub sink," Ron said in a defeated tone.

"Some <u>one</u>?" she said as she peered into the sink. "It looks like some gang."

"I'm going to report you!" Dr. Jordan screamed at her.

"Report me for what? I didn't do it."

She found our janitors and instructed them to clean up the mess. The rest of us stood watching a short distance away, like a crowd gathered around a fatal automobile accident.

"I guess it says something about us that none of us smelled it," Shelly said.

"I wonder why they would waste all that fertilizer," Julia said. "They must not have been able to make it to the garden."

Dr. Jordan overheard what was being said. "You let your patients defecate on their garden?" he asked in a near whisper.

"It's not restricted just to patients," Shelly said. "Their families can use it too."

The surgeon's face paled beneath his scraggly beard. "This place is a pigsty!" he said. "You people have lost all sense of decency and cleanliness!" He spoke so forcefully, droplets of spittle flew from his mouth.

"I wasn't decent when I came over here," Shelly told him. "As for cleanliness, you seem to be attracting as many flies as the rest of us."

Dr. Jordan stopped his frantic swatting and turned on her, but Ron intervened. "That's enough," he said before it could go any further. He took Dr. Jordan to Dr. Fitch's air-conditioned office to wait until the sink was cleaned.

When the janitors had completed their part of the task, Jean filled the contaminated sink with a strong bleach solution and left it to soak. Since there was no other place to scrub, she had a new garbage can filled with water to use until the sink was sufficiently disinfected.

"How do you expect us to follow aseptic technique with everyone scrubbing in the same water?" Dr. Jordan asked when he returned to the

O.R. “And in a garbage can to boot.”

“Would you rather use the sink?” Jean asked.

“Get me the head nurse!”

“I am the head nurse.”

He left the O.R., refusing to return until we started taking our work seriously. The sink was returned to service the next morning, but Dr. Jordan was busy with a personal crusade to teach our patients not to defecate on their vegetables. I was watching his attempts at conversion from the window of triage when the Seabees brought in the sawhorses they had built for us.

“Would you consider another project?” I asked when we had the occupied stretchers resting on the wooden supports.

“We’re still working on the damage Uncle Ho did to the air base,” one of the Seabees said. “And we got those screens to put in the shacks out back.”

“We need some toilets, too,” I said. “They don’t have to be fancy, just fast.”

They exchanged amused looks. “We can build ’em,” one of them said. “But you aren’t going to teach gooks to use ’em.”

“Maybe not, but we have someone who will certainly try.”

When I mentioned the plan to Dr. Jordan, he immediately began work on elaborate architectural drawings. Dr. Fitch not only sanctioned the project, he enthusiastically joined Dr. Jordan in the planning. Three weeks later the outhouses were a reality.

“He’s almost pleasant lately,” Jean said as she watched Dr. Jordan coaxing people into them. “Thank god for Seabees.”

“I just hope no one tells him they’re saving it up until he goes home at night,” Julia said as she ground out a cigarette.

The dedicated reformer had to be talked into taking time off to attend a Sunday afternoon party Margaret’s boyfriend Keith had arranged in Hoi An, a small city fifteen miles south of Danang.

“Did you clear it with Doctor Fitch?” I asked when Margaret inquired as to whether I was going. I reminded her the acting chief did not allow us outside the ten mile perimeter of Danang without express permission.

“I even invited him,” Margaret replied.

Shelly refused the invitation. “It’s bad enough being assigned to the same house with Margaret,” she said. “She’s only inviting us because a bunch of old men want an afternoon’s entertainment with some American women.”

Jean was spending the day with Rick, but Julia decided not to pass up an opportunity to see something outside of Danang, which was the same reason

I accepted. Because the roads were too insecure for land travel, we would be transported to Hoi An by helicopters Keith had arranged.

"Come on, we can't keep these machines waiting all day," Margaret shouted to us. "There's a war to be fought, you know." She stood on the helicopter pad located out by the bridge. Two large helicopters sat just behind her with their wide blades drooping almost to the ground.

"You could treat us with a little respect," Dr. Jordan told her as he boarded one of them. He had two cameras and a set of binoculars hanging around his neck. "After all, we did give up two months of our time to help you people out."

"I thought you were here to help the Vietnamese," Margaret said.

Dr. Gregory smiled and took a seat opposite his colleague inside the chopper. Despite frequent reminders from the crew, Dr. Jordan had to be repeatedly pulled to safety when he ventured too close to the open doors to get a better photograph of the jungle below.

It was exhilarating to fly above the green landscape, where vapors of steam rose into the air to greet us. The gunner stationed at the rear door sporadically returned fire when puffs of smoke erupted from the dense foliage, but the trip was otherwise uneventful.

Several jeeps were waiting for us at the landing pad in Hoi An, and we were quickly transported to a villa in the center of the small town. It had cavernous rooms with high ceilings, the same as Shelly's, but there was a pleasant courtyard surrounding it. Tables and chairs were set up, and two men in Australian bush hats entertained the guests with music from a guitar and concertina, which they sang to.

Most of the men looked to be over fifty, with meticulously groomed silver hair and tanned faces. They wore tailored dark slacks, light blue shirts and expensive loafers, the same attire I had seen on Americans in fancy hotels and restaurants in Saigon.

Margaret was playing hostess, using manners and a smile I had never seen. Her blond hair hung loosely down her back and she wore a bright sun-dress that flattered her trim figure. Her eyes followed Keith, who made the rounds talking to everyone present. There was ice for the drinks and the conversation was polite.

"The men seem a little old," I whispered to Julia when we met at the refreshment table.

"They're all high-ranking CIA," she said quietly. I looked to where Keith stood next to Margaret. He was younger than the other men, but he was dressed the same. His hair was as red as Shelly's and he had a charming smile.

"Margaret dates a guy from the American Consulate?" I whispered.

"Don't try to figure it out," Julia said. "Margaret defies all logic."

Julia joined the Aussies singing. She wore a mini-dress and the older men almost drooled watching her. They all used bogus job titles rather than say they were with the CIA; resettlement officer, linguist, even an agricultural advisor.

When I tired of talking to them, I wandered off to the rear area of the courtyard. I was sipping at my drink, looking over the back yard when someone behind me spoke.

"Could I show you around?"

When I turned to see who had spoken, I had to lean back to look up into the face of the man smiling down at me.

"I saw you leave the others and wanted to make sure you were O.K." His name was Dan Cowan and his hair was chocolate brown rather than grey. "You don't want to go wandering too far back here," he said. "Hoi An isn't Danang."

"I was curious about the trench." I pointed to a long, zigzag ditch that ran the entire length of the rear of the house. "What's it for?"

"To jump in when Charlie comes to town," Dan said. "Would you like to see it up close?"

I nodded and we walked across a strip of grass to the concrete shelter. He jumped down into it and reached up for me as if I were a child.

There were machine guns at regular intervals along the trench, with a plastic lawn chair sitting behind two of them. "The Aussies believe in comfort," Dan said. When he smiled a deep dimple appeared in his left cheek.

"What are these?" I started to pick up a wire leading off into some high grass beyond a barbed wire fence.

"Hey, don't pull those." He grabbed my wrist and I let the wire drop. "They're attached to claymore mines," he said. "If you pull the wire you'll set them off." He carefully rearranged it to where it was before I touched it.

"I'm sorry."

"That's all right," he said gently. "I'm sorry if I scared you."

"Where are the mines?" I asked when we moved on.

"Out there in the elephant grass." He pointed to the field of tall grass. "If Charlie tries to sneak up on us he's in for a surprise."

We continued down the trench to a blockhouse at one end. It was heavily sandbagged and was stacked with helmets, flak jackets, ammunition, water and C rations. "We spend a lot of nights out here," Dan told me. His wrinkled cotton slacks and shirt did not fit with the others at the party any more than his age. "Charlie's like a dog," he said with a short laugh. "He can't pass Hoi An without lifting his leg."

"I guess you must be a civilian?" I didn't want to ask directly if he was with the CIA.

His hazel eyes let me know he understood the real question. "I'm with the Marine Corps," he said. "I'm just assigned to this place."

"Isn't that unusual?" I wondered if the Marine title was genuine, or just a cover like the others. But his hair was cut in a whitewall crew cut and he wore dog tags around his neck.

"Complicated, but not unusual." He had to walk sideways in the trench because of the width of his shoulders. "I'm with the pacification program," he said. "We're securing an island not far from here that used to be infiltrated with Cong." His face softened when he spoke of the island. "We've managed to get some agricultural programs started and we built a school."

"It sounds nice."

"Maybe you could visit sometime. It's just across the river." Hoi An had even more waterways than Danang.

"I would like that." It was my first time outside the ten mile perimeter of Danang and it felt wonderful.

He swung himself up out of the trench and reached a large hand down to help me. When we returned to the courtyard, Julia was singing a rousing rendition of Waltzing Matilda with the two Australian musicians.

"The Aussies are a lot of fun to have around," Dan said. "The one playing the concertina goes by Bird-dog. He got the name because he likes to walk point when we go out on patrol; claims Australians have a better nose for Cong."

Keith and Margaret had trouble rounding everyone up when it came time to leave. Hoi An was not considered secure after dusk and all civilians, with the exception of the CIA, had to vacate the area.

"Could I visit you sometime?" Dan asked on the way to the chopper pad. "Maybe see your hospital." He drove the jeep I rode in and Bird-dog sat in the back with Julia singing.

"You can visit me," I said. "But I'm not so sure you would want to visit the hospital."

"It can't be that bad."

"Come smell for yourself." His dimple showed when he turned to smile at me.

"Goodbye me darlin's," Bird-dog called as we lifted up into the air. Dan stood waving until the jungle closed in on him.

The trip didn't take long, but Julia managed to lose one of her sandals out the open door of the chopper, where we sat with our legs dangling. In her inebriated state, she insisted the pilot set down so she could look for it.

"Lady, I can't land in the middle of the goddamned jungle!" the pilot shouted back to her above the noise of the rotating blades. "You shouldn't be hanging your legs out the door!"

"They were my best shoes," Julia said. "I waited months for Sears to ship them to me."

"Wait a couple of weeks," Margaret told her. "One of our patients will show up wearing it."

Julia considered a moment, then threw the other shoe out the door. "Might as well give her a matching pair."

The chopper was hovering over the landing pad in Danang, just before setting down, when Dr. Gregory got up and stepped out into midair. It wasn't far to the ground, but he scraped his face and elbows on the rough wire mesh of the pad. "I'll be all right," he assured Ron when he hurried to his assistance as soon as we set down. "I can still operate." He held up both hands, which he had miraculously managed to protect from injury.

"Fitch will kill me for letting him get hurt," Ron said when Dr. Gregory was out of earshot.

"He'll probably kill all of us if he finds out we went to Hoi An," Margaret said. "We didn't have his permission to leave Danang."

"I thought you told me you invited him to the party?" I said.

"I did. But I didn't say he accepted."

I was too happy to care. The smell of the hospital was out of my nostrils for the first time in months, and I was remembering Dan standing on the chopper pad waving, wondering if he really would come to see me.

CHAPTER THIRTEEN

The quiet of the previous month was broken when a thunderous rumble woke me from my sleep. More noise followed, causing my window and door to rattle.

"It's destroyers off the coast giving support to our land troops," Jean said when I went to her room to see if we should evacuate the building. "Their guns make a lot of noise and shake things around, but they're not aimed at us."

"I have a brother on a destroyer somewhere out there," I said. "He's a career man in the Navy." I returned to my room with a new worry. If American ships were firing at the enemy, wouldn't the enemy be firing back?

Another orthopedic surgeon was now assigned to Navy Hospital, freeing Tom to do some cases at ours. When I saw him in the O.R. the next morning, I asked how I could find out if my brother's ship was in the area.

"All ship movements are classified," he said. "You can't find out where they are, or where they're going."

The few letters I exchanged with my brother had to go all the way back to the States, then back to Vietnam through our respective Fleet Post Office addresses. They were more than two months old by the time we received them.

Tom's corpsman, Fast Eddie, had come to the hospital with him to assist with his cases. The two were inseparable; Tom cut and Fast Eddie clamped without having to be told. They were like two parts of the same machine, four hands working steadily without any hesitation as to what must be done next.

"When your brother's ship goes in for maintenance, it most likely will go into Taiwan," Fast Eddie told me as we finished up the case we were doing.

His eyes were so round and innocent, I still found it difficult to believe he led a double life: his role as a corpsman at Navy Hospital, which he executed with undisputed competence, and his second one as husband to an illegal Vietnamese wife, who was rumored to be pregnant.

"How often do they go in for maintenance?" I asked.

"Depends on how much shooting they're doing. Destroyers have to get their big guns refired if they're using them a lot."

Casualties were beginning to arrive and I turned my attention to them. But as I worked I could not help wondering if any of them were injured by the guns on my brother's ship.

"I've told the chest surgeons they won't be able to finish their study unless we get some supplies," Jean told us at the end of the day. "I have barely enough for emergencies."

The chest surgeons had only two weeks remaining of their tour, and all of us agreed that their contribution to the team had been invaluable. After a brief discussion, we decided to defy the orders of our leaders and get whatever was necessary for them to complete their work.

"I guess I could make a run to Navy Hospital," Shelly said. "The C.O. is off my scent since I haven't been cumshawing."

"I could try going out to that Green Beret Camp where Leo used to get things," I offered. Leo's last trip to the camp had been just before his departure, and the men had given him generous quantities of medical supplies they were unable to use because of the attack on the air base. There was no time for them to practice medicine on the locals when there was fighting to do.

Gail volunteered to go to her sources at the Army Hospital, and Greg asked to accompany Shelly to Navy to pick up the latest batch of outdated blood. We were gathered in the parking lot coordinating our plans when Dr. Fitch came out and demanded to know where we were going.

"You're not off duty for another hour." He held up his watch for us to see.

"The O.R. is down to emergency rations," Jean told him. "We can't do cases unless we get something to work with."

"I will get whatever is necessary," he replied in his patient missionary tone. "But it will be through proper channels."

"The chest surgeons have several cases to complete before they leave," Jean argued. "We need the things now."

Dr. Fitch was not dissuaded. "I will take care of it."

"Can you take care of it by morning?" Dr. Gregory had come out of the hospital with Ron and stood waiting for an answer. Dr. Fitch was momentarily distracted by the red and blue abrasions on his face from his premature exit from the helicopter.

We had kept the trip to Hoi An quiet and worried that Dr. Fitch would find out. But Dr. Gregory gave no indication that anything was out of the ordinary as our chief studied his abraded face.

"It might take me a little longer than one day to get a shipment," Dr. Fitch said when he stopped staring. "But I guarantee I'll get what you need to complete your study."

"I hope so," Dr. Gregory said. "Or I'll have to recommend to the AMA that it stop sending physicians to this hospital."

Our chief's hand trembled as he reached up to his beard. After only a few moments deliberation, he gave in. "All right," he said, turning to us. "You can get what you need this one time, but only because it's a special case."

The Green Beret gave me twice what I requested, with one condition. They asked that during the next lull in fighting we nurses attend a party at their camp, located south of Marble Mountain.

"We don't have anything fancy for a club," one of the men in the supply hut told me. "Just a lot of lonely guys who would like to say hello to some round-eye women."

"You let us know when," I said. "And we'll be there."

"Yes, ma'am." He saluted out of habit, even though he knew I wasn't military.

I was especially grateful for the carload of supplies when we arrived at work the next morning and found several fresh casualties already waiting for us in triage. One of them was a young man who was shot through the chest and had a collapsed lung. He was having difficulty breathing and was taken directly to the O.R. from x-ray, where Dr. Gregory, his resident and the medical students from Hue set to work. Chest tubes were almost in place when the patient's heart suddenly shifted in the chest cavity from the air leaking into the chest.

"Push oxygen to him," Dr. Gregory told Becky, who was at the head of the table. She pumped as hard as she could on the breathing bag but could not get air into the collapsed lung. Shelly and I were about to take over when one of the medical students went to her aid. He managed to force enough air in to fully inflate the good lung while Dr. Gregory finished with the chest tubes. Without direction, another medical student had begun compressing the patient's chest to help the weakened heart pump sufficient blood through the body. When the offending air was removed through the chest tubes, the lung inflated fully and the heart returned to its normal position and began beating more vigorously.

Several members of the Vietnamese staff had gathered in the room to observe. An expression of pride was on their faces as they watched Becky and the two medical students doing the resuscitation almost single-handedly. Only Lan looked displeased, standing to one side clicking his claw.

"Number one, huh?" one of our anesthesia students, Mr. Shat, said to Shelly when the patient began to improve. He was the same student who had run away after the previous resuscitation.

"Better than number one," Shelly replied.

"So much for the spirits," I said to her.

Gail came into the room with the patient's x-rays. "I think you'd better take a look at these," she said as she held the films up to the windows.

"Uh-oh, looks like we have a bit more work to do," Dr. Gregory said. The unmistakable outline of a bullet appeared mid-chest.

"It looks like it's in the heart," Dr. Gregory's resident said in a voice that bespoke inexperience. "How in the world can you go after that?"

Dr. Gregory studied the films more closely. "I think it's lodged in the myocardium," he said, referring to the muscular wall of the heart. "He's sure as hell going to die if we don't get it out of there. We might as well give it a try."

Shelly left to get blood and I went to the head of the table to help Becky. We would give the patient only morphine and oxygen, since his condition was too unstable to risk anything stronger.

The surgeons made an incision from the top of the patient's sternum to his abdomen, then began the difficult task of cutting through the ribs with our rusted rib-cutter. Neither complained, even though they were accustomed to accomplishing the task in only minutes with a power saw. The instant the chest was open, a deluge of clots gurgled to the surface. I worried that we would not have enough blood, and if we did, that it was not right to use so much on one patient. But the Vietnamese team had done so well resuscitating the young man, it was important to give it our best effort.

"His blood is starting to look like Hawaiian Punch from all the fluid I've pumped into him," I told Shelly when she came in with additional units of blood. I had started two I.V.s on the patient and had plasma and intravenous fluid pouring into them. "Do you think you could get me some fresher stuff?" I asked when I saw the dates on the bags she handed me. "He'll ooze like crazy if we load him up with this old crap."

"I'll try," she said. "But he doesn't have any relatives to donate. Not that the peasants would give it to him anyway," she added while she helped me hang the blood we had. Dr. Gregory looked disapprovingly at her over the anesthesia screen. "I'll be right back," she said and left the room.

"Don't pull the plug until I catch up on the blood loss," I told the surgeons. They weren't sure how far into the heart muscle the bullet had penetrated, and I was afraid of a rapid hemorrhage when they removed it.

I had pumped in all the old blood Shelly had brought when she returned with a unit still warm from the donor. "Terrific," I said, connecting the red life to one of the I.V.s. "Where did you get it?"

"I'm O negative," she said and left the room.

The room was sweltering in the late morning heat, and the surgeons looked near fainting as they strained to see into the deep cavity illuminated by only one overhead light. The bullet had not penetrated the inner chamber of the heart, which made it possible to remove it with a minimum of hemorrhage, but the case had tied up an O.R. and a surgical team the entire morning. Ron was handling the rest of the casualties, but our considerable investment in one patient had all of us in a somber mood.

"Jesus, it looks like there's been a massacre in here," Shelly said when she came back in to see if we needed anything. Bloody sponges and slippery clots littered the floor.

"Can you get us something to drink?" I asked. "We're all about to pass out."

Jean decided the decrepit air-conditioner jutting out of the wall was doing nothing but making noise. "Nothing like a little breeze off the garden to perk you up," she said when she opened the windows. The smell of human feces crept into the room, along with flies that headed for the blood on the floor with the determination of kamikaze pilots.

We were beginning to close the thoracic cavity when the patient started moving his hands. "It looks like I'll have to give this guy some anesthesia," I said.

Shelly had come into the room with the drinks we ordered. "Crack in just enough ether to keep him on the table," she suggested. I opened the vaporizor only slightly and she crawled under the surgical drapes to hold the patient's wandering hands while the surgeons finished up.

The drinks were warm beer, purchased from one of the vendors who sold food outside the hospital gates. "He didn't have any Coke today," Shelly said from beneath the table. "I figured beer was better than nothing."

The Vietnamese medical students giggled when Jean offered them one and all refused. But both Dr. Gregory and his resident stepped back from the operating table so Jean could pull down their masks and hold the bottles to their parched lips while they kept their gloved hands sterile. "I hope I don't get drunk," the resident said after a long swallow.

"You'll sweat it out before it has time to get to your brain," Jean reassured.

"Mouse, hand one down here," Shelly said from her cave beneath the operating table and its sterile drapes. "I'm about to die from heat stroke."

The last of the skin sutures were being put in place when Dr. Fitch hurried into the room. "I just heard what you're doing," he said. "Let me give you a hand."

"No need," Dr. Gregory said pleasantly. "We're just finishing."

"Too bad you missed it," I said to our chief. "It's not every day we do heart surgery."

"Hey, this peasant is getting ugly," Shelly called from beneath the table. "What're you doing to him, Mouse?"

"Waking him up. We're almost done."

"I'd better hold his hands until the surgeons get away from the table," she said. "It's no telling what he might grab." Dr. Gregory laughed heartily.

The young man opened his eyes and was breathing on his own by the time we were ready to move him. I left the endotracheal tube in place and we carried him to intensive care, where Margaret had an entire bed waiting for him. She had even found a sheet to cover its stained mattress.

"I'm not sure what to tell you as far as post-op care goes," Dr. Gregory said. He looked skeptically around the crowded, ill-equipped ward.

"Why not the routine for cardiac surgery?" Margaret said in her crisp style. "A bowl of clots every three hours and a bed next to a window for oxygen. Nothing out of the ordinary."

"Don't forget to keep the worms out of his airway," Shelly added.

Dr. Gregory pulled the perspiration soaked cap from his head and ran a hand through his wet hair. "You people are something," he said. "I don't know how you manage to keep your sense of humor."

"With doctors like you," Shelly told him.

CHAPTER FOURTEEN

To our dismay, Gertie was not adapting as well to the hospital as she was to the Navy club, despite her long years of experience in anesthesia. She seemed content to watch over patients Shelly or I had first anesthetized, but that would present problems if one of us was sick or out of the country and we needed her to run an operating room on her own, or supervise students.

"I think Gertie's found the ultimate cure for senility," Shelly said. "War." We watched through the window of the lounge as she arrived for work in the jeep of an officer years her junior.

"I hate to spoil her fun," I said, "but I think it's time we broke it to her that she's not a Doughnut Dolly." I was overdue for an R&R and was working on coordinating a trip to Taiwan to see my brother. "If I can find out when my brother's ship is going into port I'm going to be on the next plane."

"God girl, my bladder's about to go off like a grenade," Gertie said as she rushed into the lounge and dove for the small lavatory adjoining it.

"The only grandmother I know with a chronic case of honeymooner's cystitis," Shelly said.

Gertie's three children were grown and had provided her with two grandchildren, but only after years of struggle on Gertie's part. Her husband had deserted the family when the youngest was a baby, leaving her to raise them on her own. Gertie had been forced to live a spare life in the small town of Two Oaks, Montana, with little time or money for herself. All that had changed when she suddenly found herself surrounded by thousands of lonely men, and drawing a paycheck she had to spend only on herself.

The first case of the morning was a spinal, which Gertie could not get in after three attempts. Watching her proved so nerve-wracking, I had difficulty getting it in myself when I took over.

"I'll be back in a couple of minutes," I told her when the case was underway. I went to the lounge and smoked a cigarette, our only luxury, while I contemplated ways to tell her she simply was not working out.

But the decision to get rid of Gertie was not mine, and I found my attention wandering to other things. The new toilets the Seabees had built were visible through the window of the lounge, and I watched as patients and their families crowded into them. There still seemed to be an abundance of fertilizer on the thriving garden, but I had to admit Dr. Jordan had been successful in his campaign to get people into the unfamiliar facilities. They always seemed to be occupied.

"Mouse, you're wanted in the O.R.," Julia said when she struck her head into the lounge on the way to recovery with a patient.

I snuffed out my cigarette and got up. "What's Gertie done now?"

"I don't know, but I could hear Dr. Jordan screaming when I passed her room."

The patient they were working on was from the shacks and needed a skin graft to cover an open wound on her leg. Ron was doing the surgery and Dr. Jordan was assisting, since his success with the toilets now allowed him time for surgery.

"What's the matter?" I asked Gertie.

"God girl, they've lost the skin graft." She was searching the floor with the Vietnamese circulating nurse, while her patient lay unattended.

"You should have had it all ready to hand to us," Dr. Jordan berated the bewildered looking scrub nurse who handed instruments. "We spend all this time taking a suitable graft and you go and lose it." The scrub nurse shrugged her shoulders and chattered in Vietnamese as she searched the operative field for the missing piece of flesh.

Ron finished debriding the wound and began looking for a sight from which to take a new graft. But the patient had third-degree burns over much of her body and had little skin to spare.

"Here it is!" Gertie pulled the withered piece of skin from a trash bucket, where it had been accidentally thrown, and held it up triumphantly.

"Rinse it off in some antiseptic and give it to me," Ron ordered.

"You're not actually going to use that!" Dr. Jordan backed away from the table in disbelief.

"She's going to have infected bone if I don't get this damned hole covered," Ron replied.

"But that's dirty!"

"So's her leg." He was already smoothing the graft in place. "She'll be pissing down it in a couple of hours." We were all familiar with Vietnamese women just pulling up one wide leg of their black pants to empty their bladders.

"God boy, isn't that the truth," Gertie said over the anesthesia screen. Dr. Jordan ran to get Jean and gave her an hysterical rundown while pointing an accusing finger at Ron.

"So what's the problem? You found the graft."

"I'm going to report you." Dr. Jordan's vocal cords were so tight he could barely speak.

"At least it's not for shit," Jean said.

Julia had come in to gather dirty instruments and get them ready for another case. The frustrated surgeon tore down his surgical mask to reveal a rigidly set jaw. He looked first at Jean, then at the others in the room. Without a word, he grabbed the basin of rotted tissue and pus Ron had removed from the wound and marched over to the window.

"Hey, that's the patient's garden!" Julia yelled when he opened the window and tossed it out onto the greenery.

"So what! A little pus can't hurt when you were already letting them shit on it!"

"Pus is not the same as shit!"

"Oh, Christ, we're back to shit again," Jean said.

"That's it, I'm finished with this disgusting pit you call an operating room!" Dr. Jordan peeled off his gown and gloves, threw them to the floor and left. We did not hear from him again until days later, when an unanticipated crisis arose with the toilets.

It had been another long day of battle trauma, and we left the hospital with the unspoken hope that there would be water in our quarters to wash the blood and dirt from our exhausted bodies. No one reacted when Dr. Jordan came running across the compound yelling for help.

"Fire! Fire!" He frantically waved his arms toward the newly constructed toilets, which had smoke billowing from the ventilation holes near their roofs. "Somebody get water!" he shouted. "Call the fire department!"

"What fire department?" Shelly said.

Dr. Fitch scurried out of the hospital with a precious jerry can of drinking water we had managed to get from the Navy Club, followed by a crowd of curious patients and relatives. We stood watching with the Vietnamese as doctors Fitch and Jordan clawed at the locked door of the toilet with the most smoke. When it finally opened, a group of terror-stricken peasants emerged. Dr. Fitch splashed the water into the open door and a cloud of vapor rolled out to engulf him. When it cleared he rushed inside with Dr. Jordan.

"They're cooking in here!" Dr. Jordan screamed. "They're living in my toilets!"

"Why not?" Margaret said. "They're the nicest buildings in town."

We took turns peering into the structures, where cooking areas had been made by placing scraps of wire mesh over the holes. "Very nice," Shelly said as she looked up at the personal belongings hanging from the rafters. "Second story storage and an ash hole for each family."

"Goddamned stupid gooks, cooking and shitting in the same place!" Dr. Jordan shouted behind us. "You can't teach them basic hygiene!"

"Maybe you could teach them to shit somewhere else," Margaret said. "The garden might be nice."

Dr. Jordan glared at her, then bestowed upon each of us the same message. "You're all insane!" he shrieked. "A bunch of uncaring disgusting degenerates!" He was so distraught, I actually found myself feeling sorry for him. "I try to do my best to improve conditions and you go around behind my back sabotaging everything I do!"

"Now, wait a minute," Julia interrupted. "We didn't tell these people to set up housekeeping in the outhouses. Can't you understand that desperate people are driven to desperate action?"

"And we did get the toilets built for you," I reminded the unhappy physician.

"But not before I initiated the drive to clean this place up." He threw open his arms to encompass the misery of the shacks and the overflowing verandas. "None of you gave a damn before I came here."

"FNG," Shelly said.

"And what's that supposed to be?" Dr. Jordan demanded.

"Fucking new guy," she replied. "That's what the military calls newcomers who think they have all the answers."

"I'm not staying another day!" Dr. Jordan screamed. "I'm going back home and blowing the whistle on all of you!" Dr. Fitch tried to calm the distraught surgeon, but he left for home the following morning, via Hong Kong, Tokyo and Hawaii.

Jean was at USAID headquarters, answering to Commander Miles about the cause of Dr. Jordan's sudden departure when she received notice that she would finally be getting permanent quarters. But it would not be Leo's apartment, which had been undergoing a refurbishing before being occupied by its next tenant.

"The nursing instructor who's been in the States on sick leave is coming back and she wants an apartment to herself," Jean told me when she returned from headquarters. "That means Leo's apartment."

"But I thought you were supposed to get it." I could feel indignation rising in me.

"They offered me another place, along with the next person on the housing list." She gave me one of her infrequent smiles. "I guess we'll be going through some more midnight attacks together."

"Me? I'm the next one on the list?"

"Actually, Commander Miles' secretary is, but she's waiting for another place she has her eye on."

I couldn't believe my good fortune. Not only would I be living with Jean, but she told me the quarters we would be moving into were right next to Shelly, Julia, and Margaret's.

"It's a new place USAID is converting to American housing," Jean explained. "Our apartment will be upstairs and the Chinese family that owns the place will live downstairs."

"Let's go see it." I grabbed her arm to hurry her along.

"It's not ready yet," she protested.

"I don't care, I want to see it!"

Workmen were replacing windows and carrying up pipes for plumbing repairs on the old villa. The Chinese family that occupied the first floor stood watching the conversion of their upper story to American housing, for which Uncle Sam would pay them a ransom price in rent.

The workmen didn't object when we climbed the narrow staircase leading to the upper floor. The apartment was spacious, with French doors like Shelly's opening onto a narrow balcony that overlooked the same street. There was one large bedroom at the front of the house and a smaller one in the rear, which I offered to take. Both rooms had already been outfitted with government issue furniture, drapes and bed linens. Even the windows had been crisscrossed with wide tape to prevent glass from flying inward should they shatter during an attack.

Next to an apartment back home, the accommodations would be considered third-rate; the bathroom had mossy smelling water provided by an open storage tank on the roof, and the kitchen had only a couple of cupboards and a broken down refrigerator that was not presently running because of a power failure. Small lizard-like geckos chased one another up and down the peeling walls, and there would be no heat in the monsoon season. But compared to men slogging through snake and leech-infested jungles where they might spill their life's blood in one horrifying moment, we would be living in decadent splendor.

The expectation of soon having permanent quarters was enough to raise my spirits higher than they had been my entire four months in-country. But another surprise awaited me the next day.

I offered to work through siesta while the others went home for lunch and a rest from the suffocating midday heat. The O.R. team had just left the hospital when Shelly unexpectedly returned.

"There's someone outside to see you," she told me. "Why don't you take siesta off and I'll cover."

"Who is it?" For a moment I dared to hope my brother had been allowed on land to visit me.

"I don't know, but he's tall, dark and handsome."

I peeked out the window of triage, where I saw Dan standing by a jeep occupied by Bird-dog and Julia, who wore street clothes. Dan was dressed in Marine combat attire, complete with flak jacket and helmet, but the Aussie wore fatigues and an Australian bush hat with a wide brim that had been rolled up on either side of his head. I ran to the lounge to change out of my scrub dress, comb my hair and put on lipstick.

"Hello, me darlin'," Bird-dog said as soon as I emerged from the hospital. "Irish here has been nervous as a whore in church ever since he met you." He nodded toward Dan, who blushed beneath his helmet. "I thought I best bring him up to see you."

"I thought I'd take you up on your invitation to see where you worked," Dan said. He removed his helmet and brushed a hand nervously over his short Marine white-wall. There were sergeant stripes on the sleeves of his uniform.

"I could show you around right now if you like," I said. "While it's not busy."

Bird-dog held up a cautionary hand. "Could we delay that until after lunch?" He was looking at a trail of dried blood that led up the front steps of the hospital and into the emergency room. "You Sheilas have stronger stomachs than us poor weak soldier boys."

"Bird-dog tells me he knows a good restaurant up here," Dan said. "Would you like to have lunch?"

Bird-dog was a bit older than Dan and claimed to be as good at sniffing out good food as he was Viet Cong. He guided Dan through a series of narrow streets that wound deep into an old section of the city I had never seen. The restaurant was small, and waiters in starched white jackets served exquisitely prepared food to a lunchtime crowd consisting mainly of well dressed Vietnamese. The few Americans present were dressed in rough civilian clothes and were attracting disapproving looks from the other diners.

"Contractors," Dan said when he saw me watching them. The men were laughing boisterously as they threw chunks of lobster to a pet monkey they had tied in a tree bordering the open veranda where we sat. The creature caught each morsel expertly in its front paws, leaving none to fall to the beggar below.

Even though the men were hired by the American government to build roads, bridges and airfields, they were not considered government employees, and answered to no one but themselves.

"Pigs," Julia said when one of them began grabbing at a young Vietnamese woman who brought drinks to their table. Unlike the westernized women who worked the bars and restaurants in Saigon, this woman wore traditional Vietnamese dress. Her ao dai was made of blue silk, with slits extending up both sides of the floor length garment to the waist. White pajama-like silk pants were worn beneath. Her expression made it clear she did not like the advances being made by the inebriated Americans.

Julia did not bother to lower her voice whenever she commented on the boisterous men, seated not far from our table. I was glad when the restaurant owner replaced the young woman with an elderly Vietnamese waiter, prompting the disgruntled contractors to leave. Dan appeared equally relieved when they departed.

"Everyone has the right to make an ass of himself," Bird-dog said to Julia when they were gone. He had not removed his bush hat in the restaurant, but he spoke in a quietly dignified manner.

"Not if it involves grab-ass," Julia answered.

Bird-dog leaned over and kissed her on the cheek, which caught her so off guard she nearly spilled her drink. "See that," he said. "These American Sheilas are all tough talk until we knock them over with sweetness." Dan smiled.

Julia's blue dress exactly matched her eyes.

"When can I see you again?" Dan asked on our way back to the hospital."

"When do you have to go back to Hoi An?"

"Later today. We have a meeting at our headquarters here and have to head south before sundown." He told me it was not safe to travel the road between Danang and Hoi An after dark, or during the day if one was to judge from the hand grenades in the wooden box between the two front seats of his jeep.

"Sunday is my day off," I said. "Unless we have casualties."

"Then I'll come back Sunday afternoon."

His hazel eyes looked out from beneath thick eyebrows as dark as his hair. The floor of the jeep was layered with sand bags to absorb shrapnel if he drove over a land mine, and his long legs had to accommodate by being forced up almost to his chin.

He walked with me to the door of the hospital but did not go in. I gave him a quick sketch to my new quarters, which I would move into on Saturday. "See you Sunday afternoon," he said and turned and walked quickly back to his jeep.

"Good-bye, me darlin'," Bird-dog called as the jeep pulled out of the compound, waving his bush hat at Julia, who waved back.

Becky stood just inside the door and smiled shyly at me. "Little co, big captain," she said, using her hands to show the disparity in height between Dan and me.

I was so looking forward to Dan's visit on Sunday, I wished I had not accepted an invitation to a party at the Green Beret camp on Saturday evening. But the men had now given me supplies on two occasions, and the way our shipments were once more being diverted I had no doubt I would have to go to them again.

All of the women on the team agreed to go, and a convoy of three troop trucks was sent to pick us up. Heavily armed Green Berets helped us into the back of the middle truck and seated us away from the open rear so we would not be a target for grenades. Gertie had to be boosted over the high tailgate because of her spiked heels and tight skirt.

"God boys, I'm glad they sent enough of you," she said as they heaved her inside.

"We never travel with less than three vehicles," one of the men told her. "Just in case there's an ambush."

"Ambush!" Gertie's eyes hovered on the edge of their sockets.

"There ain't nothin' to worry about, ma'am," another of the men said.

"We won't let anything happen to you."

"She looks disappointed," Shelly said next to me.

After going past Marble Mountain, we turned onto a rough dirt track leading toward the beach, a different route than I customarily took into the camp. I was happy when the bone rattling ride was over and the trucks pulled through the gates of the sprawling complex located almost on the sand. Rows of tents dotted the landscape, but we drove past all of them to a cluster of wooden buildings. The trucks stopped in front of one designated as an officers' club and we were led into a room set with tables and chairs. It was not as elaborate as the Navy Club in town, but there was a piano to one side and a bar with bottles of liquor against its back wall.

"We have a place set up outside," the grey-haired colonel who greeted us said. We followed him through the club to an outdoor patio decorated with paper lanterns.

"I thought you said we were paying back a favor to the guys," Margaret said when she looked around at the men sitting at the tables. "Not entertaining the geriatric ward."

"These aren't the guys I was referring to," I said. "It was one of the enlisted men who invited us."

I was talking to a balding lieutenant colonel when a young man dressed in muddy fatigues approached the party from the direction of the beach. He wore sergeant stripes on his uniform, the same as Dan. "I just wanted to say hi," he said, keeping in the shadows on the periphery of the patio. "I haven't seen an American woman in so long I couldn't believe my eyes when I walked past here the first time."

"Have a seat," I said. "You look like you could use one." It looked as if he hadn't showered or shaved in weeks. And his fatigues were stiff with dried mud.

The young man looked toward the colonel and shifted from one mud-caked boot to the other under his icy stare. "No thanks, ma'am, I'll just be moving along to my own club," he said. "I only wanted to say hi."

"You've already said that, sergeant," the colonel said.

"Yes, sir." He turned to leave.

"Hey, where's your club?" I asked the sergeant. None of the men who had given us supplies or escorted us to the party were anywhere to be seen, except for the sentries when we drove through the gate.

"You're asking for trouble going to an enlisted men's club, young lady," the colonel I had been talking to said when I stood to leave. "The troops just came in from two months in the boonies."

"I'll take my chances," I said. "We promised the guys."

All of the women followed the delighted sergeant down the hill to a club situated as near the beach as any buildings were allowed because of security. It was built from plywood and had only crates for chairs, but they were offered to us with the heartfelt enthusiasm of a roomful of cheering men. Cans of lukewarm beer were pressed into our hands and apologies were made for dirty uniforms and unwashed bodies. Some of the men went to their barracks for cameras and we posed for dozens of photographs.

"No one's going to believe this back in the world," one young man said.

"Shit, man. They ain't goin' to believe it in the next rice paddy," another laughed.

Someone had brought a guitar and people began singing, not rousing songs of patriotism, but soulful ballads about what they had left behind, like the Green, Green Grass of Home.

A small knot of men sitting apart from the larger group laughed each time the word grass was mentioned and waved marijuana joints in the air. When the singing ended, the men told us stories about their work with the Montagnards in the highlands.

"They'll do anything for us as long as we treat them right," one of them said. "They can sneak up on anything with those damned crossbows of theirs."

"Now if we could just teach them to handle an M16," another said.

It saddened me to hear the peaceful hill people were being drawn into the fighting. I thought about the old man with the loose intestines and was glad I did not have to look into his wizened face now that his fellow villagers were being taught how to kill.

On the way back to town two of the men talked about an outlying hamlet they planned to visit the next day. It was one of the places they visited with their Medical Civic Action Program. The men didn't seem to see the irony of engaging in search and destroy missions when the fighting was intense, then tending to some of the same people's medical needs when there was a lull in the action. I found the dual role so curious, I asked if they would take me along on their MEDCAP mission the following morning. Dan would arrive in the afternoon.

The early morning sun had already heated the jungle to a blur of greens and browns as we skimmed at tree top level. The hamlet was no more than six miles from Danang, but there were no roads to it, only narrow paths cut through the thick vegetation. When the helicopter dropped us at a portable landing pad, we donned helmets and flak jackets and climbed aboard a truck driven by a South Vietnamese soldier. I sat in the rear with my two Green Beret companions who called out, "Sin Tuc, Sin Tuc," as we bounced along the rough path.

"It means 'medicine man'," one of them told me. "That's what the locals call us."

People poured into the path behind us and ran along in our wake, laughing and waving. Some hobbled on crutches fashioned out of tree limbs.

We stopped at a shell-pocked building and unloaded boxes of medicines and bandages. I was given the job of extracting decayed teeth, without novacaine, while the men took care of the more unsavory task of cleaning and dressing jungle sores. With no dental training, I was clumsy and slow, but the people were cooperative as I struggled with the unfamiliar task. When I gave them a cough drop as a reward for holding still, some got in line a second time to have another tooth extracted.

When the teeth were finished, I dispensed malaria pills, antibiotics and aspirin. Young children led elderly grandparents suffering from the ordinary ailments of aging - arthritis, diabetes and cataracts. There was little I could do for them, but they seemed content with aspirin and an encouraging word. I was impressed by the regard the young showed their elders; the same behavior I witnessed daily in our triage. Children would squat for hours next to an injured relative waiting for him to have surgery, or perhaps to die.

We were headed back to the landing pad before noon, feeling pleased with ourselves for what we had accomplished. The clearing with the helicopter pad was just ahead when gunfire rang out nearby.

"Get out," the men ordered without raising their voices. They pushed me to the floor of the truck, then rolled me over the lowered tailgate to the ground. I was pulled underneath the vehicle before I could make the fatal mistake of standing up.

More shots sounded from the bush across the pad, but the men did not return fire. We lay quietly listening until the sound of helicopter blades could be heard. After cautioning me to stay put, one of the men slithered through the grass toward the landing pad.

"They see him," the one with me said quietly when the chopper dipped sideways then straightened. Gunfire erupted near the landing pad. "I don't know if they'll come in after us."

The Vietnamese driver was rolled up into a ball next to one of the truck's large tires.

"You mean they'll just leave us here?" I whispered.

"No, but they might have to call in the Jolly Green." The Green Beret lay on the ground with his M16 propped in front of him, ready to fire.

I had heard Rick and Jerry talk about the special squadron of helicopters that rescued downed pilots. Rick had been complaining that the Jolly Green Giant was called upon to rescue a group of visiting Congressmen who had ventured into an insecure area against advice. When they were pinned down by Viet Cong, the rescue unit had been called away from searching for a downed pilot to extract them.

"I wish I'd not come here," I said more to myself than to the man lying next to me as the helicopter departed.

"Don't worry, we'll get you out O.K." I didn't bother to tell him I meant Vietnam.

Only an occasional shot rang from the distant tree line, to let us know they were still there, my companion informed me. "They're trying to draw us out," he said. "We'll just have to sit tight and hope they think there's a bunch of us."

The other soldier belly-crawled back to the truck, where our vigil continued. Swarms of mosquitoes attacked, but we did not dare slap them. When I heard the thwack-thwack-thwack of several helicopters in the distance, I felt as if the U.S. cavalry was riding over a ridge to our rescue. Everything in Vietnam seemed to include helicopters; the sound of their blades could bring visions of bloodied patients, dying Marines or even a pleasant afternoon party in Hoi An. I thought of Dan and wished he was with me.

When I looked skyward, I saw three choppers; two of them Cobra gunships that swung low over the far tree-line and peppered it with machine gun fire before climbing quickly back into the sky. After two more passes, the third chopper, which hovered in the background, set down on the landing pad. The other two continued their assault on the tree line while we scrambled on board and rose sharply into the air.

"Stay down!" the door gunner yelled to me when I lifted my head. I pressed myself against the floor and did not move, even though hot shell casings were spitting from his machine gun onto my bare arms and legs. It wasn't until we were safely away that I realized they had burned my skin wherever they touched.

"Sorry we got you into that," one of the Green Berets said. "We've never had any trouble in that hamlet before." He dug into his medical bag and found ointment to put on my burns.

"Nothing like having your own medic along," I said, hoping my voice did not betray the fear I still felt. The gunner looked back at me and apologized for the burns. "That's all right," I said. "Just so we got out of there."

"You medical people are all nuts," he said as he turned back to scanning the jungle below. "You'd get your asses shot off for a bunch of no-good gooks." I avoided looking at the Vietnamese truck driver huddled on the floor not far from the gunner.

Dan was waiting for me in civilian clothes when we set down in Danang. "Where the hell have you been?" he asked the moment I stepped from the chopper.

"On a MEDCAP," I said. "I didn't think you would be here until later this afternoon."

He turned his attention to the two Green Berets with me. "What the fuck were you doing taking a woman out in the bush like that?" he demanded.

The men looked uncertainly at me. "It's all right," I told them. "Thanks for taking me along." They nodded and left without comment.

"You didn't have to talk to them like that," I said when they were gone. "And how did you know where I was anyway?"

"I went over to your quarters and Jean told me," Dan replied. "Pat, you can't go around taking risks like that. People are getting killed over here."

"No shit. I happen to have figured that out all by myself in triage."

He said nothing more as we drove to my new quarters. "I'm sorry I got myself into a mess," I said when we were in my room. "But I do know what's happening over here, and I am capable of taking care of myself."

"You're no match for machine guns." He took one of my hands and started to raise it to his lips. "You're hurt," he said when he saw the burns on my arm. "What happened?"

"Nothing." I pulled my hand away.

He put his arms around me in an embrace so firm I could not get away. "I was afraid for you," he said. "Those guys had no business taking you out there with them."

"I asked them to take me; they didn't hold a gun to my head."

"Just the same, I ..." He stopped when I began to tremble.

We sat down on my bed and I told him about the ordeal at the landing pad. "Don't lecture me," I said when I finished. "I already learned my lesson."

He was quiet for some time. “I know we’ve just met,” he said. “But you’re already very special to me.”

I didn’t want him to see my tears, or to tell him how afraid I had been. I hid my face in his chest and he kissed the top of my head. Then he lifted my chin so he could kiss my lips. It seemed entirely right when we made love and drifted to sleep on a narrow bed only two lovers would find heavenly.

CHAPTER FIFTEEN

The departure of the chest surgeons left a noticeable gap in our team. Their study had given us added work, but they had always been willing to put their elective cases aside when there were casualties to be done. Ron now had to do the majority of the surgery, as well as supervise the Vietnamese medical students. Dr. Fitch did cases when absolutely necessary, but the shacks were teeming once more with patients waiting for secondary orthopedic procedures.

The frustration of too much work and too little staff reached crisis proportions when Dr. Fitch allowed a reporter from the Concerned Citizens group that liked to take pictures of burn victims to use the O.R. as a staging ground for an article he was writing. The reporter set up shop in the small doctors' lounge off the central corridor and monitored our every move.

"Where will the article be published?" I asked Ruth on one of my trips to her ward to treat a patient with tracheal burns.

"The group has its own magazine." She was removing dressings from a woman with burns over most of her chest. The woman made no sound while Ruth worked, despite the fact that her breasts were now only charred remnants of flesh. "They've already published one critical story about our hospital," Ruth said, "accusing us of being lazy and incompetent."

I asked Ruth what we had done to incur such criticism from the pacifist organization. "I think it's because we're actually taking care of the Vietnamese they're only beating their breasts about," she told me. "And we're teaching them how to care for one another when we leave here." She completed the dressing change on the woman and moved on to the next patient. "They despise the American government so much they don't like to admit government employees are actually engaged in humanitarian work."

"What country are they from?"

"America."

It was hot in the burn ward and the stench of decayed flesh was everywhere. It was a testimonial to my adaptation to the hospital that I could stay there long enough to carry on a conversation.

"They resent our rapport with the military and don't like the idea that they help us with our patients," Ruth continued. "It interferes with their portrayal of them as a bunch of murderers out raping and pillaging."

Ruth told me the group had started with good intentions. But with all the publicity they were now receiving, they seemed to be losing sight of their objective of stopping the production and use of napalm, as well as helping its victims. "Nobody wants to see napalm banned more than I do," Ruth said. "But they've gotten so off the track they spend most of their time and money on self-promotion."

Considering Ruth's description of the group's attitude toward the military, I thought it ironic that the reporter ate dinner in the Navy Club every night. But what was even more curious was his custom of wearing combat boots, army fatigues and aviator glasses.

He clacked at his typewriter from dawn to dusk for an entire week, talking to no one but Lan. The interpreter had long conversations with him.

"The little V.C. bastard is in there telling him how awful we all are," Shelly said when the two of us passed the doctors' lounge carrying a stretcher.

It was my turn to cover siesta, along with Ron, and I put a spinal in a patient he was doing an amputation on for a badly infected leg. We were completing the case when an ambulance arrived with new casualties.

"None of them are urgent," I told Ron when I came back from checking on the new arrivals. "They can wait until the rest of the crew gets back at three."

I was starting I.V.s on the new patients in triage when I heard someone choking in the outside corridor. When I went to investigate, I found a small child had been brought in by some unknown person and left lying in the screened porch. Her face was severely injured and she was choking on the blood running down her throat, as well as the swelling of the injured tissue.

I gathered her up in my arms and ran with her to the O.R. that had the best suction machine and light. Ron had completed the amputation and left, and a Vietnamese nurse was cleaning up. The man with the amputated leg was lying on the table waiting for the janitors to transport him to recovery.

I asked the nurse to help me move him so I could work on the child, but we could not lift him and his spinal was not worn off enough for him to help us. I went to the doctors' lounge, hoping to catch Ron, but found only the reporter from Concerned Citizens.

"Could you help me with an emergency?" I asked from the door. "I need to get a patient off the operating table so I can work on a child."

He looked up from his typewriter but remained seated. "I'm here to report on your war crimes, not to participate in them." His words were measured and cold.

I heard the child coughing and the Vietnamese nurse calling for help. "You don't understand," I said hurriedly. "I need your help to take care of a child."

"I understand perfectly. Why don't you ask your military friends who shot her to help you?"

The child's color was deteriorating when I arrived back in the room. With sheer determination, the small nurse and I managed to ease the amputation patient to the floor, where he lay protesting while I put the child on the table and began work.

Her mouth and nose were ragged flaps of tissue and filled with blood. I suctioned it as best I could, then clipped her swollen tongue to what remained of a cheek so it would not fall back in her throat. There was no time to get the American made laryngoscope we kept locked in our lounge for safekeeping. I had to insert an endotracheal tube blindly, with only experience to guide it. When the airway was properly established, I sent the nurse to the doctors' house, located within the hospital compound. Ron came back with her and began work.

He did a tracheotomy, since the child would have long term airway problems, and inserted rubber tubes into what remained of her nose to preserve the nostrils as well as possible during the healing process. Her damaged tongue was sutured to the side of her mouth to keep it out of her throat. Her eyes, which were badly swollen but appeared uninjured, were treated with an antibiotic ointment and taped shut.

"That's about all I can do for her now," Ron said. "Take her to recovery and I'll help get this old fart out of the way." There had been no time to move the elderly amputation patient, who shrieked his complaints from the floor all while we worked on the child.

I was on my way back from the recovery room when I heard the clacking of typewriter keys. The frustration I felt earlier now boiled into rage.

"How the hell can you sit there writing when there's a little kid who needs help?" I demanded as I stood facing him.

"It is my job to tell the people back home about all the victims of the war," he said coolly. "Not just one."

"If you really cared about the people you'd get off your ass and help them, not concoct stories to make yourself look good."

He was on his feet. "How dare you!"

"Without this war you'd probably be out of a job."

"Who'd be out of a job! You're the one getting rich off the government's war machine!"

"Rich, my ass! I could make three times the salary at home I'm getting in this pus pocket!"

He smiled and sat down. "Nurse describes hospital as pus pocket," he said aloud as he typed.

"Bastard," I said, and left the room.

Ruth was in the lounge when I went in to have a cigarette. "Bad day?" she asked.

I told her about the reporter and she nodded sympathetically. "Don't let him get your goat," she said. "Nothing makes them happier than being able to quote us saying something stupid."

"Yeah, I know."

When Jean and Julia returned from siesta I told them about the confrontation with the reporter. "I'm not opposed to a little revenge," Jean said. "Why don't you get a few patients from the shacks."

"Ones with old casts," Julia said. "Very old." Her smile was as wicked as my mood.

Julia and I hauled the stretcher of the first patient into the doctors' lounge and sat it in front of the table where the reporter worked. Jean brought in the cast cutter and Julia began cutting through plaster that was so old it reeked of mildew.

"You can't do that in here," the reporter objected.

"We use this room to remove casts all the time," Julia said without interrupting her work. "We'll stay out of your way."

She pried open the cast to reveal a purple leg that dripped green exudate. "Looks like that leg needs to go to the spirits ahead of the rest of her," I said from the doorway.

The reporter's eyes were watering and perspiration ran down his face. "That's gross negligence," he said. "How could you let such a thing happen?"

"How could you let a child suffocate?" I retorted.

"We care for people in a decent environment," he shot back at me. "Our organization takes them back to the States where they're properly looked after."

"And you get a lot of publicity."

Julia got up from the floor and gathered up her tools. "I'll get a room ready for an amputation," she said.

"Wait a minute," the reporter called after her. "You're not going to leave that reeking old hag in here, are you?"

"Reeking old hag," I repeated. "Be sure to put that in your article." He looked at the leg again, swallowed hard and began gathering up his papers and typewriter. "Come back again and we'll let you watch somebody vomit roundworms," I called as he lurched unsteadily down the corridor.

"Mouse, you're rotten," Jean said behind me.

When Shelly and Gertie returned to work at three, I went to the recovery room to check on the child who had triggered the incident. She was lying at the end of a bed containing two other children. Her small arms waved frantically in front of her as she searched for someone or something familiar. She was not over five, and it was pitiful to see her lying there unable to speak or to see. With her tongue sutured to the side of her mouth, she couldn't even cry.

"Have any relatives shown up?" I asked Margaret.

"The only place you will find a relative for this half-breed is at one of your American bases." Margaret pointed to the child's wiry black hair.

"But she has to have a mother." The child was breathing so fast I couldn't count her respirations.

"In Cabbage Patch perhaps, but she's probably glad to be rid of her. I've already told the orphanage nun she has a new candidate."

Margaret went on with her work while I attempted to comfort the child. She grabbed my hand when I took hers, digging her small fingers into my flesh. I was still there when the nun from the orphanage came in to see her.

"Hello, I am Sister Nicole," she said to me in a voice that hinted at a French accent. Her white habit was perfectly laundered and she wore spectacles with wire rims that made her look much older than she was.

"We will take her when she is well," she said to me. She spoke in Vietnamese to the child while she stroked her forehead. The child stopped waving her arms and her respirations returned to normal. "People do not want children like this."

"I'm glad you will take her," I said, then added impulsively, "Could I visit your orphanage sometime?"

"You are welcome any time." I had no plans for my afternoon off after covering siesta and offered to take her home. "But I have my bicycle," she said.

"We could put it in the back of our hospital van."

She accepted on the condition that I wait while she completed a few errands. I stayed with the child until she was ready.

"Please be careful," she cautioned as we loaded her ancient bicycle. "It is the only one we have." I placed the bicycle carefully across the back seat.

"You have a long ride," I said when she directed me across the bridge and down the road leading to Navy Hospital and the beach.

"Not so far," she said. "Only ten kilometers."

The nun turned her head away from Sophie's flapping dress when we passed Cabbage Patch, but not before her face turned scarlet within the frame of her starched white veil. Just past the MAG 16 helicopter installation, she told me to turn left down a dusty lane. The orphanage was situated on a sandy knoll overlooking the South China Sea.

We went into the largest of the buildings, which opened onto a sunny courtyard. It was surrounded on all sides by a covered veranda crowded with wooden cribs bearing the names and addresses of Americans. Each crib held three or four small children, who sat watching us with their heads resting listlessly on the side-rails. Their wasted legs dangled limply between the narrow slats, and the eyes in their small faces were bottomless holes.

"Welcome to Holy Angels." A petite nun in a white habit was hurrying across the courtyard to greet me. Sister Nicole introduced her as Sister Marie, the mother superior. Despite her slight stature, the nun's handshake was firm.

"I wanted to thank you for taking so many of our children," I said to her. "I don't know what would become of them if it weren't for your kindness."

The mother superior bowed slightly. "We do our best." She paused to look around at the many cribs. "At times it is difficult to provide enough food and clothing." I followed her eyes to the skimpy shirts and diapers the children wore.

"Don't you receive help from American organizations?" Long before I had come to Vietnam I had been dropping money into Sunday collections intended for homeless victims of the war.

"We are supposed to receive rice, powdered milk, oil and flour," the nun said with the same French accent as Sister Nicole. "At times we get it, but most times not. Much of it goes to the black market."

"Have you notified the sponsoring agency?"

"Yes, many times. They insist we are receiving the things because they have shipped them," she said in a tone that was weary of the subject. "I cannot make them understand." I asked if she received any money and she waved a hand toward the names on the cribs. "The people who donate wish to have their names displayed." Her expression was slightly embarrassed. "We are grateful for even small amounts."

Toddlers in ill-fitting clothes chased each other around the courtyard. Older girls worked over children in the cribs.

I walked closer to the cribs and felt a chilling dampness engulf me as soon as I left the sun in the courtyard. "Why do you keep them in the shade?" I asked when I saw mold growing up the sides of the cribs.

"They are too weak to stay in the sun. Dehydration is always a problem."

I looked into the crib I was standing near and discovered the source of the sickening odor hanging in the air. Each of the children had a puddle of liquid stool dirtying the thin woven mat on which he sat. Flies feasted on the offal, then crawled into the mouths and noses of the unobjecting children. Bellies were so distended from protein deficiencies that I could see the delicate blood vessels stretching from groin to breast.

Sister Nicole rolled up the sleeves of her habit and began changing diapers. "We try to keep them clean," Sister Marie apologized. "But so many have dysentery."

I made a mental note to find a place to buy peanut butter, which could be used to treat their protein deficiencies. The mother superior took me to a room filled with crude bassinets made from scraps of wood. Several nuns and young girls worked over squalling infants, speaking to them soothingly as their hands flew through the motions of routine care.

"Are they babies of American men?" I asked when I had recovered from the sight of so many unwanted infants.

"Many." There was neither bitterness nor judgment in the nun's voice. "We find them abandoned in the marketplace, or near the road by the helicopter base." She did not mention Cabbage Patch by name. "Some mothers whose husbands are killed bring us babies they cannot care for."

Shelly had told me the nuns were the offspring of Vietnamese women and French colonialists and most were educated in France. Their mixed blood gave them a soft appearance, with smooth café au lait skin and almond shaped eyes that were rounder than pure Vietnamese, the same as the orphans they found abandoned.

"Do the children have any medical care?" I asked when we left the nursery.

"Only when doctors come from Navy Hospital. They try to visit when they are not so busy."

"Maybe I could bring a doctor from our hospital," I offered. I knew Ron would be willing to help if he could find the time.

"Thank you, but doctors are not what we need." I looked at the nun in bewilderment. It was obvious to anyone that the children were in need of treatment. "Not that I am ungrateful for your offer," she said quickly. "But what the children truly need is love. We do not have the time to hold them and play with them. Some become so lonely they stop eating and soon die."

"I'm sorry." I wanted to help, but I was already feeling depressed coming from our hospital to an even grimmer part of the war.

"It is not so bad," the nun said as if reading my thoughts. "Some of the doctors are taking children home with them and soldiers come many times to play with them."

The next building we entered had large windows overlooking the beach. Bright sunlight fell across the silky black heads of young girls bent over the most beautiful needlework I had ever seen. They looked up as we entered, bowed slightly and returned to their work.

"These are our students," Sister Marie said proudly. "We were a school before the war. But when children were brought to us for shelter, we found ourselves an orphanage as well."

"What are they making?" I tried to get a better look at the intricate designs being embroidered onto heavy white fabric.

"We buy linen from Ireland and make tablecloths and napkins to sell through our mother-house in France," Sister Marie explained. "It is the way we manage to keep our school and buy food for the little ones."

It was shocking to think that the black market's tentacles would reach even into the mouths of hungry children. I was becoming more and more persuaded that Americans had to be involved in the illegal diversion of goods. Incompetence and the Vietnamese could only be blamed for so much.

We looked briefly into a room with neat rows of tables and benches, where the school-aged children met each morning during the school term. Then Sister Marie led me away from the complex of concrete buildings to a cluster of long, grass-thatched shelters sitting very near the water.

"This is where we sisters live in the hot season," she said. The temperature seemed to drop several degrees as we entered an enclosure that smelled like a hayloft on a hot summer day. A window at each end allowed a gentle ocean breeze to drift through the haze of twilight created by the low ceiling and close walls. Rows of neatly made cots were the only furnishings.

"It's lovely," I said.

"In the monsoon season we must move to the big buildings, but we are always happy to return here," the nun said as she looked around fondly. "It was our first home."

"It's nice that you have solid buildings for the monsoon," I said as we walked back toward them.

"Yes, we thank God for the wonderful Seabees." She pronounced it Seabeeze, like the buzzing of bees.

A small wooden table and two chairs had been placed beneath a tall sea pine in the courtyard and the mother superior motioned for me to be seated. "I will bring tea," she said and disappeared into one of the numerous doorways.

I was immediately surrounded by a band of toddlers who came running from their play. They shoved and pushed as they clamored for a spot near me. Two of them were on my lap when the mother superior returned.

"They are quite accustomed to Americans," Sister Marie said as she shooed them away after setting the tea on the table. "I am afraid the soldiers who come to visit have sweets in their pockets."

"I'll remember the next time," I said with a laugh. "I thought they just liked me." A few of the children wandered back to the courtyard while we drank our tea, their faces still hopeful for a piece of candy.

I asked Sister Marie what she needed most and she told me blankets and clothing. I had already written to church groups back home requesting the same items for the children in the shacks and promised the nun I would share whatever was sent.

"Especially for the babies," she said. "We need things to keep them warm before the next monsoon."

When the mother superior's eyes were averted for a moment I slipped a twenty dollar bill under my teacup. But the shrewd little nun didn't miss anything. "Thank you for the donation," she said when I got up to leave. "Americans are most kind."

She stood in the red dust waving to me when I drove down the lane. Watching her in the rear view mirror, I marveled at her unpretentious manner. While struggling to feed starving children in the midst of war, she still attempted to provide them with an education. I had begun the day with a hypocrite who thought he was a saint and ended it with a woman who didn't realize she truly was.

CHAPTER SIXTEEN

I named the little girl Fuzzy because of the hedge of black hair bordering her swollen face. It had been only a few days since her injury, but already she had been moved from a bed to the floor of the intensive care unit.

"Don't you think she should have I.V.s a while longer?" I asked Margaret. The child was trying to eat a bowl of thin rice gruel with her damaged tongue still sutured to the side of her mouth. "She could choke on that slop."

"You provide the I.V.s and I'll run them," Margaret said. "I had to buy that slop myself."

"Sorry."

"She's moving to the veranda soon, anyway. My nurses don't like half-breeds."

The Vietnamese nurses in the ward avoided the corner where Fuzzy squatted. It was the same treatment children of American G.I.s faced in the streets, where their fight for survival meant shining shoes, begging or prostitution.

"Doctor Fitch has been looking for you," Shelly said when I returned to the O.R. "We have a new surgeon he wants the surgery crew to meet."

The new arrival was not just a surgeon, he was our permanent chief of staff. Dr. Fitch would be relieved of the position of acting chief and return to his status as just a physician assigned to the hospital.

"I'm sure you will be pleased to hear Doctor Cannon is a specialist in thoracic surgery," Dr. Fitch told the assembled staff.

Ron was delighted. "Glad to have you on board," he said to Dr. Cannon. "You can have every chest case that comes through the door."

Ron had lost weight since I first met him, from long hours in the O.R. and the stupefying heat of the dry season. Jean and I had dropped several pounds from our already slight frames, as well. But Shelly and Julia seemed to retain all of their curves.

"Now wait a minute," Dr. Cannon said to Ron. "You have to give me a little time to get my sea legs before you put me to work." It was said in a joking manner, but our new chief did look as if he might need time to adjust to the tropical heat and humidity. Besides being well past middle-age, he was one of those overweight physicians who admonished his patients for being fat.

"Of course," Ron said quickly. "We're just glad to have a thoracic surgeon." I admired our general surgeon's ability to keep so much attention focused on the hospital and the care of the patients when that was not where he wanted to be. The photos he carried of his wife and two children were almost worn through from the many times he took them out of his wallet to show us or to sit quietly looking at between cases.

Dr. Fitch took the new chief on a tour of the O.R., stopping to introduce him to various Vietnamese staff along the way. Dr. Cannon repeated his name to them in the loud, exaggerated voice that Americans often use when unfamiliar with the native tongue. "DOC-TOR CAN-NON," he said, emphasizing each syllable as he stood very close to his listeners. "LIKE BOOM-BOOM."

The Vietnamese looked both embarrassed and confused, but Dr. Fitch said nothing. When they completed the tour and left, Jean asked Lan to explain to the staff what the unknowing doctor had meant. Our interpreter did so with much laughter about the stupidity of Americans.

"Do you think Fitch will have the guts to tell him what boom-boom means?" I asked Shelly.

"I hope not. I'd rather have Sophie tell him the first time he drives by Cabbage Patch."

Our new boss wasted no time taking command. A notice was immediately posted above our mailboxes announcing a general meeting to be held the following afternoon. The agenda included a discussion of the supply situation and some new rules regarding the vehicles assigned to us.

"Maybe he'll give us another vehicle," Shelly said. "I'm tired of trying to coordinate plans with four people." She had recently purchased a used motorbike so she could go out to see Tom when someone else was using the car. But it broke down often, or stalled because of the watered down gas she bought off the local economy. Tom worried about her being stranded in insecure territory after dark.

"I'm supposed to make an oxygen run out to the air base tomorrow afternoon," I said. "I hope the meeting doesn't last long."

"Maybe you won't have to go anymore. Boom-Boom seems anxious to attack the supply situation."

"Fine with me. I'm getting wrinkles from smiling at supply sergeants."

There was an air of optimism as we did the casualties the next morning. Ron was so happy about having a chest surgeon he offered to work through siesta to do a secondary procedure on Fuzzy that would make it easier for her to eat.

The little girl had been moved out onto the veranda now that the swelling in her eyes had sufficiently subsided to allow her to see. Her tracheotomy tube had also been removed and her tongue freed so she was able to say a few garbled words. When I had arrived at work that morning Fuzzy had followed me inside. I would not allow her into triage or the O.R., but she squatted just outside their doors and each time I emerged carrying a stretcher she took hold of my scrub dress and followed me to the recovery room or x-ray.

"It looks like this kid is getting pretty attached to you," Ron said when I had Fuzzy anesthetized.

"I know," I said. "She's awfully sweet."

Ron pulled on his surgical gown while I arranged my equipment so I would be out of his way while he worked on Fuzzy's mouth. "Maybe you could take her home with you. She sure as hell won't have anyone looking out for her being half American. And half black at that."

"She'll be going to the orphanage as soon as she's well enough." I tried to smooth Fuzzy's matted hair before wrapping it in a towel to keep it out of the surgical field. "I wouldn't mind adopting her," I said as I considered the notion. "But she needs a family, not a single woman."

"My wife has been alone with our two a whole year now," Ron said. "And I still have another year to go." His eyes were so pained above his surgical mask I was sorry I had reminded him of his family.

When the tissue around Fuzzy's mouth had been rearranged, she didn't look so bad. She still had rubber tubes protruding from her battered nose, but Ron would make all of that look better with further surgeries. Scars were commonplace in Vietnam; Fuzzy's biggest problem was her mixed race.

I didn't want to leave the little girl until she was recovered sufficiently from her anesthetic. The other members of the team were already in Dr. Cannon's office when I entered, and he looked at his watch to let me know I was late. Dr. Fitch gave me a disapproving look from where he stood next to our new chief's desk and chair.

"As you know, I have been sent here to deal with some specific problems," Dr. Cannon began. "One of those problems has already been resolved and I am happy to announce that a new nursing supervisor is on the way."

We had been functioning for several weeks without a nursing supervisor after Mrs. Layfield had suddenly returned to the States, just as Leo had promised. Dr. Cannon didn't realize that her absence had not caused a problem since she had done so little while she was here. Still, the room buzzed with approval at the thought that the team was acquiring another member who might be a positive addition.

"She can't be worse than Layfield," I whispered to Shelly.

"Now to the next order of business." He consulted a notebook lying on the desk in front of him. "It has been brought to my attention by Commander Miles and others that certain individuals have been wasting time and gasoline gallivanting around to various military installations." Dr. Fitch shifted nervously from one of his sandaled feet to the other. "This is supposedly done on the pretext of procuring supplies."

Dr. Cannon paused to look first at Shelly, then down the ranks of cumshaw artists like a general reviewing his troops. The only person who met his gaze without flinching was Ruth, who stood in the crowded office with her arms folded and a pleasant smile on her face.

"I am also aware that certain, shall we say arrangements, have been made to insure acquisition of these items." His raised gray eyebrows were as yellowed as his few strands of hair. "Therefore, I am ordering all such fraternization to cease immediately."

Dissension rumbled through the group. "Is he accusing us of sleeping with the military for the benefit of the American government?" Margaret said behind me. Dr. Cannon looked sharply in her direction but could not pick out the guilty party.

I raised my hand and waited until he recognized me. "Are you accusing the women on this team of screwing the military for supplies?" I asked.

"Get him, Mouse," Shelly said.

Laughter erupted but was quickly stifled by a chilling look from the chief. "I can see we also need to do something about the battlefield language which appears to have taken root." Dr. Fitch solemnly nodded his agreement. "But in answer to your question," he said to me, "I did not accuse you of anything specific. I prefer not to know what favors you have been trading in your illicit operation."

"I don't mind being accused of screwing," Julia said behind me. "I just don't want to be accused of doing it for the government."

Jean raised her hand. "Excuse me, doctor, but without the military helping us the O.R.s would have to shut down. We can't get everything we need through USAID."

"That is no longer true," Dr. Cannon replied. "I have just sent a request to Saigon for all you could possibly need."

"FNG," Shelly mumbled.

"I will be calling these little get-togethers twice a month to keep you informed of current matters," he said as he looked over the crowd. "If there are no further questions you may return to your duties."

"What about the jeeps?" Shelly asked.

"Oh, yes, vehicles." He made a check mark on his notebook. "Hereafter, they will be used for official business only. You will be issued a full tank of gas from the motor pool at the beginning of each week. That is more than enough to transport you to and from work and to the club for meals."

"Now, wait just a second," Ron said without first raising his hand. "We have to go to the PX for things like soap and toothpaste." He had been using Mrs. Layfield's jeep after her departure.

"Shopping trips shouldn't be necessary more than once a month, doctor." He looked disapprovingly at Ron's modified scrub suit.

"I'm not talking about necessary. It's nice to be able to drive out to the PX for a book, or go to the beach on the weekend," Ron said as he adjusted the bifocals slipping down his nose. "There's not a lot to do around here." The rest of us voiced our agreement.

"All right, all right, I'm willing to bend a little. You may use the vehicles for luxuries, as long as you buy your own gas."

"But the local gas is watered down," Shelly objected. "The cars will stall."

Dr. Cannon's yellowed eyebrows had lowered almost completely over his eyes and his lips were drawn into a thin line. "Why don't we just wait and see if that happens?" he said without looking up at us. Shelly didn't push the issue, fearing her motorbike might be ruled illegal.

"What about Mrs. Layfield's jeep?" Ron asked.

"I will be happy to have it, thank you," Dr. Cannon said with a smile that made it clear the jeep would not stay with Ron. He would be back to sharing one with Dr. Fitch and all the visiting doctors.

We filed silently out of the room and gathered in the lounge for a gripe session. "I never thought I would see the day when I wanted Fitch back in charge," Shelly said. "We must write Leo and thank him for getting an asshole replaced with a fistula."

"At least we'll have a new nursing supervisor," Julia said. "Maybe she can clean up the medical wards."

"Or maybe she'll be another Boom-Boom," Shelly said.

"All this bitching is not going to help," Jean said impatiently. "How long can you keep the anesthesia department running with what you have?" she asked Shelly and me.

"We're down to almost nothing," Shelly replied. "Mouse was supposed to go to the air base this afternoon for oxygen and Tom has a bunch of things for me at Navy. But I'm not going out there against Cannon's orders."

"Same here," I said.

"The hell with it," Jean said. "I'm not going to sit around waiting for a shipment from Saigon." She went to Dr. Cannon's office and was back in only a few minutes.

"Is he going to let us cumshaw?" Shelly asked.

"No." Jean was changing into her street shoes to leave work.

"Then what are we supposed to do?" I asked.

"I don't know about anyone else," Jean said. "But I'm going out to the air base to arrange an R&R and forget about this place for awhile."

By Monday the O.R.s were at a virtual standstill. Dr. Cannon seemed oblivious to the situation and further alienated us by having our mailboxes moved from his office to our already cramped lounge. Even Ruth complained about being denied the luxury of standing in the only air-conditioned room in the hospital to read letters from home.

The surgery team did what cleaning it could, then sat in the lounge daring Dr. Cannon to say anything. No new casualties were admitted throughout the day and our chief stayed in his office. When the mail arrived, there was a note in it for me that I had two large boxes at the USAID office. They were from the churches back home, where I had written for clothing and blankets, and were so heavy I accepted an offer from Commander Miles' secretary to help get them to my car.

Fuzzy was waiting for me on the front porch next to a woman the military referred to as a "one-armer". She was one of the many women and children recruited by the Viet Cong to throw grenades at passing American convoys.

Because of their age or inadequate training, the recruits frequently held the grenades too long after pulling the pin and ended up with a traumatic amputation of an arm. Whether the women truly were V.C. sympathizers, nobody knew.

Becky had told us stories about entire villages being forced to spend the whole night planting land mines along a route where American or South Vietnamese troops would be traveling the next day. They no sooner were allowed to return to their houses by the Viet Cong, when American advance teams came through and forced them out of their beds to dig up everything they had planted. The mines often exploded while they were trying to remove them, killing the person doing the digging and seriously wounding anyone in the vicinity. More than once we had received the mutilated bodies of women with their injured or dead babies still strapped to their backs.

There were men who became “one-armers” too, but their injuries were not caused by the Viet Cong. They had learned that a grenade thrown into a river could kill hundreds of fish, which then floated to the surface where they could be easily harvested.

Fuzzy watched Ron help me carry the boxes to the porch, where she squatted next to the one-armed woman. The little girl pulled at the string holding one of the boxes together, then looked up at me with what might have been a smile. I opened one of the boxes and dug through it until I found a red dress that looked her size. She jumped to her feet when I handed it to her, immediately stripped naked and pulled it over her small body. The Ba with the amputated arm looked up approvingly from her stretcher as Fuzzy smoothed the ruffles of the dress. Fuzzy tried to tell me something I could not understand because of her garbled speech. I stooped over to get closer to her and she pointed to the Ba, then to the red dress I had given her.

“Thi, thi,” I said, trying to make the child understand the clothing was too small for the Ba. But Fuzzy was not going to be dissuaded. She kept pointing at her new dress, then to the woman’s ragged pants and shirt. I dug back into the box of children’s clothing and found a colorful quilt to spread over the woman, who shivered in spite of the heat. Even in the midst of the hot season, death was a cold experience.

“Dep, dep,” Fuzzy said to the woman. The Ba seemed pleased that Fuzzy was telling her she was beautiful.

After hauling the boxes into the lounge, I selected several blankets and articles of baby clothing. I was feeling as happy as the day I met Dan when I stepped into the first of the shacks.

My eyes were still trying to adjust to the darkness when long talons flashed from the shadows, snatching away a good portion of the clothing in my arms. I could see the faded outline of a woman scampering away, but before I could follow another was in her place grabbing away the clothing and blankets. Then another appeared, and another, until I was fighting to stay upright as they scratched and clawed for the few remaining items.

"Get away! Di di!" I dropped the last items and threw up my hands to protect my face. Sharp fingernails continued to flash from the darkness and I felt the warmth of my own blood trickling down my arms.

Just as suddenly as it began, it was over. I was left standing by the door with nothing of what I had brought with me anywhere in sight. A few children cried, but there was no other sound. The inhabitants of the shack lay on the floor staring at me with vacant eyes, as if a stone had been thrown into a pond that left not a ripple. The clothing and blankets had evaporated, leaving me to wonder if any of it had happened.

I stumbled outside, where the bright sunlight reassured me it had. Blood ran down both my arms and my uniform was torn in several places. I felt someone watching me and looked up to see two Vietnamese nurses on an upper veranda. They said nothing while I attempted to wipe away the blood and cover my torn scrub dress.

Few people seemed to notice as I made my way back to the lounge, where Julia jumped up. "Mouse! What happened?"

I told her about it while she washed my scratches.

"We need to get Lan," she said when she finished. "I'll go find him."

I had changed into a clean scrub dress when Julia returned with the interpreter. I asked him to have the janitors go through the shacks and bring us any unclothed children they found. The interpreter looked curiously at my scratches but did what was asked without his usual objections.

The children were dressed within the safety of the locked lounge then returned to their mothers. When all of them were outfitted, I took the remaining items to the orphanage, where the nuns chattered excitedly as they pulled each piece of clothing from the boxes and ran to find the perfect child to put it on. There was some satisfaction watching them, but not enough to lift the depression that had crept steadily over me since the incident in the shacks.

I had come from a humble farm family, one that might even be considered poor. But nothing in my past had prepared me for the primitive struggle for survival I had witnessed that morning. I was appalled that I could be so naive, after months of living and working among the people, to walk into a den of hungry lions with only a few pieces of meat.

Leo had been right, the things we were accomplishing were but a drop in the bucket of misery called Vietnam. If it was truly the intent of the United States to win the hearts and minds of the people, it could not be done while destroying their homeland and shoving them into hovels of disease and despair.

CHAPTER SEVENTEEN

We were still doing only emergencies when Jean returned from her week of R&R in Hong Kong. Her first day back we received more than a dozen casualties who needed immediate attention, and there was still no shipment from Saigon. Shelly hesitated for a moment, then went to the locked lounge and returned with a plastic bag of I.V. solutions, needles and other emergency items.

"I was saving these in case any of us got hit," she told me. "I figured it would be enough to keep us alive until someone got us to Navy Hospital."

While I appreciated the prudence of having things on hand to treat our own injuries, I would have preferred to believe we would never have need of such things. Somehow I had managed to convince myself I would always be the nurse, never the patient.

We did the emergency cases and returned to the lounge, once more daring Dr. Cannon to complain about our idleness. When we heard his voice outside the door we prepared ourselves for a confrontation. Instead, he introduced us to the newly arrived nursing supervisor, Teresa Lane.

"Are you finished for the day?" she asked. Her manner was inquisitive rather than judgmental, and was surprisingly cheerful after her long plane ride from Saigon.

"No, but we need someone to do a loaves and fishes number on these," Shelly said, holding up the few things left from her emergency supply. Dr. Cannon's face reddened, but he returned to his office without comment.

The new supervisor looked to be in her thirties and had been recruited from a prestigious university hospital. No alarm registered in her serene face as we told her about our supply problems and Dr. Cannon's orders forbidding us to cumshaw. "Can you make do until I can have a talk with him?" she asked when we finished.

"When we say we have nothing, we have nothing," Shelly said. "We couldn't even do an emergency tracheotomy right now."

"And it's no better on the medical wards," Julia interjected. "The Vietnamese staff won't take care of the patients or help clean the wards because they're afraid of catching a disease." Julia told Teresa about the lack of immunizations for the Vietnamese staff.

"Then I don't blame them for being afraid," the nursing supervisor said. She had a plump frame and wore oversized round-rimmed glasses that made her eyes look enormous. A starched white nurse's cap like Margaret's sat atop shiny brown hair. "I'll give the wards priority as soon as I do something about the O.R.s"

"Speaking of the O.R.s," Jean said. "Why don't I show you around while things are quiet?"

They stopped in the screened porch to look over long lines of people waiting for surgery which they would not get. Jean told them they must come back another day, but they refused to leave. Teresa shuddered visibly when she saw the scraps of paper they held and learned they were their only medical document.

"Don't you have light bulbs either?" she asked, looking around the dark porch.

"We don't have electricity out here," I said from behind.

"The O.R.s do," Jean said. "At least when the power is on."

"Deplorable." Teresa shook her head and started toward the surgery suite. "I'll meet with Dr. Cannon as soon as possible."

"It had better be soon," Jean said. The sound of truck engines could be heard outside, which meant casualties. Teresa not only helped us unload the new arrivals, she did not shrink from the terrible injuries that had so appalled me my first day in Danang.

"What do we do now?" I asked when the patients were in triage.

"Do you think you can get enough from your military sources to take care of them?" Teresa asked.

"Cannon would have our heads."

"I'll take responsibility." The supervisor's manner convinced us she would. "Get what you need, do the cases and plan to meet with Doctor Cannon tomorrow." She walked briskly away in the direction of our chief's office.

"Not bad for her first day in this mule-shit pie," Shelly said.

Margaret surrendered her lone tank of oxygen from ICU, and some I.V. solutions and needles she kept locked in a cupboard for the same purpose as Shelly. I offered to do the more urgent cases while Shelly made a trip to Navy Hospital for the other things we needed. More casualties arrived in the meantime, and it was well past dark before we finished. I thought about the emergency items Shelly and Margaret had kept for team members as we drove through the darkened streets with no protection.

There was heavy fighting during the night and Teresa helped me in triage the following morning. I showed her how to ration supplies and helped her cut the sleeves out of her uniform so she could better tolerate the heat. She abandoned her cap and white nylons, changing into rubber thongs like the rest of us.

We finished the emergency cases in time to do another procedure on Fuzzy before it was time for the meeting she had scheduled with Dr. Cannon. The Ba with the amputated arm had died and Fuzzy clutched the quilt I had given her to her breast. I held onto it during surgery, and when I took Fuzzy to the recovery room afterwards I spread it on the floor to lay her on.

"That won't last until she's awake," Margaret told me. "Someone will roll her off it the moment you leave."

I reluctantly laid the little girl on the dirty floor and took the quilt with me to the meeting for safekeeping. Dr. Cannon gave me a disapproving look when he saw it tucked under my arm. He sat at his desk, with Dr. Fitch standing directly behind, and Teresa off to one side of the crowded room.

"I'm afraid we have an unexpected complication on our hands," Dr. Cannon began when we were all present. "For some reason, Saigon has failed to fill the emergency order I submitted."

"Although we expect it any day," Fitch added.

"I realize I told you not to ask the military for anything," Dr. Cannon continued. "But our new nursing supervisor has asked me to reconsider that position." He looked at Teresa, who looked steadily back. "I have decided to temporarily suspend the ban I imposed so you can get the necessary things to run your respective departments. But with the express understanding that anything we are given is to be repaid as soon as our shipment arrives." Nobody made any movement. "Well, go ahead," he said. "I'm giving you carte blanche to get whatever you like." Still there was no action.

Teresa turned to face us. She removed her owlish glasses to wipe perspiration from her face, which looked considerably older than it had the previous day. "I would consider it a personal favor if you could manage to keep your departments running until we can work something out with USAID." Hers was an eighteen month tour with the Agency for International Development, the same as the majority of the people she addressed. "I know we can get things straightened out with just a little time and patience."

Ruth, who had not met the new supervisor before the meeting, was the first to step forward. "I'm sure you will rectify our supply problems," she said as she shook Teresa's hand. "I'll be happy to do anything I can to help you in the meantime." The rest of us followed the cue of the most respected member of our team.

Not only did Teresa get the hospital functioning again, she demonstrated beyond any doubt she was not another Mrs. Layfield. When the apartment downstairs in Shelly, Julia and Margaret's villa became available, Margaret moved downstairs so Shelly and Julia didn't have to be roommates. "No more sleeping on the couch when Tom's in town," Julia said.

"I've always told you to just put a bag over your head," Shelly countered.

Teresa was told she could jump up the list of those waiting for permanent quarters and move in with Margaret. Gertie was content to remain in temporary housing, as long as she had an abundant supply of bedmates.

Teresa spent most of her time at the hospital. But music and laughter drifted between Julia and my quarters next door every weekend Bird-dog was in town. And when Bird-dog was in Danang, so was Dan.

"I didn't know you were Catholic," I said when he asked if he could go with me to Mass on a Sunday morning.

"I haven't been going to church much over here," he said. "I got a letter from my mother this week reminding me to."

Rather than drive out to Navy Hospital's chapel, Dan suggested an Army installation across the river from the marketplace. He parked his jeep next to the Bamboo Hut and we climbed down the river bank, where he hired an old Ba to take us across the water in her shallow boat. She said nothing during the trip, but smiled shyly when Dan took my hand in his.

The river smelled of fish and of raw sewage emptying into it. But the water was calm and the early morning air not as heavy with humidity as later in the day. The Ba propelled the boat with a long pole she dipped in and out of the water while standing on a rear platform. It took us only a few minutes to reach the other side, where Dan paid the woman and helped me climb the steep embankment to the Army compound.

There was no separate building for a chapel so Mass was held in the officers' club. White sheets were spread over the bottles of liquor at the bar and across a row of slot machines shoved to one side of the room. The club reeked of alcohol and stale cigarette smoke, but the chaplain seemed not to notice. He said Mass with the same ceremony one would expect in an elaborate cathedral. When we returned to the river bank, the Ba was waiting to take us back to the other side and collect another generous tip from Dan.

"Tien is off today," I told Dan when we were out on the water. "And I can't cook."

"Don't tell me you didn't learn to cook growing up on a farm?" He wore civilian clothes and his shirt was the same green as his eyes.

"I know how," I said. "But the power is off so much we can't keep anything in the refrigerator."

None of us spoke Vietnamese well enough to shop in the marketplace, nor did we have the inclination to do so. Tien spent a good portion of each morning bartering with vendors, who considered it a matter of pride to cheat her whenever possible.

We paid her a hefty wage to do our shopping, food preparation, cleaning and laundry. The laundry all had to be done by hand, but Tien's sister, who lived with her in a shack behind Shelly's villa, shared in the labor.

"I don't think it's a good idea to eat off the local economy," Dan said when I told him our food came from the marketplace. "You'll catch something."

"We have no choice. USAID won't let us buy food from the military depots." The PX stocked only snack foods that came in tins or jars.

"Then eat at the club." Dan had been with me to the Navy Club in town on two occasions. Even though he was a sergeant, his civilian clothes and the ID he showed the sentries gave him immediate access.

"I'm tired of soggy hamburgers." I didn't tell him I also avoided the club because I no longer saw Jerry for steak night. The flight surgeon had not been happy when I told him our Wednesday night dinners were off because of Dan, but he continued to give us whatever he could spare from his clinic for our hospital. Rick was at our quarters with Jean every Wednesday after steak night, as well as most Sundays.

I assured Dan that Tien soaked all the vegetables she bought at the market in bleach before peeling and preparing them. Meat was cooked long enough to kill any organisms and our drinking water was boiled. In addition, all meals were cooked and served at Jean's and my house so we would only have one kitchen to oversee. Shelly, Julia and the others from the villa next door didn't mind coming to our quarters for meals. And Jean took responsibility for inspecting the kitchen on a weekly basis to make sure Tien was keeping it clean and not using spoiled food.

Dan helped me up the river bank to his jeep, parked next to the Bamboo Hut. "Why don't we have lunch here?" I suggested.

"Is it safe?" Dan looked skeptically at the ramshackle building built out over the river.

"The French onion soup and bread are," I said. "They're cooked long enough to kill the bugs."

He blanched visibly when he broke open a loaf of French bread and found several dead weevils imbedded in it. "Just pick them out," I said. "They're dead."

I removed the bugs for him, but he still ate little. While he drank a beer and looked out over the river, I told him about the orphanage I continued to visit on a regular basis. "It sounds depressing," he said.

"Maybe I've told you too many of the sad things," I said. "I need to take a case of peanut butter out to them. Why don't you come with me?"

Dan laughed. "Vietnamese don't eat peanut butter."

"The nuns give it like medicine to treat the kid's protein deficiencies. I buy it at the PX."

"You're just feeding their worms."

"So their worms get peanut butter."

He smiled across the table at me. "Don't you ever get tired?" he asked.

"Every day," I said. "But as long as I can get up and face it again in the morning, I might as well keep going."

Since meeting the nuns, I was not as troubled about our long term accomplishments. Getting through the day took all the attention and energy I had. Perhaps it was resignation to the situation, or it might be a sign of maturity, but my expectations had undergone a radical revision in the past months. One grew up fast in war.

Dan talked about the island he had pacified and the children who attended the small school he started. "I have a Vietnamese woman teaching them," he said. "I would like to help, but I don't have the time."

"What are you so busy doing?" I teased. "Or aren't you allowed to tell CIA secrets?"

He smiled and his dimple appeared. "I don't know any secrets."

I had never been in love; there had been no time in my life for such a frivolity. During high school I had a job that kept me busy nights and weekends, and when I graduated I worked two so I could save money for nursing school. After completing the three years necessary for my R.N., I decided to continue an additional two years for a degree in anesthesia.

Dan was the first person I had dated more than a few times; in part because he was the first one to interest me. Sitting across the table from him I knew I wanted to be wherever he was, even in a war.

Dan changed the subject to his younger sister, who his mother talked about in her letters. "I always promised my mother I would be there when she was an adolescent," he said. "And here I am on the other side of the world." The look that came over his face was far different than the Marine mannerisms I was accustomed to. His parents divorced when he was young, and his mother remarried a nice man who fathered his younger sister. But in the interim Dan and his brother had helped his mother survive.

"It's hard for you to be away," I said when he fell silent.

"Sometimes I think I was pretty selfish to sign up to come over here."

"Why did you?"

"I don't know," he said, looking out across the water. "I was going to college on a football scholarship. It was fun in the beginning, then the war protestors started shutting down buildings on campus and protesting at all the games. I got listening to them and decided to come over here and see what was happening for myself."

"Don't tell me you went from being a protestor to a Marine."

"Hell, I wasn't one of them," he said. "I just said I listened to them enough to get curious."

"So what do you think now that you've seen things for yourself?"

He took another sip of his beer. "We can win it," he said with no hesitation in his voice. "If Washington will let us."

"And are they letting you?"

He looked at me and laughed. "Are you shitting me?" He finished the last of his beer and set the bottle down firmly. "Time to get going," he said. "Where's that orphanage?"

Sister Marie was happy to see us and flitted about the courtyard arranging chairs for us to sit on. When she left to get tea, several children surrounded us to collect the candy they knew I had in my pockets. A boy of about two years climbed onto Dan's lap.

"He likes you," I said.

Sister Marie allowed him to stay when she returned. "He has been very lonely," she said. "This is the first he has made a friend."

"What's his name?" Dan asked. He was rubbing a hand up and down the child's back who leaned into it like a contented cat.

"He has no name," Sister Marie replied. "American soldiers found him in a burned village and brought him to us."

"Why don't you give him a name?" I said to Dan.

"I wouldn't know what to name a little boy," he said, sounding much like one himself.

"You could give him yours," Sister Marie suggested. "We have used all the Vietnamese names."

"Danny would be nice," I said.

Dan looked down at the small boy, who was curled up in his broad lap as if he belonged there. "O.K.," he said. "If that's all right with you, Sister."

She spoke to the child in Vietnamese and he smiled for the first time. "He is pleased with his new name," she said.

With the exception of the infants crying in the nursery, the orphanage had fallen strangely silent. When I looked around to see what had caused it, I saw all of the children working their mouths in exaggerated motions.

"Peanut butter time is a nice time to visit," Sister Marie said.

Danny was given his portion and Dan laughed as his tongue chased the unfamiliar substance around the roof of his mouth. He was still chewing when he followed us outside to Dan's jeep.

"Jesus!" Dan dove for a group of ragged children crawling over the front seats.

"Dan." I was embarrassed by his language in front of Sister Marie, until I saw the reason for his concern. The children were playing catch with the hand grenades he kept between the two seats.

"Holy shit!" I said, then turned away from the nun.

Sister Marie rounded up her charges and shooed them away.

"I'm sorry," Dan apologized. "I have to carry them on the road between Danang and Hoi An. I forgot about them when I parked the jeep out here."

"Such things happen," Sister Marie said kindly. "We are fortunate no one was hurt."

I was still trembling when we drove away. "Next time we come here put them someplace safe," I said.

Dan looked across the jeep at me. "I don't think I want to visit there again, Patty. Seeing all those kids makes me kind of sick."

"I know," I said. "But they need help."

"I left some money under my teacup. I hope Sister Marie isn't offended when she finds it."

"She already knows," I said. "Americans all think alike."

It was still early afternoon and we decided to join my hospital friends at the beach. After a game of volleyball, Dan and I walked along the sand enjoying the luxury of a day away from the war.

We went as far as possible, to where a snarl of barbed wire restricted us from continuing. Several G.I.s in combat attire were sprawled on the sand just on the other side; their chests bare and their helmets and shirts tossed on the sand beside them. Their boots were covered with mud and their faces drank up the sun as if they had not seen it in months.

"Hey, I know that guy." I pointed to a second lieutenant standing with his boots ankle-deep in the surf as he looked out to sea. His hair was caked with mud and his uniform spattered with what looked like old blood. "I met him out here just after his wife had a baby. Lieutenant Tamasi, I think."

I called to him, but he didn't seem to hear. One of the haggard men got up from the sand and came over to where I stood on the other side of the wire. "The lieutenant's had kind of a bad time, ma'am. I think he just wants to be alone." The young G.I. told me Lieutenant Tamasi's platoon had walked into a mine field, killing several of his men. "Some lost legs," he said. "A lot died."

"You were with him?" I asked, looking over the other men lying on the beach.

"Yes, ma'am." He looked down at a dark stain on his own uniform. "We got hit pretty hard."

Lieutenant Tamasi turned and walked along the beach without even a glance in my direction. His face wore the vacant expression combatants called the thousand yard stare.

"He's feeling pretty bad because our Vietnamese guide led us into the trap," the G.I. said. "We got a few days R&R here at the beach before we head back to the bush. The lieutenant will get his shit together by then."

"He can't go back like that." I looked down the beach to where he sloshed through the water in his combat boots. "Why don't they send him to Hawaii so he can see his wife and baby?"

"He's not due for an out of country R&R yet."

"It looks to me like his mind is overdue."

"Minds don't count."

The young man rejoined his buddies and Dan took hold of my arm. "I think we should leave now," he said.

"Some guys fold for awhile when something like that happens," he said as we walked back down the beach. "I think the Marine Corps has the right idea. They put us through hell during boot camp, but we come over here ready to take whatever comes at us."

I stopped to look at him. "Have you seen guys killed?"

"Yeah, and I handle it a lot better than that candy-ass lieutenant."

"I know sergeants have no love for officers," I said in a disappointed voice. "But I would expect you to at least have some compassion."

"Hey, he let his men get led into a minefield...."

"A Vietnamese guide did that," I interrupted. "A traitor." Dan shrugged and continued walking. "Dan, being a Marine doesn't make you invincible," I said as I turned to look up into his face. "When you talk tough like this I'm afraid you'll start believing it so much you'll do something stupid."

He put an arm around me and guided me back toward where our friends were. "I'm not a stupid guy," he said. "And I am sorry about what happened to the lieutenant."

"How could the guide do that?" I asked before we reached the others. "Lead them into a minefield he knew was there."

"He was probably Cong."

"Do you go out on patrol with the Vietnamese soldiers you've trained?"

"Sure, but I know my men. I practically live with them." The troop barracks were close to Dan's compound in Hoi An.

Bird-dog was playing his concertina and Julia sang and danced in the sand. Everyone was drinking Foster's beer provided by Bird-dog.

Dan opened a beer and handed it to me. "I don't like people making you sad," he said. "It takes the sparkle out of your eyes."

"I didn't know there was any left."

CHAPTER EIGHTEEN

"I'm having an awful time teaching Gertie how to use ether, Shelly told me. "All she talks about is how they did things in Two Oaks, Montana."

I offered to trade places and went to the O.R. where Gertie was working while Shelly took over triage. Gertie was attempting to start an I.V. on an old man, who let out a terrified scream each time she harpooned him with a needle. Several discarded angiocaths lay on the floor and she was unwrapping still another.

"Gertie, you can't go through angiocaths like this," I said. "We have to cumshaw them and they're hard to get." The special plastic needles could survive the jostling our patients received while being transported from one place to another without becoming dislodged. They were perfect for transfusing blood, and they could be reused if we were careful not to damage them when inserting them into a vein.

"I can't help it if the patient has bad veins," Gertie said. Tufts of grey hair stuck out wildly from beneath her surgery cap.

"Why don't I give it a try?" I suggested when she missed still another attempt. "Some days its just hard to hit them."

"God girl, I have days like that all the time."

When the I.V. was started, Gertie sat down at the head of the table and placed an anesthesia mask over the old man's face. He cried out for mercy when she cranked the ether vaporizer wide open.

"Back off on it," I said; the fumes were making even my eyes water. "You're giving too much."

"I've done this before, you know," she said testily.

When the patient was finally asleep, I returned to triage to help Shelly, and also to give Gertie some independence. "She's going through angiocaths like she does men," I told Shelly. "Do you think you could get us some more?"

"Not this month," Shelly said. "They're running short on them for our own guys."

We were working long days since Teresa got a shipment of supplies to us. "If they don't keep this supply situation straight, I'm not staying my whole eighteen month tour," I said.

"Don't tell anyone," Shelly said quietly. "I'm getting out of here as soon as Tom's tour is up." She had only volunteered for Vietnam to be near Tom, so it didn't surprise me that she would leave when he did.

When I went back to check on Gertie, I found one of the patient's arms hanging limply over the side of the table. I picked it up to put it back on the armboard, where it should have been secured with tape, and found it cold and mottled.

"Gertie, have you been having any trouble with this patient's blood pressure?" I asked when I couldn't find a pulse in the arm. I had ducked down behind the anesthesia screen so I wouldn't alarm the surgeon with my question.

"Blood pressure? What blood pressure?" Gertie said loudly. "He hasn't had one for the last half hour."

"Jesus Christ," Ron said from the surgical field.

I felt for a pulse in the carotid arteries of the man's neck and found none. "I think this patient may be in cardiac arrest," I said as calmly as possible.

"God girl, I think he's just plain dead."

"You mean I've been operating on a corpse?" Ron said in a stricken voice. If the power had not been out, he would have noticed the blood getting dark as its oxygen content dropped.

"There's no point trying to resuscitate him," I said when it became apparent he had been in cardiac standstill for some time. Ron dropped his instruments into the open belly and left the room without a word. "Gertie, why didn't you call for help?" I asked when he was gone. "Shelly or I would have come."

"You listen here, I was giving anesthesia before the two of you were born!" She yanked down her surgical mask to make her point. "I don't need you to tell me what's going on! I knew this patient was dead before you even came in the room!"

Her face was so contorted I worried that she would have a stroke. "O.K., Gertie," I said soothingly. "I just wish you had called for one of us."

Julia had been assisting Ron and now collected dirty instruments. “If you had told me you were having trouble, I would have gotten you help,” she said to Gertie.

Tears welled into Gertie’s eyes and she began wringing her hands. “I tried to get help,” she said. “But the circulating nurse didn’t know what I was saying, and you know you can never find that interpreter.”

“Why don’t you let me take over here,” I offered. “You go to lunch and take siesta off.”

Jean had the body removed and called for the next case. But she was upset that the interpreter had not been available when he was needed. “That damned Lan hasn’t been here all morning,” she said. “He’s either going to come to work on time, or he’s not going to work here.”

She went to her Vietnamese counterpart, Mr. Hai, who hurried away on his motorcycle to find the missing interpreter. In the meantime, Jean decided to go to USAID headquarters to make sure Lan was not submitting hours on his time card that he was not actually working.

Mr. Hai returned with the interpreter at almost the same time Jean returned from USAID. She had discovered that our government was routinely paying Lan for twenty or more hours a day, without ever once questioning the validity of his claim.

Mr. Hai stood at Lan’s side when Jean held up a copy of the interpreter’s time sheet and demanded an explanation. “How could you be putting in twenty hours a day interpreting when the American team is here only twelve?” she asked. “And some days you’ve claimed twenty-four!”

“Sometimes I work more,” the interpreter said as he clicked the claw on his little finger. “But I am generous to Americans and not ask for more money.”

Jean started to laugh at the absurdity of the statement, then became angry. She pointed out to Lan the impossibility of working more than twenty-four hours a day. Lan looked embarrassed at having made such an obvious blunder, but only for a moment.

“Your government pay me,” he said. “Who is stupid?”

“Not me,” Jean said firmly. “You submit more hours than you work one more time and I’ll have you fired.”

Both Lan and Mr. Hai promised to start spending more time at the hospital, but their sullenness made it clear they did so reluctantly.

“Why shouldn’t they want to screw the Americans government?” Shelly said when she heard about the time sheet. “They’re both V.C.”

"You don't know that," Jean said.

"Hai sure knew where to find Lan in a hurry. He was probably out in Cong territory planning a midnight raid."

I received a note from headquarters that I had received a large box. It was filled with equipment from a hospital in Minnesota where I had once worked. The staff had collected everything that was not being used and sent it to me after reading a letter I wrote them about the desperate situation in Danang. There were scrub gowns and surgical drapes, glass syringes, metal basins, needles and even razors; all of which had been replaced by disposable plastic and paper. Laryngoscopes and endotracheal tubes they considered outdated looked better than anything I had seen in six months, and at the bottom of the box were several beautifully illustrated textbooks for the medical students from Hue. Shelly and I took them to the students, who accepted them with profuse bows.

"I wonder how long it will take to sell them?" Shelly said on our way back to triage. "They should bring a good price on the black market."

"Is there anybody you trust?"

"My dog, and he's dying." Shelly's monkey had disappeared the night of the attack on the air base and never returned. Tom's corpsman, Fast Eddie, had immediately remedied the situation by bringing her a mangy puppy.

"Why don't you take the mutt to a vet?" I asked.

"I didn't know Fitch was taking new patients."

There were no casualties admitted, so we spent the morning arranging our new instruments and supplies on the shelves of our anesthesia office. With the shipments Teresa had managed to get through, we actually looked well stocked.

Gertie offered to cover siesta and after much trepidation we agreed. But it was with express instructions that she was to send someone to Shelly or my house if any casualties came in.

We returned to find Gertie involved in a case Dr. Cannon was doing on a small boy who had come in with a coin stuck in his throat. "How long has this been going on?" I asked when I went into the room.

"God girl, they didn't give me time to call you," Gertie said breathlessly. "The boy's sister brought him in right after you left and Doctor Cannon said he had to operate right away."

The patient's color did not look good and air was hissing out of an incision in his trachea. I was surprised he did not have a tracheotomy in place.

"He's not being ventilated adequately," I told Dr. Cannon. "You're going to have to stop and put in a trach."

"We'll have him closed up in a minute," Dr. Cannon replied. "The coin's not in the trachea; I'll take a look in the esophagus."

I was appalled that he had not determined where the coin was before going after it, especially when that could be easily determined by symptoms and x-ray. One never opened a trachea unless such a procedure was clearly indicated.

"You just take care of things at your end of the table," he said when I questioned him about why there were no x-rays done before surgery. "And let me do the doctoring." Jean came into the room when she heard him raise his voice. "If you had some decent instruments around here I wouldn't have had to make an incision at all," he told her.

"We send any cases that need bronchoscopy instruments out to Navy Hospital," Jean said. The hollow lighted instruments could be inserted through a patient's mouth to retrieve foreign objects from the esophagus, trachea or lungs without having to make an incision, but our hospital didn't own any.

"Thanks for telling me," Dr. Cannon said. "I could have used that information earlier." Jean had taken siesta off with Julia, Shelly and me, and so had Ron. The case was the first Dr. Cannon had done since his arrival.

"It's not doing this kid any good to discuss instruments," I said. "He's turning blue."

Doctor Cannon extracted the coin from the child's esophagus and told us to wake him up. I was already in the process of doing so, but his heartbeat was irregular and weak, and his color would not improve even on straight oxygen. Shelly came to help just as he arrested. The two of us tried to resuscitate him, but there was no response after more than thirty minutes of effort.

"I want you to know I consider this an anesthetic death," Dr. Cannon said when we gave up.

Gertie started to object, but Shelly stopped her. "It wasn't your fault," she told Gertie. "Let's just get on to other cases."

"You're going to let him get away with that?" I demanded when Dr. Cannon left the room. "You know he killed this kid."

Shelly gestured for me to lower my voice. "Shit, Mouse, that guy's not a surgeon," she said quietly. She pointed to the ragged incision in the child's throat that had been closed with stitches that looked worse than any intern's. "Look at that thing," she said. "It looks more like a shark bite than an incision."

"But how could he fake credentials?" Jean asked. "He had to pass an FBI security clearance the same as the rest of us before he came over here."

"Not necessarily," I said. "USAID was in such a hurry to send me over, I was shipped out before my FBI check was completed."

Ron came into the room and inspected the incision before the body was removed. He agreed with Shelly that Dr. Cannon's surgical expertise was questionable, and promised to assist on any future cases he did so he could observe.

Sister Nicole was waiting in the screened corridor with the child's sister, who was not much older than him. When she saw her brother's limp body, her mouth fell open to emit a scream, but no sound came out. Sister Nicole told us the boy was the last relative the girl had. The war had claimed her father, who was in the Army, and a land mine killed her mother. As I watched the nun lead the girl away, I felt certain Dr. Cannon had claimed her brother.

"We're going to have to do something about Gertie," I told Shelly over dinner that evening. "Even if Cannon was at fault, she didn't handle that case well."

"Maybe we could trade her to the enemy," Shelly said.

"Be serious. We can't let her keep going the way she is." But Gertie was so happy to be in Vietnam we did not want to have her fired and sent home.

"Why don't we put her with our best anesthesia students?" Shelly suggested. "We could tell Gertie she's to supervise them, but they could do the cases the way they know they should be done. She might actually learn something while she thinks she's teaching,"

"But what if she tells them to do something wacky?"

"They could pretend they don't understand her, the same as they do us when we tell them to do something they don't want to," Julia said.

Julia had been carrying on a battle with the Vietnamese scrub nurses not to sit on the sterile instrument table. But every time she left the room they kicked off their shoes, moved the instruments to make room and perched on the table. With the back of their scrub gowns only partially closed, it was gross contamination.

Gertie was delighted with her new supervisory role and became much more pleasant to work with. The only remaining problem was Dr. Cannon, who seemed to avoid the O.R. whenever Ron was available to assist him.

Shelly decided to ask the thoracic surgeon at Navy Hospital about him when she went out to visit Tom that Friday evening. Julia and I went along to see a movie Navy Hospital had borrowed from a hospital ship in the area.

The film had been chosen for its abundance of scantily clothed women, ribald humor and rough language, and was shown in the officers' club. The men whistled and cheered whenever a woman appeared on the screen, but when a particularly voluptuous one came out on a balcony in black lacy underwear, they made the projectionist back up the film and show it again; then again and again. The previous viewers had done the same and the segment was so worn it eventually broke. The men threw popcorn at the screen while the enlisted man acting as projectionist worked to splice it. As soon as he had it repaired, they made him show the segment again, and once more it broke. When he finally managed to piece it back together, minus several frames, the power failed. The men threw popcorn at the screen and cussed their bad luck until the power came back on. Then choppers sounded overhead, and the projector had to be shut down while everyone listened to see if they were incoming medevacs.

With all of the interruptions, the film was not half over when a rocket attack began close by. We grabbed our drinks and ran for the bunker located behind the shabbily built club.

"Shit, this is nothing," one of the doctors said after half an hour of listening to the now subdued fighting. "I'm getting a fresh drink."

The rest of us were following him into the club when a tremendous blast shook the building and made the floor ripple under our feet. "Incoming!" someone shouted, and we scrambled back to the sandbagged bunker.

When we emerged sometime later, we found the club in shambles. Shattered glasses lay everywhere and liquor poured onto the floor from broken bottles. "Break out the paper cups," someone said. The bartender complied, but the power was out for the remainder of the evening and the movie abandoned. Some people returned to their quarters, but the rest of us took our drinks to the roof of the club to watch a firefight taking place at Marble Mountain, about a half mile away.

Puff the Magic Dragon, a converted C-47 aircraft, was providing air support for ground troops and put on a spectacular display. Two Gatling guns fired several thousand rounds a minute out the side of the aircraft, with every fifth bullet a bright red tracer to mark the direction of fire. As it circled over the target, the aircraft really did resemble a huge dragon spewing fire across the night sky.

Some of the doctors set up expensive photographic equipment to capture the scene on film. Shelly took the opportunity to question the thoracic surgeon about Dr. Cannon, who he assured her could not be a certified chest surgeon.

It was nearing midnight when Shelly gave up waiting for Tom to return from the O.R., where he had been summoned early in the movie. Flares lit up the sky as we drove towards town, racing against the clock to get to Danang before the bewitching hour.

"Hey, that flare chute is about to land," Shelly said as she slowed the car. She pointed to a parachute drifting slowly to the ground just ahead of us. "The silk it's made of would make a number one nightie."

"I'm not risking my life for a damned silk nightie," Julia said. The flare was headed toward the ditch, which could very well be mined.

But Shelly insisted it wasn't far away and would take only a minute to retrieve. She disappeared into the darkness and Julia and I sat holding our breath, waiting for an explosion.

Several minutes passed with no sign of her. Julia called out softly and got no answer. Then she turned on the headlights, even though it would make our vehicle a target for enemy fire. Minutes passed and suddenly Shelly appeared in the beam of the headlights; a soldier carrying a rifle right behind her.

"Just a little misunderstanding," she said as she climbed back behind the wheel.

"Climbing a fence around a secured area is more than a little misunderstanding, ma'am." I squinted my eyes to see the armed man still standing in the glow of our vehicle's lights. "You proceed on into town now," he said with a tip of his helmet. "And don't go stopping anywhere you might get yourselves hurt."

"What the hell was that all about?" Julia asked when we were once more headed for Danang.

"The chute got hung up on a fucking fence," Shelly said. "How did I know it was around MAG 16?"

She told us the sentry had caught her halfway up the fence and almost shot her. "God girl, he thought I was Cong," she said with genuine fear in her voice. "When I heard that rifle click behind me I though I was dead."

"You're nuts," Julia said.

"Imagine him mistaking me for a peasant," she said, reverting to her Mae

West voice. "When's the last time you saw a Vietnamese with red hair and a set like these?" She stuck out her chest for emphasis.

"All that, and you didn't even get the chute?" I asked when I realized she didn't have it with her.

"I can order a nightie from Sears."

By the time we reached Danang there were flares lighting up the sky, and the rumble of heavy artillery sounded from where destroyers fired on the land. The Vietnamese guards USAID had recently hired to protect our houses had locked the high metal gates at both Shelly's villa and mine before disappearing to wherever they went once they thought we were asleep. We had to climb over them, which caused a good deal of commotion.

"Sorry I woke you," I said when I heard Jean complaining in her bedroom as I passed by. "We had an exciting night."

"So did we. Cannon's been sent back to the States."

"What?" I hurried into her darkened room so fast I tripped over a chair.

"A couple of FBI agents showed up just after dinner and escorted him to a waiting plane," Jean said while I uprighted the chair. "Ron says he faked his papers and they just caught up with him."

"You mean he's not a doctor?"

"He used to be, but not a surgeon."

"I knew it!" I felt my way to my roommate's bed and sat down on the end of it.

"Hey, watch where you're sitting," a male voice said.

"Rick's here," Jean said with an embarrassed giggle.

"Gee, I'm sorry," I said as I jumped back up. "I didn't know."

"Well, now you do," Rick said from beneath the covers.

Teresa filled us in the on the details over lunch the following day. "The whole office is buzzing about it," she said. "Even Commander Miles." Doctor Cannon had lost his medical license several years earlier and was receiving psychiatric treatment when he signed up for Vietnam. "He told USAID he had years of experience in foreign service," Teresa told us. "That's why they hired him."

"Good old USAID," Julia said. "They would hire Hitler if he told them he had experience with relocating people."

"It's a wonder they caught him when they did," Teresa said. "Think of what he might have done?"

"He did plenty," I said, remembering the look on the little girl's face when she saw the body of her brother.

Dr. Fitch resumed his role as chief, but it was Teresa we went to when we needed anything. She managed to get the ban on gasoline for our vehicles lifted, and was going after the supply problem with a vengeance now that we were once more facing shortages.

"Sometimes I think it would be easier just to write to some Congressmen," she said as we dressed for work in the lounge. "If we could get the story to the right people it might mean an end to our problems."

"Or a beginning," Jean said. "USAID doesn't like people who write letters to Washington."

"Now here's someone who knows how to get a story to the right people," Shelly said. She was reading a newspaper mailed from her home town weeks before. "First civilian heart surgery in Vietnam performed successfully," she read aloud. "The dedicated American surgeon pulls his mask from his weary face as he leaves the operating room of a primitive hospital in Danang, Vietnam, having just completed major heart surgery with the help of only two Vietnamese nurses."

"Let me see that," I said, reaching for the paper. A photograph of Dr. Fitch in full surgery garb was spread across the front page. "Why, that son of a bitch," I said. "He took credit for our heart case and he didn't even help."

"I think it's funny," Shelly said with a laugh. "The only part they got right is the description of the hospital."

Jean and others in the room looked over the article and laughed along with Shelly. "But Dr. Gregory and his resident should get credit for that case," I said.

"Oh, who cares who gets credit as long as it got done?" Jean sounded aggravated. "How much credit does Ruth get in the press for all the work she does?"

"Mouse is one of the few people I know who still expects the world to be fair," Margaret said.

"Come on, let's go kick the bastard in the balls before you have a stroke," Shelly said when I picked up the paper to look at the article once more.

Dr. Fitch was at his desk typing a memo to Saigon when we entered. He looked surprised when I laid the paper in front of him, and flushed crimson when I pointed to the photograph.

"There's obviously been some mistake," he said after a few moments of pretending to read the story. He pulled nervously at his beard as he spoke. "Some reporter probably got word of the case and mistakenly put my name and picture on it."

"Bullshit," I said. "There were no reporters around here that day."

"Maybe we should send Doctor Gregory a copy of the article," Shelly suggested.

"Go ahead," Dr. Fitch said. "I can only tell him the same thing I've told you."

Shelly picked up the paper, crumpled it slowly in her hands and tossed it in the basket at the side of Dr. Fitch's desk. "The best place for trash is a trash basket," she said. "Let's go, Mouse, there are real cases to be done."

"He should be thrown out of the country for that," I said when we were in triage.

"And replaced with another Boom-Boom?" Shelly said.

"Maybe you can forget about it. But this place is really getting to me."

"Then take an R&R. I can hold down the fort with Gertie and the students."

I began an all out assault on Navy intelligence to find out when and where my brother's ship would be going into port. With the ominous rumbling of ship's guns reminding me of his presence each night, I wanted to make sure he was all right.

CHAPTER NINETEEN

"Even if I knew where your brother's ship was I couldn't tell you," the lieutenant at Navy Intelligence said. "We can't give out that information." The office was located at the deep water piers, some distance from Danang. "I'm sorry you drove all the way out here," he said as I prepared to leave. "Ship movements are classified."

I drove back to Danang, hoping to get a message to my brother through the Red Cross. But Teresa informed me that was only for emergencies such as a death in the family; homesick sisters didn't count. I was about to give up when an unexpected tragedy hardened my resolve.

The USS Forrestal, an aircraft carrier cruising off the coast of Danang, caught fire killing over a hundred men and severely injuring hundreds more. The injured were flown by helicopter to Navy Hospital for treatment, and those who perished in the fires were taken to the morgue at the air base to await identification from dental records sent from home.

"Most of them were pilots," Tom told us when he came to see Shelly after days of nonstop work caring for the injured. The boundless energy he always seemed to exude had been exhausted. His face was so pale the freckles on it looked three dimensional. "They were asleep after bombing raids up north and caught in their bunks," he said. "Their sleeping quarters were located directly beneath the deck where the biggest fire occurred."

"Aren't they all burn patients?" I asked. It was not unusual for physicians to work outside their specialty when there were a lot of casualties. But I was surprised an orthopedic surgeon would be taking care of burn patients.

"They're all burned," Tom said. "But they also broke their arms, legs or backs trying to escape the flames."

The grizzly task of identifying bodies by dental records took weeks to complete. I observed coffins being loaded onto planes whenever I drove out to the air base for oxygen, a painful reminder that my brother was not as safe off the coast as I would liked to have believed.

My reception at Navy Intelligence was much friendlier the second trip. "I didn't realize you were a nurse," the same lieutenant said when I used a new approach for the information. "We've sent a lot of men to Danang for treatment."

"I know," I said. "The carrier fire."

"I want you to know how grateful we are to all you nurses," he said in a voice that cracked with emotion. "You and the docs have done an outstanding job."

My first reaction was to tell him I was not a military nurse and had no part in the care of the men he referred to. But my cumshaw instincts told me to keep quiet.

"That's why I would like to see my brother," I said. "I want to make sure he's all right, and he wants to do the same with me."

The lieutenant sat at his desk for a few seconds looking out the window where the burned hulk of the carrier could be seen tied to the pier. "Let me see your I.D. again," he said.

I handed him my passport. "You can see that my brother's last name is the same," I said. "His first name is Jack." He asked for the name of the ship, then disappeared into a back room.

"You can't write this down," he said when he came out with a scrap of paper on which the name of my brother's ship and the port it was going to were scrawled. The date was there too, only one week away. We were alone in the room, but the lieutenant looked anxiously around him as I read the information. When I had it memorized, he crumbled it into a tiny ball and swallowed it.

"I don't suppose you could let him know I plan to meet him there?" I said hesitantly.

The young officer looked around again. "Ma'am, I could be sent to Leavenworth for what I just did," he whispered in a frantic voice.

"O.K., but just in case, I'll be at the Palace Hotel." He laughed when he heard the name of the hotel Fast Eddie had told me sailors used while on liberty in Taiwan.

Teresa approved my request for an R&R without question.

"Get the chief!" the desk clerk shouted the moment I walked into the

Palace Hotel. Other hotel personnel gathered around and chattered in Chinese as they looked from me to the elevator. When the doors opened, my older brother strolled out and gathered me in his arms.

"How did they know who I was?" I asked above the cheers of the staff.

"I gave them a picture of you from my wallet," Jack said when he released me. "They've been watching for you since I got here yesterday."

The desk clerk held up a faded photograph from when I graduated from nurse's training. "Same-same," he said, pointing from the picture to me.

Jack was dressed in his blue chief's uniform and looked much older than I remembered. As he studied my face, I suspected he was thinking the same about me.

"How did you know I would be at this hotel?"

"I got a message a couple days before we left Nam," Jack said, shaking his head at the memory. "It nearly scared the shit out of me when the old man called me up to the bridge. I thought sure someone had died."

"Did you get into trouble?" I was also worried about the lieutenant at Navy Intelligence, who obviously had sent the message.

"Hell, no. The old man chewed my ass for not telling him I had a sister in Danang and gave me five days liberty."

"Five days! I thought we wouldn't have time for much more than a hello and good-bye."

Jack told me his destroyer had been just off the coast of Danang. "Your guns have been keeping us awake," I said.

"We shake your shacks pretty good," he said with a laugh.

"Is your ship the only one out there?" The staff had gone on about its business, and we stood alone in the shabby lobby.

"Shit, no. There's a whole bunch of destroyers, and a battleship is on its way over." Jack paused for a moment. "Although I don't know what the hell good it'll be. You can't maneuver those big mothers very easy, and you have to be able to get out of the way fast if you're fired on."

"So why are they sending it?"

"Ask the fucking brass in Washington. The only thing it would be good for is to pull a couple thousand water skiers." He laughed heartily at his own joke.

My brother hadn't changed, except that he had more gray hair and his face was wrinkled from years of duty in the steamy engine room where he worked. He still chain-smoked and exhaled slowly while watching some distant horizon. And he still repeatedly apologized for his profanity.

"Now don't let any goddamned sailors try getting friendly with you," he said as he carried my bag to my room. "I'm right across the hall in case you need help."

"Don't worry, I'm used to men trying to get friendly."

"And don't mind my mouth. I've been in the fucking Navy so long I can't talk decent anymore."

"Maybe I've been around Marines too long," I said. "It sounds perfectly normal to me."

"Christ Almighty, don't go talking about jarheads. Marines are nothing but trouble."

I decided not to tell him about Dan, at least for now. "See you later," I said as I entered my room.

The cheap sailor haven seemed palatial after six months in Danang. There was hot water and the toilet flushed the first time. It was heavenly to have a bathtub, other than the South China Sea, and I peeled off my clothes and soaked in water so hot it steamed up the entire room.

"I've already made the rounds of the clubs," Jack said after dinner in a G.I. joint not far from the hotel. "There's only one that plays American songs instead of that ching-chang shit."

The club Jack took me to was filled with sailors on liberty. Taiwanese women in short skirts, tight sweaters and dime store make-up crawled over them like ants at a picnic. There were plastic palm trees and blinking lights that reminded me of Christmas. Loud music from a local band made conversation nearly impossible.

"It's nice to see the guys having a good time!" I shouted as I looked around the smoke-filled cave. "Even if it is with prostitutes!"

We were escorted to a small table on the fringes of the noisy room. "It sure seems strange, sitting here talking to you," I said. "Did you ever think when we were growing up on the farm that we would be in a war together?"

"I don't like you being over here one bit," Jack said. "I was against your coming from the beginning."

"I know." He had been one of the few members of my family to voice any objection, believing a war was no place for a woman.

"So tell me what you're doing?" he said, squinting across the table through his cigarette smoke. "You sure as hell are thin."

"I'm working hard," I said. "We have lots of casualties." His brow furrowed and I wished I hadn't referred to people his ship could possibly be responsible for injuring. "I've met a nice man," I said, desperate to change the subject. I told him as much as I could about Dan, leaving out the parts that might upset an older brother. He listened quietly, with the same sad expression on his face as when I had mentioned the casualties.

"You're in love with him, aren't you?" he said when I finished.

"Yes, I guess I am."

He leaned across the table to me. "He sounds nice, Patty, even if he is a fucking jarhead. But you want to be careful getting involved with a guy in a war."

"What about you? You have a wife and three kids."

"I had them before I got sent over here."

"Not the first time. You had only one then."

"I know, but it took me two tours to figure out what a bunch of lying bastards are running this mess." He opened a fresh pack of cigarettes and frowned when I took one. "I'm staying in the Navy because I'm close to retirement," he said. "But I won't let my boys join."

"That doesn't sound like the old career man I used to know."

He ordered another round of drinks from the Chinese waitress, who dipped low enough over our table to show off her small cleavage. "There won't be anymore career men when this one's over," Jack said. "The brass won't find men willing to die for them so easy in the future."

"You think the war is wrong?" The last time I had been with him he sounded like a recruiter.

"This isn't a war," he said. "We're just killing people." He touched one of my hands in a fatherly gesture. "Take the two of us," he said. "You're over here busting your ass to save people I might have shot. Does that make any sense?"

"I thought you were aiming at the enemy."

"Shit, we just barrel-ass in there and blast away at targets we're given. No one knows what the hell we're hitting."

I watched the young men laughing and drinking all around us. They looked like Jack had a few years ago, before he grew as weary as he now looked.

"Jack, do you think we'll win?"

He thought for some time before answering. "I'm just a know-nothing enlisted man," he said slowly. "But I've been in the Navy a long time and seen a lot. And from where I sit, no American is willing to squat in a hole eating a ball of rice and cockroaches for twenty years like the gooks we're fighting. And without bombing the hell out of their harbors up north, which we aren't going to do, there's no way we can stop them."

"Then why are we here?"

"The same reason we got ourselves into a lot of fucked-up messes; for a few people getting rich off it, and a lot of old men who want more medals to pin on their chests. It doesn't mean shit to them that one swipe of their red pencils can wipe out the lives of hundreds of young men."

I thought of Dan and shuddered. "Don't say that."

"I'm sorry, Patty. But you're asking to get hurt getting involved with that guy."

He called the waitress to order more drinks but I declined. "I've had enough," I said. "I'm going back to the hotel."

"I'll walk with you, but I have to come back to help the owner audition a band after this joint closes. I've been doing that since I dropped anchor."

I thought my brother was joking until an elderly Chinese man rushed over to our table when he saw we were about to leave. Jack reassured him he would be back and the old man bowed and returned to his table next to the kitchen.

"He wants to make sure the guys like the band," Jack explained as we left the club. "I ask them to play American songs I think the men would like to hear. If they don't know them, they get their Chinese asses kicked out."

He waited outside my door until he heard the lock click. But there was no sleep to be had. Traffic in the uncarpeted corridor continued through the night; the staccato click of spiked heels interspersed with the heavy thud of military shoes. On the other side of the paper-thin walls I heard the details of payment being discussed.

"You pay first," a female voice said.

"No, I pay you afterwards," the male voice insisted. "That's the way Marines do it."

"Marine same-same sailor. You pay first."

"O.K., O.K. But I pay for just one time."

I was relieved my brother wasn't there as the sounds of mating filtered through the partition. When the headboard finally quit hitting up against my wall, I rolled over to go to sleep. But after only a few minutes the female began to protest.

"No, no. You pay money first."

"Afterwards," her partner said. "Didn't I already give you half?"

"You give me ten dolla. Cost twenty dolla, two times."

"O.K., my wallet's right there in my pants hanging on the chair. You take the money as soon as we're done."

"Oh, no," I said when the thumping of the headboard resumed. There were only a few seconds of silence after it stilled, then the woman's plaintive voice. "Only five dolla in pants," she said. "You give me five more."

"No, I only give you fifteen," the Marine said. "You get the rest from the American government."

"I no think so G.I."

"Honest, I'm here from Vietnam and the government pays part of it; it's called combat pay. You go to the big Navy base and they give it to you."

"You come with me."

"I can't. I'm waiting for a phone call from my mother back in the States."

"Navy base long way," she complained.

"Take a taxi with the money I gave you. The government will give that back too."

The sound of clacking heels had barely disappeared down the corridor when I heard a bag being hastily packed. "Bastard," I said to the wall.

The next three days passed quickly, visiting the elaborate museums in which the Taiwanese took great pride, and taking bus trips to the outlying areas. The countryside was beautifully green, with no bomb craters or defoliated forests. On Sunday I went with my brother to Mass at the Navy base.

I couldn't help staring at the faces of the blue-eyed altar boys who were the offspring of American servicemen stationed in Taiwan. They looked so pale and innocent compared to the young faces wizened by war to which I had become accustomed. Jack was quiet on the taxi ride back to the hotel.

"I know you're trying to help people," he said over a final cup of coffee. "But I want you to get out of Nam before things heat up."

"If things get bad, I'll be on the first plane out."

"If there is a plane."

"Stop worrying, Jack. You just quit shaking our shacks with your big guns so we can get some sleep."

He insisted I move to a better hotel, even though I had only one day left of my R&R. The move was accomplished in enough time for me to go with him to the pier where his ship was docked. When he took me in his arms, I felt his tears on my cheek.

"I'll be fine," I said in a voice that was not at all convincing.

He backed away, self-consciously brushing tears from his eyes. "Tell that guy of yours to look out for you," he said before he turned to leave.

“See you at home,” I called after him. But he was already lost in the crowd of people gathered to bid their farewells or to greet arriving ships.

My new hotel was much nicer, and far more expensive. Since it was my last night I went to a good restaurant and ate dinner alone, savoring the peace and quiet. I was the first passenger of the R&R flight at the air base the following morning, where some of the men arrived still buttoning their clothes. “I hope they have fifty bucks left,” a guy next to me said. “The military makes them pay for their own clap cure.”

The return trip was noisy with unending tales of sexual conquest. In addition to me, there were female stewardesses on the civilian flight. But the men were too relaxed from their R&R to be inhibited.

“The last woman I had was so ugly I kicked her out before daylight,” one Marine said. “I wouldn’t even let her cut on the light to get dressed.”

“What time was that?” a man across the aisle asked.

“About three this morning.”

“Jesus, I picked one up out in the hall about then. She was ugly as shit, but she settled for ten bucks.”

“Ten bucks! Man, I had her first for five!”

The stewardesses blushed as they listened to the talk, but they kept up a steady service of steak, eggs and coffee. When a volley of gunfire sent the plane zigzagging to avoid being hit, they quickly took their seats and buckled up.

“Looks like Uncle Ho sent a greeting party,” one of the men said as he looked out the window.

“Man, I’m glad I spent that last ten bucks,” another said.

We were on final approach when the captain came on the intercom. “All of us at Pan Am would like to wish you well and hope you are home soon.” Cheers of gratitude and exuberant applause erupted for the civilian airline crews that volunteered to provide R&R flights at great risk to themselves.

But the cheering ended when we sat down on the runway and puffs of smoke mushroomed outside the windows. “Welcome back to the war,” someone in the rear said.

CHAPTER TWENTY

My first week back would have been dismal if it had not been for the excitement of Becky's approaching wedding. Our favorite anesthesia student was being married in a traditional Buddhist ceremony and had invited the American members of the anesthesia staff. But when Saturday finally arrived, we were inundated with casualties. Shelly and I offered to finish them so the Vietnamese staff would not be late for the afternoon ceremony.

Most of the patients had been flown in by helicopter from a remote jungle area after being injured while fleeing a firefight in their village. They escaped along paths cut through the jungle by the North Vietnamese to transport supplies, a primitive road system known as the Ho Chi Minh trail. In order to discourage pursuit by parties who happened upon the well camouflaged byway, the North Vietnamese had booby trapped it with punji sticks.

The weapons were made by whittling bamboo into sharp spikes, which were then driven into the ground at an angle and covered with grass and leaves. The bayonet-like spears could penetrate even combat boots, lodging themselves so securely in the muscle and bone of the foot that they required surgical removal. To make sure the victims were sufficiently disabled, the tips of the sticks were coated with manure, which would be deposited deep within the tissues to cause infection. Because our patients wore only thin sandals, the sticks had gone right through their feet, leaving them so impaled they were completely immobilized.

"Don't try pulling them out," Ron cautioned us in triage. "They all need to go to the O.R." Some of the patients had tried removing the sticks before being rescued by an American reconnaissance patrol and had caused so much damage to vital blood vessels that their feet would have to be amputated.

The work was tedious. We first had to remove the sticks, then debride the deep wounds to make sure all the shredded tissue and manure were removed.

Copious amounts of antibiotics had to be used in the irrigating solution to give the wounds a final wash.

With the help of two newly arrived AMA physicians, Ron managed to complete the cases soon enough for us to go to the wedding. We changed into clothing we had brought to work with us just in case, but both Shelly and my hair was a matted mess from perspiring under surgical caps. There was not enough time to go home and shampoo it, if we had water.

"There's a beauty shop down by the river," Shelly told me. "Are you game?"

"We'll get lice."

"Not if we make them use our own combs."

"But they probably use water from the river."

"So?" Shelly said. "We go smelling of fish, or go smelling of sweat."

The small shop was so close to the river bank I watched a child relieving himself while his mother washed laundry just a few yards downstream. I was reconsidering my decision to have my hair done when one of the operators came to me and bowed. She motioned me to a chair, after first wiping it carefully with a damp cloth, and bowed once more.

I stepped over a murky trench that ran down the center of the room, emptying into the river just across a muddy strip of land. Boards had been placed over the open sewer at strategic places so customers and operators could get from one side of the shop to the other. Unfortunately, the dryers were placed right along it and our feet were splashed every time someone emptied a basin of water. We were waiting for one or both of us to be electrocuted.

Shelly's red hair caused a sensation among both the opeators and their Vietnamese customers. "I'll probably leave with more dirt than I brought in," she said as they paraded by to touch it.

The power went off several times while we sat under the wheezing dryers, but we finished in time for Becky's wedding. "I look like Orphan Annie," Shelly said, back on the street. Her red hair was curled so tightly it stuck out from her like a tree in full bloom. My short dark hair had been coaxed into something resembling a pageboy, a style popular with the local women.

A slight breeze offered relief from the afternoon humidity as we walked to the temple, located not far away. Shopkeepers called out to us to examine the wares they had spread on the sidewalks in front of their establishments, and children ran alongside begging to shine our shoes. Wind chimes tinkled from unseen places and elders peered from darkened doorways like wise old owls. The sweet smell of incense drifted from homes, where the photographs of deceased relatives could be seen on elaborate family altars. I was reminded of a woods in the fall of the year by the pungent odors.

Margaret was already seated in the temple next to her boyfriend Keith, the American in charge of the consulate where Becky's fiance worked. She wore a pale pink suit, with shoes to match, and her blond hair was pulled up on her head in a simple but elegant style. Keith was dressed in a suit and tie despite the oppressive heat.

Soft music played on a string instrument and incense floated from an altar decorated with gifts brought to the wedding. Gertie could not attend because of a date, but she had sent a bottle of Johnny Walker Scotch which sat with the other gifts at the foot of a statue of Buddha. Leo had not forgotten Becky's wedding and sent an electric iron and hot plate, items coveted by the Vietnamese.

Becky usually wore western style clothes, but she floated into the temple in a traditional Vietnamese ao dai made of shimmering red silk, white being the color of mourning. An ornate head piece towered so high on her head she actually looked tall. Tran wore dark slacks and a white shirt covered with silver embroidery. Public displays of affection were forbidden by Vietnamese culture, but I saw him look toward Becky with a fondness that could not be hidden.

"Remember not to point your toes at their dead relatives," Shelly said after the brief ceremony. We were in a cyclo on our way to the home of Becky's uncle, who was hosting the wedding reception.

"For Christ's sake, there aren't going to be dead relatives there," I said to Shelly. "Only their photographs."

"I meant don't point your feet at their pictures."

It would be our first time in a Vietnamese home, and Shelly was brushing up on what we had been told was and was not acceptable by Margaret's boyfriend. When sitting across from the family altar of past relatives, Keith had instructed, one must remember to hold the feet in a sideways position. Pointing the toes at photographs of the deceased was considered a sign of disrespect.

We stayed at the reception just long enough to drink tea and politely sample the small cakes served to us. "You shouldn't have eaten those cakes," Keith told us as we left the reception. "They'll be making an exit as soon as your stomachs realize what you've done to them."

"They were baked," I said.

"Not the icing. I'm sorry I didn't think to warn you." He was so politely formal wherever he was, I wondered why he was attracted to Margaret and her sarcasm.

"I hope he's wrong," I said on the way back to our quarters. "Dan's due in Danang in less than an hour."

"And I'm suppose to go out to Navy to see Tom," Shelly said.

The spasms hit just as we pulled into the alley between our two houses. When Dan arrived I was still in the bathroom. Jean explained my predicament, and he left for the large CIA compound located in Danang to catch up on some paper work. He came back at dinner time, but I was too ill to leave the house.

Shelly and Julia came over early the next morning to tell us we had casualties. There had been heavy fighting during the night, but I had been too weak to crawl beneath my mattress. When I woke, there were small bits of plaster and dust covering my bed and stuck in my hair.

"I don't know if I can work," I said. "My legs are so weak they feel like they can't support me." The diarrhea had only subsided a few hours earlier.

"Drink a couple of Cokes," Jean suggested. "You'll be all right once you get some glucose in you."

"I slept in my living room," Shelly told me while I sipped at a can of warm Coke. "My toilet's backed up from the work-out I gave it, and I can't stand the smell in my room. Of course, the living room wasn't much better," she added. "My dog is so sick he crapped on the floor every time there was a burst of gunfire."

"Why don't you put that thing out of its misery," Jean said. It was Sunday, Tien's day off, and Jean was fixing us tea before we left for the hospital.

"I already did," Julia said. "I threw it out this morning. It'll be in someone's stew pot by dinner."

Dog was considered a delicacy by many Vietnamese, as any American who adopted one for a pet soon found out. They watched the malnourished animals grow fat on the generous scraps fed to them by foreigners, then stole them to eat.

We stopped by the marketplace on the way to work to buy a stalk of bananas for our breakfast. We found another tall stalk propped in the lounge when we went in to change.

"Oh, oh," Jean said. "Ruth only buys bananas when we're in for a long seige."

The burn ward nurse was already working in triage. Teresa was there, too, carrying stretchers and starting I.V.s. I set to work despite feeling exhausted from my all-night battle with my intestines.

Dan came in around noon to see if I was all right and to ask me to lunch. He looked around the room full of casualties and took a step backward. "I guess you don't have time," he said.

"We could use some help," I said. "If you're not busy."

"Sure," he said quickly. "But you have to show me what to do."

He helped unload ambulances and transport stretchers, and by the time the cases were finished his face no longer looked like an intern's watching his first autopsy. We went outside to have a cigarette and Fuzzy ran to meet me. There was another one-armed woman lying on the porch, who the little girl had befriended the same as she had the first. She had even given her the quilt the other Ba had used until she died.

"Who's your friend?" Dan asked. Fuzzy clung to my skirt while I told him about her and her injury. "You could be treating a little V.C.," he said when I finished. "She's lucky she didn't end up a one-armer like her friend." He nodded toward the woman lying on the stretcher.

"Fuzzy is just a child."

"That child might be responsible for the deaths of several Americans." He continued to watch both her and the one-armed Ba.

"That's crazy," I said. But I was already wondering whether that was why Fuzzy had befriended two women who lost their arms throwing grenades. "Even if she is a 'so called' V.C.," I said defensively, "she's not responsible for anything she's forced to do."

"Why do you assume she was forced?"

"Look at her; she's only five years old." My voice rose, and Fuzzy looked worriedly up at me before going to squat next to her Ba. "Teaching a child to kill is obscene," I said more calmly. "If you teach them to love, they'll love."

Dan's expression softened. "I'm sorry about the kid's face," he said gently. "But she wouldn't have been around an area where she could get hurt if she wasn't there for a reason."

I dropped my cigarette to the concrete porch and mashed it out with my foot. "Remember that logic if I ever get hurt."

"Why do you always have to personalize things?" he asked in an irritated voice.

"Because to me it is personal. Ideologies tend to lose significance when you're working on broken bodies all day."

Dan looked at the Ba, who was shivering beneath her quilt. "This place is depressing," he said. "I don't know how you can work here."

"I'd rather be doing this than shooting them."

His eyes narrowed, then filled with such a terrible pain I wanted to turn away from them. "I'll wait in the jeep," he said.

Fuzzy was still watching, and I went over to where she squatted to tell her everything was all right. Her frightened expression disappeared and she pointed to her mouth, then to the mouth of her one-armed friend. I took her with me to the vendor who sold food just outside the hospital gates. Shelly and I had driven him outside the compound when we caught him selling food to our patients waiting for surgery. It was difficult enough having to contend with betel nut and roundworms obstructing airways of anesthetized patients, we did not have time to also worry about bellies full of food that could be regurgitated up the esophagus and down into the lungs.

The vendor looked closely to see if I was wielding a stick like the one I had used to chase him off, and bowed when he saw that my hand contained only money. Fuzzy selected tea, several small rice cakes and a loaf of bread, which he wrapped in a piece of dirty paper. I walked back with her to the porch, where I left her to share the food with her one-armed friend.

Dan sat in his jeep looking straight ahead. "I'm sorry I was so cruel," I said when I got in beside him. "I don't know why I said that."

He looked over at me and sighed deeply. "I'm sorry I called Fuzzy a V.C." We decided to go to the Navy Club for dinner, but first went to my house to wash away the blood from triage and change clothes. "Just for the record," Dan said when we were in my room. "I've never killed anyone."

"Would you though?"

"Of course I would if he was going to kill me," he said. "What the hell would you expect me to do?"

"I didn't mean self-defense."

"This is a war, Patty. It's all self defense."

He was angry again, and I was once more feeling guilty. "Let's get ready for dinner," I said. "I've had enough war for one day."

"So have I." He came across the room to where I was changing and took hold of the dress I was about to pull over my head. He took it from me, dropped it to the floor, then kissed me with such passion I was left speechless. "Let's skip dinner," he whispered as he held me closely to him.

There was no war while we made love. Or while we lay in each others arms, far away from unhappiness and pain. The minute world we created had no room for orphans or one-armed women with eyes that told us how horrible life could be.

Dan had a meeting at his Danang headquarters the next morning, after which he came to my hospital. I was in triage once more, sorting through the latest carnage. One of the patients was a woman whose uninjured infant had been brought in with her. While I pumped blood to prepare her for surgery, Dan held the baby.

"Do you think he's hungry?" he asked when the baby started to cry. He wore his Marine uniform and paced back and forth with the small infant in his oversized arms.

"Probably," I said as I continued to work on the mother. "It looks like they've been lying in a rice paddy for awhile." Both mother and child were covered with thick slippery mud.

When the woman went to surgery, I went to our locked lounge and found some fruit juice for the baby. He was only a few months old and we had no baby bottles because nearly all children were breast fed. I soaked a piece of gauze in the juice and the child sucked at it hungrily.

Despite all efforts to save her, the mother died in the operating room. I couldn't find Sister Nicole to take the baby to the orphanage, so I took him home with me when we went to lunch. "Tien won't mind," I told Dan when he suggested it might not be a good idea. "I have to watch out for him until I find Sister Nicole."

We were leaving the hospital when I felt Fuzzy's hand on my leg. I looked down into her sad eyes and realized she was jealous of the baby in my arms. I invited her for lunch and she ran to say good-bye to her Ba before piling into the back seat of Dan's jeep. On the drive through town she tried to smooth the wrinkles from the red dress I had given her, as well as to rearrange her tangled hair without benefit of a comb.

"Are you going to make a habit of picking up strays?" Jean asked when we trooped up the stairs to my apartment. The others were already gathered around the table for lunch and Tien was busy serving.

"It's just for today," I said.

"That's how Ruth got started," Margaret said. "Now she has three or four of them living with her."

Dan helped Fuzzy into a chair and I handed the baby to Tien. She was not pleased by Fuzzy. She put a bowl of plain rice in front of her, then served chicken and vegetables to the rest of us.

"I wonder why she doesn't like her," I said as I put part of my meal into Fuzzy's bowl. Tien was clucking happily to the baby in the bathroom while she bathed the mud off him.

"Because she's a worthless girl," Margaret answered. "Tien already has one of those."

"Fuzzy's not worthless."

"Tien's a wealthy woman with all the money we pay her," Julia said. "I don't think she's too thrilled about having to wait on a peasant."

Fuzzy chomped happily at her food, oblivious to the talk about her. "It doesn't look like she has much difficulty eating anymore," Jean observed. "Ron did a great job with her." The rubber catheters were gone from Fuzzy's nostrils and her nose and lips were beginning to look better.

"She'll be going to the orphanage next week," I said. "As soon as she gets rid of the last of her stitches."

When Tien came back into the room, she had the baby scrubbed clean and diapered in a dish towel. "Dep, dep," she said. Fuzzy gave him a look that made it clear she did not find him beautiful. When Tien inquired about the baby's mother she seemed delighted to hear she had died.

"You will never get that Johnny away from her now," Margaret said, using her common name for all male babies.

"Johnny," Tien repeated. She carried the baby back to the kitchen.

"Tien's husband was killed in the war," I explained to Dan. "She has only one daughter."

"And she's not likely to have any more," Margaret said. "Not unless we all go home and let these people live in peace."

"I wouldn't exactly call communism peace," Dan said across the table.

"Is that?" Margaret pointed to Fuzzy's scarred face and the child lowered her head.

Dan put down his fork and looked squarely at Margaret. "The only chance these people have is if we drive the communists back up north where they belong." His jaw was set at a determined angle.

Margaret rested her elbows on the table and leaned forward to face him just as squarely. "So that's what you're doing here, sergeant. Keeping the land safe from those terrible communists up north." Dan said nothing. "Are you sure that's what the people want, being kept safe from the dreaded Reds?"

"You're European, why don't you tell me," he said. "Or haven't you ever bothered to look over the Berlin Wall?"

Margaret's eyes flashed with indignation. "Perhaps you should look over it yourself," she said. "It's the Americans who sat on their asses allowing it to be built."

Dan laughed. "Good god, Margaret, you're accusing America of interfering over here, and at the same time you're accusing us of not interfering enough in Europe. I think you need a history lesson."

Margaret folded her napkin in such a slow, deliberate fashion it seemed to take hours. When she spoke, it was in a voice that held none of its usual sarcasm. "I lost family in the bombing of London," she said quietly. "I would say I'm quite well versed in history." She got up from the table, pinned her nurse's cap in place and left.

"Sorry, I didn't know," Dan said.

"None of us did," Jean said, still watching the stairs Margaret had descended.

"Maybe that's why she hates Americans so much," Shelly said. "She certainly blames us for the war over here."

"But this time she's right," Julia said. "I don't believe the Vietnamese give a damn about democracy," she said, exhaling smoke in Dan's direction. "They just want to be left alone to plant their rice and raise their children."

Dan did not respond for several seconds. "You girls have a whole different view of things," he said finally. "I think I'll just keep my opinions to myself from here on."

Tien did not relinquish her Johnny when it was time to return to work and Fuzzy eagerly took over the vacant spot on my lap in Dan's jeep. He dropped us off at the hospital and told me he had to leave immediately for Hoi An.

"I have to get my troops ready for a patrol tonight," he said.

"Are you sure you're not just trying to get away from my friends?"

He reached back for his helmet in the rear seat and put it on. "Your friends are fine," he said. "As long as we don't talk war." He leaned over to kiss me good-bye and drove quickly out of the compound.

I watched him go, thinking back over our lunchtime conversation. In the almost seven months I had been in Vietnam, it had become increasingly clear that the Vietnamese were less enthusiastic about ridding their country of communists than their American benefactors. Perhaps it was their long history of occupation by the Chinese, then the French, and now Americans that caused them to appear resigned to invasion by foreign forces. Or perhaps it was because the vast majority of Vietnamese were illiterate and truly did want to be left alone to raise their children and plant their rice, as Julia said. Whatever the reason, they did not have the passion for democracy that America was attempting to force feed them.

More boxes arrived later that week from the churchwomen I had written back home. There was one that contained nothing but toys.

"Let's take them out to the orphanage," I said when Dan showed up unexpectedly Saturday morning. "I can't wait to see the kids get their hands on them."

"If we can go to the beach afterwards," he said.

When he turned down the dusty lane leading to the orphanage he said, "I hope it's peanut butter time."

The nuns squealed as delightedly as the children when they opened the boxes. Dan got down on the floor to show the children how to operate complicated American toys, but one child stood apart, refusing to join in the fun. It was the young girl whose brother had died at the hands of Dr. Cannon.

"She is not happy with us," Sister Marie said to me. "But she will be better when school begins again." I told the nun I would be bringing Fuzzy out the following week and she promised to make room for her in her already crowded kindergarten classroom.

"Do you think Tien would mind if we took Danny to your house for awhile?" Dan asked when I suggested it was time to leave. The two of them had been playing a game and Danny did not want to stop.

"I thought you wanted to go to the beach."

He looked down at Danny, who clung to him the same way Fuzzy did me. "Maybe another day."

"I guess she wouldn't object to a boy," I said. "But it's up to Sister Marie."

The nun readily agreed but asked if we would take three other children as well. "They are having such a difficult time," she said. "And we cannot give them the time they need."

Oversized feet were coaxed into undersized shoes, causing the children to waddle like penguins. We waited while their somber faces were scrubbed and each was dressed in clothes from the boxes. They were so quiet on the trip into town, I decided to stop by the hospital and pick up Fuzzy. She could perhaps cheer them up, and it would give her an opportunity to meet children with whom she would be living.

"Good Christ! She's turning the place into a refugee center!" Margaret yelled when she saw us. Tien looked just as unhappy, until I handed her the clothes I had saved out of the boxes for Johnny.

"How often is this going to happen?" Jean asked when she came out of her room and saw the crowd around the lunch table.

"Some of the children aren't adjusting too well to the orphanage," I said.

"Well, I'm not adjusting too well to them."

"O.K., I won't bring any home after this," I said. "Except maybe Danny."

"Danny?" Margaret looked first at the small boy sitting next to Dan, then at him. "Congratulations, sergeant, I didn't know."

"Don't be so crude," Julia said.

The meal was chaotic, with hands flying across the table and overturned iced tea dripping into our laps. They were behaving like normal, noisy children, and even I was relieved when it was time to take Fuzzy back to the hospital and the others back to the orphanage. They waved at everybody passing our jeep on the way, and shouted gleefully when American G.I.s waved back.

"I'm glad you took me out there again," Dan said on the drive back to Danang. "It's easy to get used to thinking of all Vietnamese as gooks."

He stuck out his arm to signal a left turn and a young boy on a bicycle snatched off his wristwatch without even slowing down. Dan tromped down on the accelerator to chase the thief, but he quickly disappeared in the maze of cyclos, motorbikes and cars.

"Now that's a goddamned gook!" he yelled.

CHAPTER TWENTY-ONE

The woman with the missing arm smelled infected when I went to the hospital on Sunday morning to make sure Fuzzy had food. I turned her stretcher around so the inflamed stump would be next to the wall, where it was less likely to be bumped by someone walking past her on the veranda.

Fuzzy took the money I gave her and quickly tucked it down the front of her dress so others would not see and steal it. I was about to return to my quarters, and possibly an afternoon on the beach with my coworkers, when I noticed activity at the pediatric hospital that was being built next to ours by the Swiss government. Although it had been under construction for months, the two story building was still surrounded by a rickety wooden scaffolding and piles of concrete block.

"Hello," I called when a nurse appeared on the doorstep in a starched white uniform. She had a broom in one hand and a bucket in the other.

"Yes, hello," she called back. She set down the bucket and disappeared into the building, returning with a young man with yellow hair that stood almost straight up from his forehead. He wore a white lab coat over a shirt and trousers.

"How can I help you?" he asked as I came up the stairs toward him. His accent sounded German, but there was a Swiss flag hanging next to the main door.

"I'm from the American team," I said, extending my hand. "Welcome to Danang."

"Thank you, thank you," he said with a smile. "I am Doctor Brandt; we have come just last night." He looked in the direction of the piles of construction materials and nervously worked a hand through his straw-like hair, making it stand even higher. "The Vietnamese sent a cable that our hospital is finished, but it is not so."

I didn't want to be the one to tell him the building was probably as finished as it ever would be. We had watched the Vietnamese workers mix large quantities of sand into the concrete to save on costs, no doubt pocketing the savings themselves, and saw them carry away lumber and pipes almost the moment they were delivered to the site. What the construction crew didn't take during the day, our patients and their relatives took at night.

I went inside with the doctor, where he pointed to a series of bare shelves. "We spend much money on medicines and equipment," he said. "And none of it is here." The nurse I had first seen appeared from nowhere and nodded her head to confirm what Dr. Brandt said. Her hair was a thick blond and she had bright blue eyes.

"We must be here before the things are shipped," she said. "They do not take them if we are here to watch."

Although I agreed they shouldn't have sent supplies and equipment until they were in-country, I told them that wouldn't have eliminated theft. A brief description of our experience with the black market was enough to convince them.

"But why do they steal from people who try to help them?" The young doctor spoke in a voice as defeated as his expression, and more nurses gathered around to listen to the grim news.

"It's only a few who steal," I lied. "Most appreciate the help."

I followed them on a tour through their hospital, where garbage and the remnants of cooking fires littered the floors. There were a few cribs that had not been stolen, but they were occupied by adult relatives of patients from our hospital who had taken refuge in the unoccupied building. Jean would have to give the Swiss team lessons on her cattle drive.

We were standing in one of the squalid wards when a woman came to us with a small child who was gasping for breath. "We must do a tracheotomy," Dr. Brandt said after a hasty examination. He hurried with the child to an examining room, but his hands stopped in midair when he reached automatically to a shelf that was empty. "We have nothing," he said, turning to me with a look of alarm.

"I'll get what you need," I said and ran for our hospital next door.

When I returned, two of the nurses were taking turns doing mouth-to-mouth resuscitation on the child. I put a laryngoscope into its throat but could insert only a tiny endotracheal tube.

"It looks like diphtheria," I said when the tube was in place. The grey membrane in the child's throat was unmistakable. "I know you did what you thought was best," I told the nurses. "But you shouldn't do mouth-to-mouth on these patients. They have too many diseases."

"We have immunizations," one of them said in the same thick accent as Dr. Brandt.

Their hair and eyes were the same as the first nurse. And they all wore starched white uniforms with an armband of red, decorated by a white cross, the same as the flag that hung outside.

"Not against tuberculosis," I said. "And they all have it." I was pumping air into the child's lungs with a small breathing bag I had brought with me from our O.R.

"But why do they have such diseases?" Dr. Brandt raked a hand through his scarecrow hair. "Surely you are immunizing the people against diphtheria."

Our new nursing supervisor had managed to get an immunization program started for the nurses on the wards so they would take care of the patients. It was now being extended to other Vietnamese staff members, but our patients and their relatives were still without protection.

"We hope to have programs some day," I said. "Right now we are kept busy just taking care of casualties."

Dr. Brandt managed a weary smile. "I do not mean to criticize," he said. "We are most grateful for your help." His nurses had taken over the breathing bag and were attending the sick child as best they could.

I offered to get them enough things to function until they could get word back to their country about their stolen supplies. But I cautioned them that they must use everything sparingly and not waste it on patients who were too sick to survive. Before they could ask the question so obvious in their eyes, I left to get the supplies. It would be up to them to devise their own method of deciding who would be treated and who would not. I was having enough difficulty living with the decisions I made in our own triage.

"Where are you going with those things?" Dr. Fitch had come out of his house on the hospital compound just as I was pushing a cart filled with supplies to the Swiss Hospital. When I told him about the newly arrived team he said he already knew. "I didn't offer our assistance because we can't spare anything," he told me. "We have barely enough for ourselves."

"But they'll be taking care of all the children," I said. The smaller victims of the war were frequently overlooked once they left our recovery room. The new medical team would be providing us a tremendous service by giving them long term care.

Dr. Fitch spread his hands palms upward. He wore his usual baggy cotton pants and barefoot sandals, and his beard and hair were now well beneath his shoulders. "We simply do not have the things to spare," he said. "I will meet with their chief tomorrow and explain the situation."

I looked at the items on the cart, some of which had been cumshawed from our various military sources. "I believe that decision should be left to the people who got these things," I said. I continued on to the Swiss Hospital, leaving him standing in the red dust of the hospital courtyard.

Dr. Brandt and the nurses were so excited about the supplies they immediately began wiping down shelves to put them on. People were shooed out of the cribs and the floors were swept and scrubbed.

"Don't work too hard," I said before I left. "If you get sick you can't take care of patients. And don't stay here after dark. It isn't safe."

"We shall leave soon," Dr. Brandt said cheerily. "Thank you for your kindness." He walked with me to the door.

I was returning the empty cart to our hospital when Shelly pulled into the compound on her sputtering motorbike. I told her about the Swiss team, and she offered to get them some additional things from Navy Hospital.

"Tom and the other Navy docs are throwing a party for their corpsmen," she told me. "They sent me into town to round up some nurses." It was rumored that Navy Hospital would soon have female nurses, but none had arrived thus far. "We're all meeting at my quarters," Shelly said.

She was gunning the engine of her bike to keep it running with the watered down gas she bought for it on the local economy. Dr. Fitch came out of his house to see what the noise was, and Shelly let the bike idle until he went back inside. "Get out of this mule-shit pie for awhile and come with us."

I told Shelly I would meet her at her villa and went to say good-bye to Fuzzy, who was squatted next to her Ba. Just as I got there, I heard American voices coming down the veranda from the direction of the burn ward. A group of Americans, led by the reporter from the Concerned Citizens group, turned the corner and stopped. The reporter didn't seem to recognize me without my surgery garb, or to recognize Fuzzy from the day he had refused to help with her.

One of the group started taking photographs of the one-armed Ba with an expensive camera he wore around his neck. "Hey, watch what you're doing," I said when he moved her stretcher for a better angle and accidentally banged her painful stump against the wall.

"I'm sorry," he apologized. "I wanted to get a better shot of her face."

"I'm sure she isn't interested," I said, pulling the canvas stretcher back to its original position.

"Ma'am, I am trying to take pictures that will bring an end to this war," he said in a voice that sounded sincere.

"She's too sick." I stood in front of the stretcher, protecting the woman from further injury.

"Don't pay any attention to her," the reporter who had finally recognized me said. "We happen to have permission to take whatever photographs we wish of this hospital," he said, standing only inches from me. "And the sicker the patients, the stronger the message."

"And the more you advance your film, the more you advance your career."

Fuzzy was drawn up into a corner of the veranda, with eyes wide with fright. I took her hand and went with her to the burn ward to see if the visitors had caused any problems.

Ruth was at work, even on Sunday, and told me the group had spent little time in her ward. "They took pictures of these new patients," she said, indicating two women swathed in bandages. "They were burned by a cooking fire they tried to start with gasoline, but the reporters wouldn't believe me. They thought I was trying to hide the fact that they were victims of napalm."

"How could anyone hide napalm?" The black, bubbling blisters caused by the chemical were distinctive even to the untrained eye.

Ever since my arrival in Vietnam, I had tried to imagine a war fought in my own country, especially if it were nuclear. People talked about surviving the deadly fallout, but I had seen enough napalm victims to know that burns would be the much greater enemy. And next to thermonuclear burns, napalm would be considered a sunburn. Ruth had years of experience, but not even her saintly ministerings could save all of the patients we received. If healthy, well-trained medical personnel like her couldn't do the job, how could inexperienced medical people suffering from injuries of their own and radiation sickness they would surely incur?

I invited Ruth to the beach party Navy Hospital was throwing, but she declined. When Fuzzy and I returned to the veranda, the visitors were still snapping pictures of her Ba. "Dinky Dao," I said to Fuzzy.

The worried expression left Fuzzy's face and she tried to smile through the scars restricting her facial movements. She was delighted that I would call other Americans crazy. "Dinky Dao," she repeated.

I left her there with her one-armed friend, the subject of a photo layout that would undoubtedly be printed long after she had died. When I turned to look back at them before driving away, I saw Fuzzy standing in her red dress waving to me. She was always so afraid I wouldn't come back, it was hard for me to leave her.

The party on China Beach was well underway when the nurses from our team arrived. Some of the corpsmen had secured a yellow Navy life raft, which they had anchored out beyond the breakers for diving. Margaret was swimming for it when I splashed into the cool water and followed.

I had gone only half the distance when suddenly I was struck in the back of my neck with such force I was propelled forward in the water. I heard myself groan as the air was squeezed out of my chest in a crushing wave of pain that radiated out all four extremities. Then there was nothing; no sound, no sight, no feeling.

"Stop fighting me." The voice came from very far away through a grey mist that enveloped me. "Stop fighting or you're going to drown."

The last command was more urgent and I tried to comply. But I wasn't fighting; I couldn't even feel my arms and legs. The prospect of being paralyzed flashed into my mind and I prayed that I was already dead.

"Please, ma'am. Stop fighting, or I can't save you." The words were said between gasps.

"Shot," I said weakly. "Must be shot." There had been gunfire down the beach and I was convinced a stray bullet had hit me.

"You're not shot. There's no blood."

My vision began to clear, and I recognized the young man who was trying to keep me afloat. It was Fast Eddie, Tom's corpsman.

Although I still could not feel anything, I could see my legs moving in contorted motions beneath the surface of the clear water. My arms moved too, skipping spastically across the water in wild flailing motions that caused them to repeatedly hit the corpsman's upper body. Blood ran down his face from where my nails had scratched him.

"You have to stop fighting," he said again.

"I'm not fighting. Don't feel anything." I had to stop to catch my breath. "Must have hit my spinal cord."

"Oh, my god, you're bleeding," Fast Eddie said. "In the back of your neck."

I wanted Dan, to see his strong arms swimming out to save me. But the grey mist was coming back, shutting out all light and sound.

I awoke still in the water, with the corpsman trying to keep me afloat while he pulled me toward shore. "It looks like fang marks in the back of your neck," he said when he saw that my eyes were open. "You must have been bitten by a sea snake."

Now I knew I was going to die. There was no antivenin for the poisonous snakes, and muscular activity hastened the spread of the deadly venom through the body. With my arms and legs flailing, it was certain to have already reached every cell.

I started to pray, not that I would survive, but that I would live long enough to tell Dan I loved him. And I wanted to tell my family I was sorry to cause them such sorrow for the sake of a stupid beach party.

The exhausted corpsman was periodically waving an arm for help to the people on shore. "The idiots are waving back," he said in a near whisper. His breath was coming in short gasps, and we were occasionally dipping beneath the surface of the water.

"Leave me," I told him. "Get to shore yourself."

"No." It was said with his last bit of strength.

I felt his grip relaxing on my chin. Dan, Dan, Dan. The words could not be spoken through the water that was seeping into my mouth and nose.

"Stay calm." Somebody had hold of my chin, forcing it upward. The female voice was familiar. "Hold on, we will have you out in a moment."

I opened my eyes and saw wet blond hair trailing over the water next to me. Margaret was holding my head up, and a second corpsman was helping Fast Eddie.

By the time they got us to shallow water, my extremities had stopped spasming and I was beginning to feel a tingling sensation in them. The people on the beach finally recognized there was something wrong and came running toward us.

"I was swimming behind her when I saw her arch up in the water then go under," Fast Eddie told them in an exhausted voice. Both of us were lying on the sand with several doctors looking us over. "She had a seizure, a really big one," Fast Eddie said. "There're fang marks on the back of her neck."

Tom gently rolled me over to look at my neck. "How do you feel?" he asked.

"I don't know. I can't feel much." The faces gathered above me were grave.

"Mouse, are you an epileptic?" Shelly asked as she knelt beside me. "Have you ever had a seizure before?"

"No, never."

"See if she wet her pants," someone in the crowd yelled. "That's how you can tell if she really had a seizure."

"Someone get that drunk out of here," Shelly ordered. "See if she wet her pants in the middle of a fucking ocean."

"We could take you over to Navy Hospital," Tom told me. "But there's really nothing they can do but keep you quiet and wait and see what happens." He was wearing only a bathing suit, but he had the same calm, professional manner as in the receiving area of his hospital.

"Put something cold on my neck," I said. The feeling was coming back and it burned unmercifully. The only cold thing available was beer, and a can was placed on the back of my neck by a baby-faced corpsman who looked at me as if I were already dead. "How about giving me one of those to drink?" I asked him. "I'm thirsty."

"Yes, ma'am." He smiled and popped open the can he had been holding on my neck, replacing it with a cooler one.

My muscular strength gradually returned, and I was helped to our car by several pair of hands anxious to help. "I'm sorry I hurt you," I said when I saw Fast Eddie standing silently nearby. His chest and face were a mass of scratches.

"It don't mean nothin'," he said, brushing a nonchalant hand across them. "You just get better now."

Jean and Shelly took turns keeping cold compresses on my neck all afternoon and evening, assuring me I would be all right. Tien came over, even though it was her day off, and made me a rice gruel guaranteed to cure anything.

I was surprised when I woke to a quiet house and found it was nearly noon the next day. Jean had gone to work, but with explicit instructions that Tien not leave me alone. The maid came into my room the moment she heard me stir and helped me get my stiff body to the bathroom.

"You look like a water buffalo," Shelly said when she came to check on me. She rubbed a hand across the enormous hump surrounding the fang marks on the back of my neck. "Tom wants to take some pictures in case you survive."

"Thanks for the optimism."

"I'm serious. He says they've found guys with fang marks on them dead in the water. They thought the venom killed them, but now they think they might have drowned from the seizures when the venom hit their nervous systems."

"It probably wasn't a poisonous sea snake," I said.

When the others came home for lunch I thanked Margaret for her role in the rescue. "Fast Eddie wouldn't let me go," I said. "Both of us would have drowned if you hadn't pulled us out."

"Actually, I would have been there sooner," Margaret said. "But I saw the two of you bobbing up and down together out there and wasn't sure if I might be interrupting something."

CHAPTER TWENTY-TWO

By midweek the swelling had subsided enough for me to return to work. Shelly had taken enough supplies from our hospital to the Swiss to have them in full operation, which was fortunate because of an unexpected influx of typhoid patients. It was the first mass outbreak of the disease we had experienced, and we were unprepared for the many who required surgery to repair bowel perforations that were a common complication. Not only did the cases tie up our operating rooms for hours, the patients required massive amounts of intravenous fluids and antibiotics to treat the dehydration and peritonitis caused by the intestinal contents leaking into their bellies.

In addition to the frustration of trying to care for the patients while handling our continuing stream of casualties, I was troubled by my inability to find Fuzzy. Somewhere between the time I had left her to go to the beach party and my return to work three days later, the one-armed Ba had died and Fuzzy had vanished.

“Maybe someone took her out to the orphanage and she’s mixed in with the other children,” Teresa suggested when I asked if she had seen her.

“I’ve already asked Sister Nicole,” I said. “Fuzzy isn’t there.”

The nursing supervisor speculated that a relative might have claimed Fuzzy, but even though I would liked to have believed that, no family member had ever come looking for her during her long hospital stay. And her mixed race made the likelihood of some stranger taking her too remote to consider.

“She was always so afraid I would leave her,” I told Jean that night. “But she’s the one who left me.”

“She might still turn up. There are a lot of people milling around our hospital she could have taken up with.”

My roommate excused herself and went to bed without further discussion. I knew she cared about Fuzzy, but she had other problems occupying her mind.

Rick had continued to come into town every Wednesday night for steak night. But on his most recent trip, he had accidentally hit a child who darted out from the shacks between Danang and the air base.

"He came from nowhere," Rick had told us between gulps of Scotch when he arrived at our house late that night. "I was just driving along, and all of a sudden he was flying over the hood of my jeep." The pilot had rushed the child back to the small clinic Jerry ran at the air base, where he was given emergency treatment. But he died while they were having him airlifted to Navy Hospital for more extensive care.

"Accidents happen everywhere," Jean told him. "Even in war."

Rick drained the last of his glass and sat looking into its depths. "I just didn't expect to come over here and kill a kid on my way to steak night with my girl." He looked vulnerable without the dark glasses he usually wore. "There's something wrong," he said. "Something wrong with me and with this fucked-up war." He picked up the bottle of Scotch Jean had set on the table after pouring him a drink and took it with him out to the balcony.

"I don't understand it," I said to Jean when he left for the base well past midnight. "He drops bombs on hundreds, maybe even thousands of people. Why is he so upset over one kid?"

"The bombs bother him too," Jean said. "But it happens to be his job." She went to fix herself a drink. "It's hard to see where the bombs are landing when you're screaming over a target in a jet," she said. "That child he hit probably represents all the ones he doesn't see."

Rick flew Phantom jets, which traveled at five to six hundred knots over their targets. He truly enjoyed flying and was in the habit of kicking in the afterburners, which boosted the power even more, when he passed over Danang on his way up North as a special farewell to Jean. The noise from the powerful afterburners nearly shook us out of our beds, but Rick thought it was great fun. Following the accident, he never again sent his greeting.

I continued searching for Fuzzy; in the shacks, through the maze of people hanging around the verandas, and even asked the food vendor outside the hospital gates if he had seen her. The child was nowhere.

"She has to be alive," Ron reassured me after one of my fruitless searches of the compound. "She was perfectly healthy other than her facial injury."

I admitted to already thinking about checking the morgue. But the outlying building lacked air-conditioning, the same as the rest of our hospital, and the smell had driven me away before I got past the front door.

I was glad when Dan called to tell me he had made arrangements for me to go to Hoi An the following week. "I'm taking you to my island," he said above the static on our antiquated telephone system. "I want you to see it before monsoon. And Bird-dog wants Julia to come with you."

The flow of typhoid patients had dwindled, but I still worried about leaving Shelly alone with Gertie for an entire weekend. "Go and have a good time while you can," Shelly told me. "You never know if you'll get another chance."

The eat, drink and be merry philosophy she espoused had disturbed me when I was new in country, but it hadn't taken me long to adopt it as a way of life. None of us really believed we would die, but we lived as if we did.

Dan had made arrangements for us to make the trip by helicopter because of the insecure roads, but when we were setting down on the helipad in Hoi An there was a sudden loud PING, followed by the grating of metal. The door gunner sprayed the bush cut back from the helicopter pad.

The chopper started to lift up into the air again, then twirled around wildly and plopped down to the grated pad with such a thud it banged our heads against its walls. Dan and Bird-dog came running toward us in a crouched position and led us to a bunker at one side of the pad. Another Aussie was there, manning a machine gun while the helicopter crew escaped.

"It's nothing, me darlin's," Bird-dog said when we were all safely inside the bunker and he had sniffed the air for Cong. "Just one little sniper with a lucky shot." He pulled off his helmet and replaced it with his bush hat, then put his arm around Julia.

"Why didn't you take it up?" Dan asked the pilot.

"Couldn't," he said. "He hit the tail rotor housing with the first round."

The shooting had not lasted beyond the initial shots, but the disabled craft had to be left sitting on the pad. The men drove us to their villa, where their housekeeper had a meal waiting that was much worse than Tien's cooking. They then took us on a sight-seeing tour of the town, with Bird-dog acting as chauffeur and tour guide.

"This, me darlin's, is the Happy House." He stopped in front of a plain cinder block building that had no windows and sat back several yards from the road. It had a grated metal helicopter pad next to it. "I'm sure Dan wouldn't want you to miss this."

I felt Dan's arm tighten around me in the back seat. "I'm sure Dan would," he said firmly. "Drive on."

"What is it, a whorehouse?" Julia asked.

"I'm afraid no one comes out of that place smiling," Bird-dog said with a wink.

I looked to Dan for an explanation, but his face was set in stony silence. Bird-dog did not stop again until we reached a grass landing on the banks of a wide river. Dan and Bird-dog hired a fisherman to row us across to a small island where dozens of children ran to meet us. Dan stooped down to talk to them in Vietnamese I found surprisingly fluent.

"Numbah-one," a small boy said to me as he pointed to Dan. "Sergea', numbah-one."

"Sergea', dep," a girl who looked to be in her teens said. Several others giggled with her and held their hands up to cover their mouths.

"Best watch that handsome sergeant of yours," Bird-dog told me. "Looks to me like these little Sheilas mean to give you some competition."

Dan still seemed annoyed with the Aussie for stopping at the place he called the Happy House. He walked on without acknowledging Bird-dog's comment, and the gaggle of children followed behind.

There was pride in Dan's face when he showed us a school and a small medical clinic he had established on the island. "My Vietnamese troops are responsible for a lot of this," he said when we complimented him. "We had to drive all the Cong out before we could do anything."

"And you're sure they're all gone?" Julia asked. She looked around at the grass huts making up the small village Dan and his men had secured. Chickens scratched lazily in the dust and old people peeked out at us from behind ragged curtains serving as doors.

"We're sure," Dan said. "This island is completely pacified."

We followed him along dikes separating dozens of rice paddies. Dan stopped occasionally to speak in Vietnamese to the people working in them. They spoke to him as they stood in knee-deep muck, with their pant legs rolled up, stooping to plant small sprouts of rice for their new crop.

"Their backs must get awfully tired," I said as I watched an old woman who looked permanently stooped.

"Not any more than yours do hauling those field stretchers," Dan said.

Julia wandered on ahead of the group and had to be reminded to stay with us. "I thought you said this place was safe," she said when Dan called her back.

"It is," he said. "But only as safe as any place in Vietnam can be."

Bird-dog put an arm around her so she would stay by his side.

"Where did all the pigs come from?" I asked. A bunch of them grunted their way across the path in front of us as we walked back to the small village.

"Uncle Sam sent them over," Dan said. "The government's trying to teach the people how to grow pork instead of just chickens and ducks."

"Show them what else your government gives them," Bird-dog teased.

Dan looked at him and smiled for the first time since the Happy House. "All right," he said. "You won't leave me alone until I do."

He led us to a cluster of low concrete structures jammed with people and their household belongings. Pigs roamed freely around them, rooting in the ground.

"We built these things according to government specifications," Dan said of the buildings. "They're supposed to be pigsties, but the people threw the pigs out and moved in."

Bird-dog laughed and tipped his bush hat back on his head. "Can't blame them, they're a heap better than their houses."

"The pigs don't seem to mind," Julia said.

An elderly man had come out of one of the buildings to scatter food on the ground for them. The large gunny sack he dragged behind him had the handshake emblem of USAID on it.

"That's right, it's bulgur wheat," Dan said when he saw me looking at the feed. "The people will trade a whole sack of it for one handful of rice." The highly nutritious grain was sent over in shiploads by the Agency for International Development for the people.

The same fisherman took us back across the water in his smelly boat. Before we got into the jeep Dan and Bird-dog checked it carefully for explosives that might have been planted underneath while we were away. Bird-dog's jeep had a kangaroo painted on its side.

It was late afternoon by the time we returned to the villa, and guests were beginning to arrive for a party the men had arranged. "Dan's boss is staying up at headquarters in Danang," Bird-dog said. "We thought it might be a good time for some fun."

Dan took me out into the courtyard to escape a noisy dart game that began almost immediately. We ended up in one of the fortified bunkers situated at each end of the trench.

"Are you really part of the CIA?" I asked after a few minutes of listening to music drifting from the house.

"Why do you ask?" He had a laugh that betrayed his uneasiness in awkward situations.

"Sergeants don't usually live in villas."

He looked back toward the house where light streamed through a set of French doors. "It's nice," he said. "But I pay my dues being attached to this outfit." He didn't say what they were, but I was already aware that sergeants couldn't get a helicopter to bring us to Hoi An. As I looked at him in the twilight, I noticed he was also growing his hair out of the traditional whitewall Marine cut.

"I was offered this job when I signed up for Nam," he said. "I thought I might as well live as good as I could."

"Are you glad you came here?"

"Most of the time." He looked at me and smiled. "You?"

"Sometimes," I said after considering a few moments. "I feel I'm helping people who need me, but I also know that I'm not doing enough."

"What else could you do, for god's sake?" he asked with genuine surprise.

"Spend more time at the hospital instead of sitting here with you, or going to the beach."

"You spend too much time at that place as it is." He looked off to where the sun was setting over a backdrop of thick jungle. "Why didn't you join the military?" he asked. "Or is it only Vietnamese casualties you feel sorry for?"

"Of course not. I just didn't want to join the Army and be sent to a stateside base for two years."

"You'd rather be a bush ape?" he said with a smile.

"I like it up here a lot better than Saigon."

"Me too." He reached a hand out to take mine. "Especially since I met you."

When we went back into the house, the dart game had progressed to a contest of who could gulp down the most beer between throws. Julia was keeping up with the male players. "The Aussies have some wild parties," Dan said. "Do you want to stay?"

"Or what?"

"Go to my room."

"I'm not very good at darts."

"We might have another night together," he said as we lay together after making love. Music floated through an open window. "You can't leave until they get that disabled chopper off the pad."

"It's all right with me," I said. "But Shelly will kill me if I leave her alone with Gertie an extra day."

"Shelly knows what it's like to be in love." I sat up to look at him and he laughed his nervous laugh. "What's the matter, didn't I tell you I love you?"

"I don't think so."

"Well, I do." He pulled me closer to him. "I've loved you ever since I saw you working at that dung heap you're assigned to."

We listened to the music, and to helicopters flying overhead. "Dan, do you think we might be fooling ourselves?" I asked. "I mean, it's different over here. Feelings are different."

"Of course they are. There's no time for all the phony crap that goes on back home."

"Do you think you would feel the same way about me if we weren't in a war?"

"I would feel the same about you anywhere." He kissed my forehead. "I love you, Patty. Here, back in the world, anywhere we might happen to be."

We made love again, and he was reaching for his cigarettes on the bedside crate when gunfire erupted nearby. "Better get dressed in case we need to make a run for the bunker," he said. He jumped out of bed and pulled on his trousers, after first handing me my dress. "Remember to stay low and head straight for the trench," he said as he pulled on his boots and shirt. "If I should fall, keep running."

I stopped dressing. "But I could never leave you if you were hurt." I felt tears welling in my eyes.

"I didn't mean to upset you." He put his arms around me and stroked my hair. Another explosion set our ears ringing. "Come on."

We were halfway down the corridor when we heard the sharp crack of gunfire very close by. Dan pulled me to the floor with him, and after a moment of waiting for more shots we crept down the darkened hallway on our hands and knees.

"Hell, it's those fucking Aussies," he said when he peered cautiously into the main room of the house.

The dart game had been abandoned for target practice. "You have to stop them," I said. They were shooting at a target across the room and people were gathered on either side of the makeshift firing range. A man who had passed out from too much partying slept in a chair directly in the line of fire, with bullets ripping just over his head. If he came to and sat up, he would be dead.

"Nobody can stop the Aussies when they're on a drunk," Dan said. "Not even the Marines."

Julia and Bird-dog were in line behind the man firing, waiting their turn at the target drawn on the wall in black and red marker. I was appalled by the antics and still wanted Dan to break it up. But then I remembered that nobody had tried to stop me when I continued to swim in the South China Sea after nearly drowning.

The helicopter pad was still out of commission the next afternoon when Dan was given a message to deliver immediately to his Danang headquarters in the pouch that was hand carried between the two facilities. "They're making you into a regular little courier," Bird-dog told him. "Join the Marines and learn to fetch and carry."

Dan dismissed him with a look that discouraged further comment. "How would you like to go back to Danang by the scenic route?" he asked Julia and me. "You would be back for work on Monday."

"I guess we should," Julia said. "Fitch doesn't even know we're here."

Sundays were generally quiet, and the men decided the fifteen mile trip by road would be safe enough. But they dressed us in flak jackets and helmets before putting us into Dan's jeep. Julia offered to drive.

"We'll bring up the rear in the second vehicle," Dan told Julia. "Once we're out of Hoi An, you don't stop for anything. If you hear shooting, or even if you hear us yelling, you keep your foot on that gas pedal and head straight north until you hit Danang. Don't drive off the road for anything, don't stop for anyone waving you down, just keep driving. Understand?"

"Understand," Julia said, imitating his military speech.

He smiled and leaned into the jeep to kiss me. "We'll be right behind you in Bird-dog's jeep. If any shit starts flying we'll take care of it."

The road was supposed to be paved, but long stretches of it were red dirt with huge potholes. I had trouble keeping myself on the seat as we pounded northward as fast as the jeep could go. We had traveled a significant distance when I heard shouts behind us.

"Someone's yelling for us to stop!" I said as I turned to look back through a cloud of red dust.

Julia looked straight ahead, not slackening her speed. "I hear!" she yelled back. "But Dan said not to stop for anything!"

"But I think it might be Bird-dog!"

"He's yelling not to stop!" she shouted. Dust was flying up behind us in such a thick cloud we couldn't see anything in the rear.

"I don't see their jeep," I said when we reached a paved surface and could see better.

My hands were perspiring and my eyes hurt from the dirt that had blown into them in the open jeep. We were on the outskirts of Danang when Julia slowed enough to take a good look behind us.

"They're not there." Her face reflected the fear I felt.

"Do you think we should go back?"

"I don't know," she said. "What else can we do?"

"The M.P.s," I said. "We'll go to the M.P.s and tell them we lost the guys on the way up here. They'll know what to do."

Julia drove as fast as possible to the M.P. station, located not far from our houses, and explained what had happened. The military police appeared skeptical at first but were persuaded by the red dirt covering us and our jeep.

"You shouldn't be out on that highway," one of them told us. "It's not secured for civilian travel."

"Please, just get someone to look for the guys," I pleaded. "Something's happened to them."

"We'll have to get someone to investigate," one of the M.P.s said. "We don't patrol down there."

"You need to hurry," I said impatiently. "It's getting dark."

"Lady, those men had no business sending you out on an insecure road," the man in charge said. "And when we do locate them they will have to explain why they did."

We heard a jeep approaching. "Hey, you Sheilas left us out there in Indian territory," Bird-dog said when he pulled up along side of us. "We could have got ourselves killed."

"What the hell happened to you?" Julia demanded.

"Little water in the gas line, that's all," he said as he lifted his bush hat to brush dirt from his hair. "We stalled for a bit, but we got her going."

I went to Dan and put my arms around him, but he pulled away with an embarrassed expression and went to talk to the M.P.s watching us with unfriendly expressions. "Nothing to worry about," Bird-dog told us. "The good sergeant will take care of them."

Dan walked with the one in charge to a guard house near the heavily sandbagged entrance of the M.P. station. I saw him pull out the card that gave him entry to clubs and helicopters.

"He really must be a spook," Julia said when Dan put the card back into his wallet and walked back toward where we stood.

"All clear," he said.

"Didn't I tell you?" Bird-dog said.

"You drive like a maniac," Dan told Julia. "We couldn't even catch up to your dust." His expression was amused, but I was still shaking with fright.

"You told us not to stop," I said. "We were scared half to death."

"I know," he said soothingly. "I don't know how we got water in our line. We don't buy gook gas; we get it at the motor pool."

"No matter," Bird-dog said. "Let's get that parcel of yours delivered so we can head on back before Mister Charles takes over the road for the night."

CHAPTER TWENTY-THREE

The influx of typhoid patients was just behind us when we were inundated with an outbreak of cholera. Dr. Brandt and his nurses were more affected than us, since the disease spread rapidly among the young. Mothers would arrive at the pediatric hospital in the morning with two or three sick children and be childless by nightfall.

In the midst of the epidemic, a new chief arrived to take over our hospital. He had originally been assigned to a large rehabilitation facility in the Delta, the southernmost region of Vietnam, but the officials responsible for sending us Boom-Boom decided to give us a chief who had already been well checked-out. Dr. Gaukel was in his sixties, bald and addicted to putrid black cigars.

The first meeting he called was to thank us for the job we had been doing, and to reassure us things would get better. "There's one other thing," he said as he exhaled a cloud of smoke so acrid it made several of us cough. "I don't go much for formality, so you can drop the doctor crap and call me Otto." He looked completely at home behind the desk Dr. Fitch looked at longingly from a corner of the crowded office.

Another physician had arrived on the same flight, an orthopedic surgeon who volunteered with the AMA's two month program. The silver haired surgeon looked like the president of a country club next to Otto, who resembled the proprietor of a pool hall in his baggy trousers and rumpled shirt. "I want you to take good care of this fella," Otto told us. "We're lucky to have a surgeon as famous as Doctor Wheeler volunteer to come over here." The latter flashed a smile that revealed perfectly capped white teeth.

"Who is he?" I whispered to Ron.

"Never heard of him," Ron answered. "But I'll pretend I have if that's what we have to do to keep him happy." Other than the cases Tom managed to do in his free time from Navy Hospital, Ron had handled all orthopedic cases since Jim Ramirez had departed.

"I don't expect any special treatment," Dr. Wheeler said in a voice as genteel as his appearance. "I came here to work, the same as everybody else."

"Welcome aboard," Ron said when he was formally introduced. "I've read about your interesting work."

"I'm flattered," Dr. Wheeler said. "General surgeons don't usually take time to read my articles."

Ron quickly introduced Jean before the conversation could get any more specific. "Jean's the head nurse in surgery and will take good care of you," he told Dr. Wheeler. The new surgeon looked curiously at Ron's chopped off scrub pants and sleeveless top.

"I'm afraid we don't have much to work with," Jean said to the new arrival. "But we'll do our best to keep you happy."

"Just keep things moving and don't hold me up," Dr. Wheeler said. "I like to work fast."

"Sounds like we'd better keep Gertie out of his room," Shelly whispered to me.

"That should be fun with you going on R&R," I replied. Shelly and Tom were going to Thailand for five days the following week, when another orthopedic surgeon was due to arrive at Navy Hospital.

Dr. Wheeler lived up to his description of himself. The surgeon could go through almost as many cases as Jim Ramirez and do them just as well. But he complained bitterly about the long turnover between cases and demanded Jean do something about the Vietnamese nurses. Not only because they were slow, but because Julia still had to constantly remind them not to sit on the instrument table while she assisted Dr. Wheeler.

"They don't appreciate the time I've taken from my practice to come over here," Dr. Wheeler said. "I could do five cases while they take off time for siesta."

"We usually take siesta off too," Jean told him. "The American team has just been staying to accommodate you."

"Well, I appreciate your consideration. But I must say I wouldn't expect anything less."

"Give him another week," I told Jean. "He'll be taking siesta off like everyone else."

But the energetic surgeon did not slow down. He demanded a full crew to keep his room running from seven in the morning until six in the evening, including Saturdays. Shelly had returned from R&R but had come back with a stomach disorder that forced her to bed because of persistent vomiting and diarrhea. Between running triage and keeping all the O.R.s going, I was about to collapse when Becky returned from her honeymoon and took over some of the workload.

I was sorting through a fresh batch of casualties when Dr. Wheeler came into triage to see how many patients would require orthopedic procedures. He examined them quickly and was on his way out when he stopped to look at a woman I had set aside. "Get this one to the O.R. stat," he said. "She's about to bleed out."

"There are other patients ahead of her," I said without interrupting my work.

"She has to be done first," he insisted. "Look at the blood she's losing."

"That's why I set her aside. I don't think she'll make it."

"I couldn't agree more when you're doing nothing to help her." He took hold of one end of the stretcher the woman was lying on. "Get the other end," he ordered.

I continued to pump blood on the patient I was attending to. "This one should go first," I said. "She's younger and a lot more salvageable."

Dr. Wheeler let go of the stretcher and straightened up. "And just who gave you the right to decide who's salvageable and who's not?"

"I've been running triage for seven months," I said. "No one else wanted the job."

"That doesn't give you the right to play God. I suggest you let physicians decide."

The patients in triage were watching us in bewilderment. "I do the best I can, doctor. If you want to take over, you can have it."

I expected another lecture as I turned back to my work and was surprised when Dr. Wheeler said nothing. When I turned to see if he had left, I found him standing face to face with three South Vietnamese soldiers holding M16s. Mr. Hai, Jean's Vietnamese counterpart, was with them. He pointed to a patient I had started an I.V. on, and two of the soldiers marched over and picked up the stretcher while the third held his weapon in firing position.

"What are they doing?" I demanded of Mr. Hai.

"This man officer in North Vietnamese Army," he replied. "Soldiers take him."

“Tell them to put that stretcher down,” I ordered. “Nobody takes injured patients out of here.”

Mr. Hai looked at me with flashing black eyes. “This soldier business.”

“He needs surgery,” I said walking after them as they carried the stretcher into the corridor. The patient lay very still, looking neither left nor right. “Tell them to put him down.”

The soldier with the drawn M16 shoved me aside with one sweep of his arm and the stretcher was carried away. Mr. Hai headed for the O.R.

I returned to triage, where Dr. Wheeler stood as if in a trance. I stepped around him and went back to work. “Aren’t you going to do anything?” he asked when he regained his composure.

“You heard them,” I said. “It’s soldier business.”

“But they kidnapped him!”

“I didn’t see you doing anything to stop them.”

He hesitated for a moment, then pointed to the woman we had been arguing over when the soldiers appeared. “She’s dead,” he said.

“I know.” I was busy starting an I.V. on another patient.

“There’s ‘morphine’ written on this,” he said when he stooped to read the tag wired to her toe. “Did you give it to her?”

“It was given in the field.”

“Who would give a patient in shock morphine?”

“Probably the corpsmen who brought her in.”

“But it killed her.”

“The war killed her, Doctor.” I was relieved when he turned to return to the O.R.

When the emergency cases were completed, I went to Otto’s office to talk to him about the incident with the soldiers. Dr. Fitch was sitting at the chief’s desk, looking like a small boy trying out his father’s razor. He jumped up when he saw me and quickly told me where I could find Otto.

The new chief was in front of the Swiss Hospital supervising a crew of janitors who were splashing buckets of water on the feces-encrusted walkways where typhoid and cholera patients had waited for admission.

“You’ll never get it all off,” I said, looking at the mess.

“Well, hell, I don’t expect to,” Otto said as he exhaled a cloud of smoke. “But at least we can move it around a little.”

He stomped out the butt of his unraveling cigar while I told him about Dr. Wheeler. “Let the rich son of a bitch go back to his Fifth Avenue practice if he’s so unhappy,” he said. “We can get along without him now as well as we can a month from now when he's due to leave."

"What about the patient the soldiers took?" I asked.

"For once I think Hai is right," Otto drawled. "That probably is soldiers' business."

He went back to supervising the removal of feces and I returned to work. But the incident was still bothering me when I joined my friends at the dinner table.

"I wonder if they took the patient to a military hospital," I said.

Margaret laughed, genuinely amused. "Mouse, haven't you been here long enough to figure a few things out? Especially when you're best chums with a spook?"

"What does that have to do with it?"

"They were probably taking him for a helicopter ride," she said. "That's how your CIA likes to question prisoners."

"A helicopter ride to where?"

"To the end of the line, if you have to ask." She paused to look around the table at the others. Shelly was still in bed with whatever bug she had picked up in Thailand, and only Julia seemed interested in what Margaret was saying. "They take two or three of them up in a helicopter," Margaret said. "If the first one doesn't talk, they push him out. The others usually spill their guts."

"I don't believe that," I said. "Americans wouldn't let that happen."

"Americans order it; ask your boyfriend."

I excused myself and got up. Margaret took her final stab.

"I knew the first time I met you how naive you were," she said. "You exemplify exactly what's wrong with this war; a bunch of ignorant Americans thinking they can change the world to fit their ideals. Only they don't know the first bloody thing about war, or what it does to the people and the countries where its fought."

"I'm sorry about your family," I said. "But it's not my fault they died. Maybe they should have done something about Hitler before he started dropping bombs on Britain."

"Stop it!" Jean slapped her hand on the table so hard the silverware danced. She looked at both of us with the scolding glare of a mother. "Take this talk somewhere other than the dinner table. I'm sick of war when I come home at night."

I pushed my chair carefully back to the table, feeling properly chastised. "I'm sorry," I said to Jean. "No more war at dinner."

"And no more orphans," Margaret added. "Keith is coming to dinner Saturday and I don't want them sitting around the table feeding their worms."

I stayed out of the O.R. as much as possible the next day to avoid Dr. Wheeler and he left the task of sorting and preparing the patients for surgery to me. As much as I disliked him, I admired his capacity for work and his remarkable patience with our adopted medical students. He not only taught them surgical techniques in the O.R., but spent long hours going over medical books with them in the evening and helping them with their English. If criticism of our Vietnamese nursing staff and our triage policies were the price we had to pay, it was one we paid willingly.

Julia helped me admit several patients in triage.

"I'm not looking forward to Dan's visit on Saturday. I want to ask if what Margaret said about questioning prisoners is true, but only if he can assure me it isn't."

"Margaret's just speculating on rumors to harass you," she said.

Dan looked at me with surprise when I asked him almost the moment he arrived.

"Where does Margaret get her information?" he asked.

"I guess from her boyfriend. He works at the Consulate." Dan nodded silently. "Is it true?" I asked after a few moments. "Are prisoners murdered during questioning?"

"I'm not involved in anything like that." His face remained calm.

"Not even at the Happy House?"

"Bird-dog was out of line stopping there. That place is off limits to all but a select few, and I'm not one of them." Dan looked directly at me. "I carry a pouch between Hoi An and Danang containing information I'm not even privy to. I'm a glorified messenger, Patty, nothing more."

"But is it true about the helicopter rides?" I persisted.

"I told you, I don't know." We were in my room and I had music playing on a tape deck I had purchased at the PX. "There're a lot of unpleasant things happening here," he said after a few minutes of silence. "Don't try to get involved in something you know nothing about."

"In other words, it's soldiers' business."

"Yes, it is."

Petula Clark was singing DOWNTOWN, happily contented in her world away from war. Dan lay on the bed and I sat next to him. But for the first time since we met I did not like being near him.

"Maybe you don't agree, but I happen to be involved in this war too," I said after some time. "I don't think anybody could get more involved than working with its carnage."

He reached over to take one of my arms. "I know," he said. "But it makes me mad when you act like only Americans fight dirty." He sat up to face me. "Shit, we have Cong dressing up like women to shoot at aircraft," he said. "And they do it from the middle of a populated area like a marketplace, because they know Americans won't return fire."

Rick had told Jean and me the same thing. Small reconnaissance planes were often shot down by enemy who surrounded themselves with women and children.

"I didn't mean that the Viet Cong and North Vietnamese are saints," I said. "We get plenty of examples of their brutality into triage. It's just that hearing about torture bothers me."

"It bothers me too," he said. "That's why I like to come here; to be with you and push all the business of war out of my mind."

"And I give you a lot of crap about it," I said. "But I'm not going to go so far as to apologize."

He laughed and kissed my cheek. "That's all right," he said. "But keep the crap in small doses." He laid back on the bed once more, looking up at the ceiling while Percy Faith played a medley of soft music. "It's not fun trying to fight a war with a television camera pointed at you," he said after awhile.

"I know that." I lay down on the bed beside him. While we listened to the music, I decided I knew no more about the job the military was doing than the reporters who came to our hospital and wrote critical stories knew about us. Second guessing Dan's role in the war was no better than Dr. Wheeler questioning my actions in triage. I was doing my best, but that didn't mean I was doing what was right. I was put there, inexperienced and imperfect, the same as the men fighting the battles out in the jungles and from the cockpits of planes. In the end, perhaps only God could judge.

"The monsoons will be here soon and there won't be any beach weather left," Dan said when I got up to change the tape. "Why don't we have one final day at China Beach."

"Can we stop at the orphanage on the way? I have a case of peanut butter for them."

I also wanted to talk to Sister Marie about Fuzzy. The mother superior knew many people in Danang because of her long years of operating a school, and she had promised me she would do her best to try to find my little friend.

"I am sorry," she said as soon as she saw me. "The child is nowhere I ask."

I watched other children scurrying into the classroom where they took lessons and felt sad that Fuzzy was not one of them. Even the child who had lost her brother to Dr. Cannon looked happy.

Dan reminded me we were headed for the beach. He said good-bye to Danny while I promised Sister Marie I would be back soon.

"No more war," he said when we drove up to miles of white sand and clear water. "Let's have one whole day of soaking up the sun and enjoying one another."

But the air held the unmistakable feel of monsoon. Clouds were hanging over Monkey Mountain, a high peak located off to the left, and the water was cooler than usual. As much as I complained about the heat, I did not like to think of the approaching rainy season. The dull grey skies and cold torrents of rain falling straight down made everything worse, especially for the casualties who must lie in it waiting to be rescued.

We were walking along the beach when a young man approached and asked if I remembered him. "I was with the lieutenant the day you tried to talk to him out here," he said. "Lieutenant Tamasi."

"Yes, of course," I said. "You had just come in from the field.

"Right." He seemed pleased I remembered.

"How is he?" I asked. "Did he ever get to Hawaii to see his baby?"

The young man looked back at the buddies he had left sitting on the sand. "I thought maybe you'd want to know," he said hesitantly. "The lieutenant got ... he got killed."

I couldn't tell if it was artillery I heard, or thunder coming from the clouds over Monkey Mountain. Suddenly nothing seemed distinct.

"He was going to Hawaii, like you said. He got hit a few days before his R&R." He stepped backward in the sand, edging back toward his buddies. "I'm sorry," he said. "I thought you probably wanted to know."

When I looked into his face I felt sorry for him. "It's O.K., I'm glad you told me."

"We should be going," Dan said beside me. "It looks like rain."

We drove in silence until we reached the bridge. "Dan, let's not argue about the war anymore," I said. "Lieutenant Tamasi's wife would give anything for just five minutes more with him, and we waste so much of our time together."

"I agree," he said. "No more arguing about anything."

By the time we reached Danang, the skies had opened to release a deluge of water that flooded the poorly drained streets. Stranded motorists sat in stalled vehicles waiting for the waters to recede and people ran by with their conical hats dripping water.

"This will slow everything down," Dan said.

"Good," I said. "I could stand a few less casualties."

"Most of them will be on the American side now. Our men aren't used to fighting in mud." I thought of Lieutenant Tamasi and felt a sense of loss so profound it made me shiver. Dan pulled a jacket from the back seat and put it over my shoulders.

"I'm sorry about your friend," he said.

We stopped by his Danang headquarters, a large walled-off compound, to pick up a pouch he must deliver to Hoi An. Bird-dog was waiting for him when we got back to my quarters.

"Good-bye, me darlin's," Bird-dog called from the back of the jeep as they drove away. He waved his bush hat and blew Julia a kiss.

"Does he always wear that hat?" I asked Julia. She huddled with me on the balcony of my house to wave good-bye to our departing men.

"Even in bed," Julia replied. "He says he wants to look proper if he's killed."

CHAPTER TWENTY-FOUR

Tien waded over to our house and put light bulbs in the wardrobes to help prevent mildew. I got out the rubber boots I had ordered from Shelly's catalog, as well as the electric blanket I hoped would keep me warm.

"Don't be surprised if you have company in your bed tonight," Jean warned when she saw me with the blanket. "The beasties like to keep warm too."

My roommate was right. When I turned back the covers that night I found my bed occupied by geckos and other small creatures. I shook the bedclothes thoroughly before crawling in.

The hospital was even more dismal. Patients hurried from one building to another trying to stay dry, and the overflow on the verandas looked even more pathetic in their flimsy clothing and bandages. I was happy the Seabees had repaired the roofs of the shacks, but wading through ankle-deep mud to unload ambulances was a nightmare I had somehow managed to suppress. The one thing that had improved was the fewer numbers of people waiting for surgery in the shacks. Dr. Wheeler had since departed, but not before making an impressive dent in our backlog of patients needing secondary correction of orthopedic injuries.

The Swiss team had also done a miraculous job. But although their hospital was now clean and organized, they had to waste precious time running to empty buckets and pans set under multiple leaks in the roof of the poorly constructed building. Sick children were crowded two and three to a crib, and they shivered from the drafts the staff struggled to plug. The entire team looked fatigued and I cautioned Dr. Brandt that they should get more rest.

"We shall," he said on one of my visits to his hospital to start a difficult

I.V. "As soon as we get the work finished."

"That's an incurable disease over here."

He smiled feebly and ran a hand through his scare-crow hair. "Perhaps I could take some time to read," he said thoughtfully. "I came here with little knowledge of tropical medicine."

"We all did."

One of the nurses hurried by, and he asked if I might take them to the club with me one night. "They should have entertainment," he said. "They are working many hours."

"Wednesday is steak night," I said. "I'll take them then."

"Steak night?" he said. "Perhaps my reading can wait."

I took the entire team the next Wednesday. Fortunately, Jerry wasn't there, but dozens of men descended on the blond, blue-eyed nurses. Dr. Brandt looked like a worried father.

Dan had been right about casualties. Our hospital was not nearly as busy, but the military hospitals in the area were working around the clock. In addition to an increase in the number of battle injuries, many men were ill with skin diseases, malaria and hepatitis. The already crowded wards at Navy Hospital were filled to overflowing, and out at the air base the Seabees began another addition to the morgue.

Dan couldn't come to Danang as often as he once had, and I made the trip across the river to the Army chapel alone most Sundays. Whenever the Ba who customarily took us across saw that he was not with me, she turned her head quickly away. Nearly all Vietnamese had lost someone they loved during the long years of war, and nowhere was the loss reflected more than in the faces of peasant women whose husbands and sons were not rich enough to bribe their way out of military service.

Otto was proving to be as valuable to our team as Ruth. He not only restored our spirits with his unfailing cheer, but he was making marked improvements in our patient care. Supplies were being delivered on a regular basis and the patients' daily food ration now included meat and powdered milk. In addition, he had moved our mailboxes back into his office warmed by a space heater he procured from the Seabees.

Shelly had returned to work, but Julia was now ill. "Why don't you go out to Navy Hospital and have Tom do some blood work on you?" I asked in her bedroom.

"He's too busy," she said. "They have so many casualties Shelly hasn't seen him in weeks."

"Same as Bird-dog and Dan," I said. "And my electric blanket is a poor substitute."

"Especially with the power off most of the time," Julia sympathized. "Ain't war hell?"

It was on one of our blacked-out nights that I left my damp room and went out to the living room to curl up on the sofa in an afghan my mother had sent me. I was reading by candlelight one of the dog-eared books our team passed around when a noise attracted my attention.

"Mouse, is that you?" Jean called from her bedroom.

"No, it's probably just cockroaches." Despite our constant vigilance, we had roaches so big in the kitchen you could hear them crawling over the pots and pans during the night.

I continued reading until, out of the corner of my eye, I caught the shadowy figure of someone on our balcony just beyond the French doors. His back was to me and he was bent over a small bundle. After restraining an impulse to call out to Jean, I slipped quietly across the room and telephoned the M.P. station just down the street. There was static on the line and I tried to keep my voice low enough so the person outside would not hear.

"There's someone on my balcony," I whispered after first giving my location. "I think it might be someone breaking in to steal something." The theft rate from our quarters had doubled since USAID had hired guards to protect us. They watched our houses, but it was to tell their friends when we were away so they could steal our belongings.

"Say again," the M.P. said above the static.

"There's someone on our balcony," I repeated a bit louder.

The M.P.s voice was calm but forceful. "Get out of the building immediately," he said. "He could be planting a satchel charge."

I lowered my body as close to the floor as I could and made my way to Jean's room. "Mouse, what the hell are you doing?" she said when I reached up from where I crouched to put a hand on her shoulder.

"Shhh. Keep your voice down and come with me. There's someone on the balcony."

She was out of bed and sprinting down the stairs two at a time before I could catch her. When I passed through the living room, I saw the silhouette was no longer outside the French doors.

We scrambled behind a concrete building located in the rear of our compound, where we found the Chinese family who lived downstairs already congregated. "Nice of them to warn us," Jean said.

We stayed there with them until we heard a jeepload of M.P.s pull up to our house. The entire area was thoroughly searched before we were allowed back inside.

"He must have heard you calling us and got scared off," one of the M.P.s told us. "Aren't you people supposed to have a guard?"

"He's not around after dark," I said. "Unless he's sleeping somewhere around here." Two small children with the Chinese family looked around the area, as if searching for him in places they had seen him. But the guard was nowhere to be found.

"I'm going to find that son of a bitch and shoot him," Jean said as soon as the M.P.s were gone. She went upstairs and returned with the gun Rick had given her to keep by her bed.

"You can't just shoot the guy," I argued, following her from one of the guard's favorite sleeping places to another. We were both in our nightgowns and the Chinese family watched as if we were insane.

"We're supposed to be protected!" Jean continued her search with her pistol pointed and ready to fire.

"We're also supposed to be working in a modern hospital. Let's go inside before we both catch cold."

Jean relented, but only because it had begun to rain. The next night an American warehouse just blocks from our quarters was blown up by a satchel charge. It did considerable damage to the building, and to the nerves of any Americans living in the area.

Dan was upset when he heard about the incident and insisted that I have a weapon at my bedside. He went to his headquarters to get one, then took me out to the beach to teach me how to use it.

"You can't hit something when you can't see it," he admonished when he saw that I was aiming with my eyes squinted almost shut.

"I can't help it," I said. "I hate guns." My brothers had tried to teach me how to hunt on the farm. But I could never pull the trigger on a deer looking inquisitively through the trees, or a beautifully colored pheasant taking flight. I couldn't imagine doing so when a human being was the target.

"Here, pretend this one's a V.C. and this one is me," Dan said. He set two empty beer cans side by side on the stump of a sea pine and came back to where I stood. "The V.C. is holding a gun to my head," he added. I fired almost instantly, hitting the can that was supposed to be Dan. "Christ, I'm glad we're only pretending," he said with a laugh.

"I told you I couldn't do it."

"You're doing fine, we'll just pretend they're both V.C." He set two more cans on the stump, and by the end of an hour I was hitting them with reasonable accuracy.

When we returned to my quarters he laid the gun on the table next to my bed. Then he made me promise to spend the nights in the compound of his Danang headquarters.

"It's all arranged," he said when I started to object. "My boss said your whole team is welcome."

"They won't go."

"That's their business. But I can't stand to be out on patrol at night wondering if you're all right."

I still wasn't convinced it was necessary, until he told me reports from all of the intelligence units in I Corps were predicting an increase in activity around Danang.

"I'll start tomorrow night," I said before he left for Hoi An. "I promise."

Just past midnight I woke to a ferocious series of explosions. "They're hitting Danang!" Jean called from her room. "Get under your mattress!"

The noise did not subside after a few minutes, as it usually did. When it did let up enough to crawl out from under my mattress, I went to Jean's room and told her about Dan's offer of shelter in the intelligence compound. The women in the house next door went with us, with the exception of Margaret.

"I thought you weren't coming," Shelly said when Margaret rode into the compound on her bicycle less than an hour later.

"I wasn't, until I saw the Chinese family that lives below Jean and Mouse loading up their belongings," Margaret said. "I consider that a more reliable prediction of trouble than the CIA."

We were assigned cots in one of the large sandbagged bunkers within the compound and given an Army blanket to cover with. There was no place to plug in an electric blanket, even if I had thought to bring it, but I vowed to at least bring a pillow if I came again.

Work was hectic the next day, and the patients in poor shape because of the exposure they suffered lying in the cold rain until they were rescued. I passed the word among my coworkers that they were welcome in the intelligence compound and more than half of them went with us the second night. Julia was still ill and vomiting almost continuously into a bucket she held in the bunker.

While gunfire continually sounded, we ate cold C-rations and listened to nervous CIA agents talking excitedly into field telephones and radios. Dire predictions of imminent attack came almost hourly, and the whole town was put on red alert. Each member of our team was given an assignment to help defend the compound, should Danang be overrun. Mine was to be an ammo runner, distributing ammunition to the various machine-gun posts within the compound. I rejected the assignment when I discovered several of the men who would be manning the guns anxiously going over firing instructions with one another while they swigged Jack Daniels from a bottle being passed around when their boss was not present. I had no intentions of running around in the dark with my arms full of ammunition while inexperienced, or inebriated, CIA agents manned machine-guns.

My new assignment was to set up and operate a first-aid station, but when I examined their emergency medical equipment I found it could treat nothing more serious than a bee sting. I reported my findings to Dan's boss, who seemed annoyed.

"I thought you would bring your own supplies," he said. "Medical personnel should be prepared to practice medicine." His manner was so coolly detached, I wondered if he had invited us to share his compound out of concern for our safety, or to have readily available to him and his men the only American medical personnel in the city.

"We might be able to get some things from our hospital," I said. "But it's not safe to go there after dark." There were flares lighting the entire perimeter of Danang, and the rumble of artillery could be heard in all directions.

"I'll send some of my men with you." His grey hair was perfectly groomed, and he wore a carefully pressed safari suit.

Otto volunteered to lead the party for supplies, along with Jean and Margaret. Julia was too sick to go, and I was to stay at my first aid station in case I was needed.

The supply party returned in less than an hour, with Dr. Fitch crammed into the jeep with them. He had chosen to stay at his house, rather than come to the compound, but had taken refuge with the patients in the hospital when the fireworks started.

When the team had arrived at the hospital, they met Mr. Hai going out the gates with a truck filled with supplies. Jean demanded to know where he was going, but he roared away with his headlights off.

"The little sneak has been letting shipments get through knowing all along he'd get it back," Shelly said. "I told you he was V.C."

"I don't think so," I said. "He helped the ARVN soldiers take that North Vietnamese out of triage. A V.C. wouldn't have pointed the patient out to them."

"Maybe the dear boy is taking care of people out in the villages," Gertie offered. She was dressed in a silk dress and high-heeled shoes from an earlier date.

"I believe you're right, Gertie," Dr. Fitch said.

"I'd still like to see what he has in that locked cupboard he keeps in our anesthesia office," Shelly said.

"Then why don't you open it?" Otto asked.

"Because Doctor Chen has forbidden it," Dr. Fitch said quickly.

"That guy who's never around?" Otto growled. "What does he have to say about anything?" The Vietnamese chief of staff had not paid even a courtesy visit to meet the new American chief.

Otto went directly to Mr. Hai the next morning, but he refused to discuss his actions of the night before. After politely requesting that he open the locked cupboard and being refused, Otto instructed the janitors to break the doors open.

"I go Bac Si Chen," Mr. Hai threatened. He stood with the rest of the Vietnamese staff outside the entrance to our anesthesia supply room..

"You go right ahead," Otto said. "I'd like to meet the guy who's collecting a salary for being my absent counterpart."

Mr. Hai was gone when the doors were finally forced open, releasing a cascade of equipment that slid out onto the floor. "Look at this," Shelly said. She picked up a blood pressure cuff that had the name of my hometown hospital stamped on it. "He's even stolen our private stock."

"And we've been accusing Gertie of wasting these," I said as I sifted through a pile of angiocaths Shelly had cumshawed from Navy Hospital. "There's enough here to supply an army."

"North Vietnamese Army," Shelly added. "Hai was probably planning to do exactly that after he split it with Chen for his private clinic."

Dr. Chen came to the hospital with Mr. Hai, bowing profusely when he met Otto. Our chief showed him the cupboard, and Dr. Chen clicked his tongue disapprovingly. I thought he looked more upset about losing face in front of both the American and Vietnamese staff than he was about the stolen supplies.

The Vietnamese chief looked much like Dr. Wheeler had standing next to Otto. He wore clothes that were hand tailored, covered by a white lab coat that looked as if it was made of silk. Several of his teeth had gold crowns on them, and one of his incisors had an inlaid heart of jade.

"We go see Commander Miles," he said to Otto. The jade heart showed whenever he smiled.

"Fine," Otto said. "But Mr. Hai goes with us."

It was well past lunch time when the three of them returned from USAID headquarters. "You're not going to like this," Otto told us when we gathered in our locked lounge to hear the outcome. "Hai told Miles he was taking care of people out in the countryside and Miles believed him."

"God boy, that's exactly what I said," Gertie crowed.

Dr. Fitch smiled at her, and Otto continued. "Chen says he believes him too."

"Why not?" Jean said. "It gives Chen a way to save face, and Miles doesn't have to get involved in finding out what Hai was really up to last night."

"I'm afraid Miles wants to get involved." Otto took the cigar from his mouth and tapped it in our can-cover ashtray. "He's ordered me to get a written apology from each one of you for falsely accusing Hai."

"What?" I nearly tripped getting to my feet. "Otto, he stole things I got from a hospital where I worked back home. What more proof do we need?"

"He claims he didn't ask for the things to help his people because you wouldn't have given them to him."

"He's right about that," Ron said.

"I'll apologize over my dead body," Shelly said.

"I've only been ordered to request an apology," Otto said after taking several seconds to relight the stub of a cigar. "What you do is your business." We started to take a vote but he interrupted. "While you're voting, there's one other thing. Miles has also informed me Hai has been selected to receive an American government grant to study nursing in the States." He paused to let the news settle. "Miles asked for a recommendation a couple of months ago and Chen recommended Hai."

"Are you shitting me?" Shelly said. "They're going to spend American tax dollars training that little V.C. piss ant when he's stealing us blind?"

"Nobody asked me about a recommendation to send someone to the States to study," Teresa said. "And I am the director of nursing." She looked more offended than angry.

"This is the first I've heard about the grant too," Otto said. "Miles only discussed it with Chen." He left us alone in the lounge to decide what we wanted to do.

Teresa took a vote on whether or not we should write apologies, which received a resounding no from everybody but Dr. Fitch, who chose to abstain. When she asked about the nursing grant, Ruth raised her hand.

"My assistant has been wanting to go to nurse's training ever since she started working in the burn ward," she said quietly. Her hair was now more silver than black and I worried that she was spending too much time working. "I think she should at least be considered for the grant." There was an enthusiastic round of applause from all of the team members.

"And what if Commander Miles doesn't go along with us?" Teresa asked.

"We all resign our positions," I said. "I'll be first."

"I'm second," Shelly said. Julia was not there to vote. She was now too sick to get out of bed.

The offers continued until Teresa held up a hand to stop us. "I like to work with people who have guts," she said with a smile, and left to give Otto our decisions.

Our chief didn't have to tell us the outcome of his second meeting with Commander Miles. The murderous look Mr. Hai gave us when he heard the decision said it all.

"I'm happy for you," I told Ruth when it was announced her assistant would be sent to the States in Mr. Hai's place. We were reading our mail in Otto's office.

Ruth smiled and thanked me. "I meant to ask you about something," she said. "Come with me to the lounge." She dug into the large canvas bag she carried to and from work and pulled out a magazine. "This is the latest publication of that Concerned Citizens group," she said as she paged through it. "A friend of mine sent it because there's an article about our hospital."

"I can imagine what it says," I said.

Ruth handed the magazine to me. "I was more interested in this picture," she said. "Could this be the little girl you've been looking for?" I looked at the black and white photo and saw Fuzzy staring back at me. SAN FRANCISCO COUPLE SPONSORS CHILD NEEDING PLASTIC SURGERY the caption read.

Fuzzy sat between an affluent looking man and woman, wearing a white hospital gown that made her look even smaller than I remembered. Her face had been changed so much I might not have recognized her had it not been for her wiry hair and large solemn eyes.

"He took her," I said after reading further. "That day he was here with all the people from his organization. I never saw Fuzzy after that." I pointed to a photograph of the journalist who had refused to help with Fuzzy the day of her injury. He was squatted on the veranda next to the one-armed Ba.

"The article says she will probably be sent to a Catholic orphanage in the Delta," Ruth said. She told me the group took patients to the States for corrective surgery, then returned them to their own country.

"But Fuzzy's from here," I said. "She would be lost in a place where she doesn't know anybody."

"I don't understand their reasoning either." Ruth's voice held the first bitterness I had ever heard in it. "All that money for airfare for all of them and surgery on just one child. Think of how many burn dressings that would buy, or artificial limbs that could be made right here in this country."

"I'm going to try to find her in the Delta," I said. "The nuns at our orphanage will help me."

"Do you think that's the best thing?" Ruth looked at me with an expression that suggested it was not. "She's already had a lot of disruption in her young life," she said. "Don't go looking for her unless you can give her something better."

I started to respond but stopped. Dan and I did not know where our future would lead, or whether we would even have one. We were two people in a war, with conflicting feelings and little time for dreams of a future.

I looked again at the article, which was as critical of our hospital as I had imagined. It didn't make me angry, however, it only made me sad. Fuzzy's face had been improved enough by plastic surgery to allow her to smile. But she wasn't smiling.

CHAPTER TWENTY-FIVE

When Julia missed three more days of work because of vomiting, I went to her villa to convince her to see a doctor. I found her buried beneath a pile of blankets, with a basin filled with vomitus on a chair by her bed.

"You look like shit," I said.

"Don't used that word," she wailed. "My rear end has a permanent indentation from sitting on the john."

"Where's Tien?" I asked, after emptying the basin.

"Taking care of that orphan you gave her. Everything is Johnny, Johnny, Johnny."

When I pulled back the covers to straighten her disheveled bed, I noticed a yellowish hue to her skin. My suspicions were confirmed when I looked into her eyes and found them jaundiced.

"Come on, you're going to Navy Hospital," I said. "This isn't Ho Chi Minh's revenge, it's hepatitis."

Julia was too weak to protest while I pulled clothes on her and loaded her into the car. She hung out the window vomiting the entire trip and was immediately admitted with the diagnosis of severe infectious hepatitis.

"We had better check on Tien," I told the others over dinner. "She might be taking short cuts in the kitchen."

"It's probably that brat you gave her," Margaret said. "Why don't you find her another one so we can try for plague?"

Since Jean had been in charge of routine kitchen inspections, we let her be the one to give the kitchen a thorough going over. She went through every shelf and cupboard while the rest of us stood silently in the background. "Jesus, what's in here?" she said when she opened the refrigerator, which was running. The odor was worse than our morgue on a hot day.

"Nuoc mam," Tien said as she ran to rescue a bottle of dark fluid Jean held at arm's length. It was the Vietnamese version of soy sauce, made by fermenting raw fish in the sun for weeks and then simmering the slimy residue. We had forbidden Tien to cook the foul-smelling concoction on our stove, but we apparently had not made it clear the refrigerator was also off limits.

Jean was not convinced the nuoc mam was the culprit and the search continued. Her persistence led to the source of contamination of our food. Tien knew that boiling killed germs, but she made the false assumption that freezing would do the same. She was filling ice cube trays directly from the tap, then using them in iced tea she had carefully boiled to kill any pathogens.

I told Julia about the discovery when I went to see her that evening. "Great," she said weakly. "I get sicker than a dog because I happen to like iced tea. I'd rather have the clap; at least I would have had fun getting it."

She was in a tiny cubicle at the end of a long ward of male patients. The private enclosure was intended for high-ranking military officers, but had been assigned to her because of her sex, as well as the infectious nature of her disease. There was no private bathroom, however, and each time she had to relieve herself the other patients were required to vacate the communal facility at the opposite end of the ward.

"Why don't you just use a bedpan?" I asked when she said she had to go.

"Because I would have to empty it myself in the same place," she replied. "I might as well just deposit it there to begin with and save myself a trip through the ward with a full pan."

"Too bad they don't have a garden," I said when I noticed a door leading from her room to the outside.

"The broad has to use the head!" a corpsman bellowed when he saw me helping Julia between the rows of cots. There was a loud chorus of moans from the lavatory, which had only screening for its upper partition. We had to wait several minutes for dysentery patients to straggle out, pushing I.V. poles ahead of them.

"I can't quit shitting," a male patient called out to the corpsman.

"Sorry, troop. You'll have to sit on a bedpan until she's through."

The young man stumbled past us, giving Julia an imploring look. "Sorry," she said. "I'll try to hurry."

"I'll bet they toss a coin for the job of standing guard," I said when I observed a pajama clad patient posted at the door. He quickly looked the other way when I caught him taking a surreptitious look through the screen.

"I'm too damned sick to care," Julia said. "If they want to look at my ass, let them." She was now so jaundiced her face looked orange next to her dark brown hair. And she had lost so much weight I worried that she would be medevaced home.

"Why don't the female nurses take care of you?" I asked. A contingent of Navy nurses had arrived only a week before, which caused a flurry of excitement among the all-male ranks.

"They take care of the critical patients; the corpsmen take care of the rest of us," Julia said. "Tom says they've really upgraded the care." A loud roar went up from the men in the ward outside. "Oh no," Julia said. "They're watching crotch shots again."

A make-shift television station had been set up on Monkey Mountain, the highest peak in the area, to provide entertainment for men in hospitals. The station had originally been intended for overseas radio communication, but some enterprising engineers from Armed Forces Radio found a way to transmit telecasts of American news programs, westerns and outdated beauty pageants. The men were partial to the latter, particularly during the talent section when cameras sometimes inadvertently caught a closeup of a tumbling acrobat just as she went bottomside up.

The television programming changed to a newscast, which was showing violent protests against the war. Troops were in the streets of the American city being shown, and protestors and police clashed in bloody battle.

"Shee-it!" a patient said as we walked back through the ward. "That's our world they're showin'."

"Makes you glad you're over here getting your shit blown away to preserve the peace, doesn't it?" a G.I. with bandages covering his entire upper body said. Someone threw a combat boot at the television and a corpsman went over and switched it off.

Julia spent her days waiting for visitors, but it became more and more difficult for me to walk through the long ward to her cubicle at the far end. The men lying there swathed in bandages, or suffering fevers that made their bodies weep, looked at women with such longing in their young faces. We were their mothers, sisters, wives and girlfriends; all the people they wanted there to comfort them. Or representatives of what they would face when they went home with missing limbs and scarred faces.

I wanted to stop and hold each of them and tell them how sorry I was. But by the time I went to the hospital each evening, there was little left of me after a day of giving anesthesia and sorting through casualties. It was effort enough to manage a frozen smile while I walked as quickly as possible to my destination.

When Julia was finally released, it was with instructions that she eat plenty of fresh oranges. After checking all our military sources and coming up with nothing, we were forced to buy them from street vendors, who had stolen them en route to American PXs and military mess halls. Even Tien could not get them for less than a dollar each.

Jean was the next to develop symptoms. Margaret thought it funny that the American team was turning as yellow as the locals, until she too came down with the disease. Teresa, Shelly and I were spared, perhaps because we preferred Coke in a can to iced tea.

We were reduced to only the direst of emergencies with the skeleton crew left to staff our hospital. Otto used the opportunity to arrange for a study much like the one the AMA surgeons had conducted on patients with tuberculosis. The candidates were all from one of the wards and would be operated on by Navy surgeons on a hospital ship anchored off the coast beyond gunfire range. Because the ship's helicopters could only be used for transporting American patients, it was up to us to get our people out to them by whatever means available. Otto asked for volunteers to help and Julia, who had just returned to work, and I took on the task.

"I don't know if this was such a good idea," Julia said as the two of us helped patients into a dilapidated fishing boat. "I'm tired of being able to do nothing for these people, but I don't want to drown trying to help them." Each of the patients was severely tubercular and had been in a dark, crowded ward for months. Julia had been transferred from the O.R. to work there by Teresa.

"I wonder if we'll even get out of port," I said when the small boat settled precariously into the water under our weight.

But that was not our only problem. The fisherman's motor coughed and wheezed but would not start. He climbed back up onto the dock and disappeared, returning after several minutes with a companion who helped him work on the engine. After much scratching of heads and chattering, the engine finally sputtered into action.

A cold monsoon rain fell as we headed out to sea, and the undersized boat looked as if it would capsize at any moment on waves so high they blocked the horizon. But we miraculously skittered down the other side of each of them and went looking for the next. Water splashed over our feet, and all of us were wretchedly sea sick.

"There it is!" Julia shouted when we reached the crest of a particularly fierce wave. She pointed to a glistening white ship with enormous red crosses painted on its sides and the name REPOSE.

"Thank god," I said. But when we pulled alongside a small platform at the lower side of the ship, I realized the worst part of the journey had just begun.

Our boat moved up and down with the large waves, but the ship's enormous size and weight made it sit stationary in the water. When we were down in the trough of a wave, the stairs, which were fixed to the side of the ship, were high above us. Every fifteen seconds or so, when we were carried up by a crest, there was a brief opportunity to step over from the boat to the platform before we dropped away again. But the water next to the ship swirled like a whirlpool, pitching the small boat so violently our patients were terrified. Julia timed the waves until she established a pattern, then courageously led the way. When she was safely on the stairs she reached back to help the others.

"Cam duc! Cam duc!" the woman I was trying to coax out of the boat yelled.

"Duc, duc," I told her. "It's O.K."

"Try one of the younger ones," Julia called to me.

I selected a young man who was holding back. "Numbah ten," he said, looking over the side of the boat at the churning water.

"Number one," I said, and pointed up to the deck of the ship. "Bac Si, number one. Het roi, dao quadi." He understood my pidgin Vietnamese enough to know I was telling him the doctors aboard the ship were very good and would make the pain in his chest go away.

He moved to the front of the boat and reached timidly for Julia's hand. When he got to the platform, he followed her up the narrow metal stairs clinging to the side of the huge ship. The other patients followed, one by one, with me bringing up the rear. Crewmen were not allowed to go down the stairs to help civilians board, but they cheered us on and pulled us up onto the deck when we reached the top of the slippery stairs.

A special ward had been set up for the chest cases, and a corpsman assisted our patients into clean blue pajamas after first giving them a shower. "The nurses don't want lice in their wards," he told us.

"It looks like they don't want us anymore than the lice," I said. Two female American nurses were watching Julia and me from a nearby passageway and their expressions were not friendly.

The corpsman blushed. “It’s kind of hard for them being restricted to ship,” he said quietly. “They’re maybe a little jealous of people who aren’t.”

“Maybe we should invite them to see the dump where we work,” Julia said. “Then they’d be happy to be confined to this floating paradise.”

The wards we passed were spotlessly clean and equipped with all of the latest technology. But the American casualties lying in the bunks were desperately injured, many missing multiple limbs. Others lay comatose, with bandages wrapped completely around their heads as machines breathed for them. I did not envy the nurses who worked over them with dedication and gentle patience.

There seemed to be labels for everyone - K.I.A., killed in action; M.I.A., missing in action; W.I.A., wounded in action. But there needed to be a new category for those rescued by rapid helicopter evacuation and the miracles of modern medicine; the men returned from near death who could never return to a normal life. They would spend their days confined to deteriorating veteran’s hospitals, or hidden away within the shelter of families from a society that did not wish to be reminded of this unpopular war. They were Vietnam’s M.I.L.s, missing in life.

Teresa called for me shortly after we returned to our hospital. “I need to talk to you,” she said. “In my office, please.”

I felt like I had when I was bitten by the sea snake. All the air was being squeezed out of my chest in one crushing motion. “Did something happen to Dan?”

“No, nothing like that,” the supervisor said quickly.

I hadn’t seen Dan in weeks, even though we continued to sleep in the compound of his Danang headquarters most nights. He telephoned when he could to reassure me he was all right, and to tell me he was going out on frequent reconnaissance patrols around Hoi An.

“Someone has written a letter to Washington,” Teresa said when I was seated in her office. “A formal letter of protest.”

“Not that crap about Hai and the nursing school grant again?”

“No, it’s about your procedures in triage,” she said hesitantly. “One of the AMA doctors has accused you of practicing euthanasia.” Before I could ask who, she said, “Dr. Wheeler has apparently written a detailed report about a woman who received morphine when she was in shock. He claims it killed her.”

“I told Otto about that patient,” I objected. “And I didn’t give the morphine, it was given in the field. Doctor Wheeler knew that."

"He also says she was denied treatment in triage."

"The morphine was her treatment, for Chrissakes. The woman was beyond anything but making her comfortable."

"Don't get upset," Teresa said when I raised my voice. "Otto just wants me to get a statement from you and we'll handle it from there."

I told the nursing supervisor everything I could remember about the patient, including the incident with the South Vietnamese Army taking a suspected enemy patient out of triage. "I don't suppose Wheeler mentioned that in his report," I said. "Since he did nothing to help me stop them."

Teresa consulted the paper in front of her. "The inquiry from Washington doesn't mention it."

"Big surprise."

"Did the woman actually receive a lethal dose of morphine?"

"She received a lethal dose of war. And I didn't give either."

Teresa sighed wearily. She had lost so much weight during the hot season her round glasses were much too large for her face. And her hair was beginning to show tinges of grey.

"You know the procedures in triage," I said to her. "We would have needed a blueprint to put that woman back together. And my guess is she would have died before we got halfway finished."

"I'm sure you did the right thing. And thank you for being so candid." She folded the letter and put it to one side of her desk, which she kept as orderly as her management of the nursing staff.

I leaned back in the chair I was sitting in and let my legs splay out in front of me. My knee-length rubber boots were caked with mud. "Why does Washington listen to someone who was here for such a short time?" I asked in a voice that sounded defeated even to me. "They never listen to anything we say."

"Doctor Wheeler is a well known physician," Teresa said. "I expect he has some political connections."

"Then why doesn't he use them to help us improve this place?"

"I don't know. People have their own reasons for what they do." She looked out the window of her office at patients scurrying through the rain. "You must admit, he was a fine surgeon."

"But was he worth all the trouble?"

"He was to the patients."

I felt both embarrassed and frustrated. "I'm sick of triage," I said, sitting up in my chair. "How about getting someone else to take over?"

"And who would that be, Gertie?" Teresa grimaced at the prospect. "Shelly is due to leave here in less than four months; there's not much point in switching places with her." I didn't tell her Shelly would be leaving much sooner. I got up from my chair and started to leave. "Where are you going?" she asked.

"Triage." I nodded toward her window, where a military ambulance, which could hold six patients on stretchers supported up its interior walls, could be seen coming through the gates. Teresa put an arm around me and walked with me to unload the newest arrivals.

When Dan arrived that weekend, I asked if he could go on an R&R.

"Sure, things have let up lately."

"I know, we've been sleeping at home for over a week."

"How about Hong Kong?" he asked. "Everyone who's been there had a great time."

"I'll make arrangements for two weeks from Monday, if I get approval from the head nurse." That would give my recovering colleagues time to return to work. When I asked, Teresa gave her blessing.

CHAPTER TWENTY-SIX

"I guess we should have slept in the compound," I said when I heard someone banging loudly on our door downstairs. Someone at the door in the middle of the night could only mean a Red Alert.

Jean stood beside me with her gun as I opened the door. "Baby sister sick, you come hospital." It took me a few seconds to recognize Becky in a dripping rain poncho that hung almost to the ground.

"I wouldn't go over there at this hour," Jean cautioned.

"I have to, Becky always helps us." The anesthesia student waited just inside the door while I ran upstairs and dressed.

Jean reminded me to take the gun Dan left by my bed, and helped me load Becky's bicycle into the back of our vehicle. I wished that she had offered to come with me as I drove through the dark, rain-drenched streets, knowing that I would be returning alone.

The electrical power was off at the hospital, and large rats squealed and scurried over our feet as we made our way down the corridor to the O.R. suite. In the dim yellow glow of a flashlight, I found another of our anesthesia students bent over a tiny girl lying on an operating table. I quickly examined the feverish child before attempting to insert an endotracheal tube through her swollen throat. When I could not get one in, Becky began to cry.

"She needs a tracheotomy," I told the other anesthesia student. "Get Bac Si Ron." The doctors' house was only yards away from the hospital.

While I waited for help, I stuck a large needle into the child's trachea to ease her fitful breathing as much as possible. She stopped breathing all together just as Ron arrived wearing only trousers and sandals. We tried for over half an hour to resuscitate the child, with no response.

"I don't think there's any point in continuing," Ron said finally. He pointed to large purple blotches that were beginning to appear everywhere we had touched the patient. "It's a good thing we've had plague shots," he said. I hated the shots because they had to be taken every few months and caused such muscle aches and high fevers it was difficult to work. But I was grateful for them now.

"No chet roi! No chet roi!" Becky cried when we stepped back from the table.

"It's too late," I told her. "Your sister was too sick."

Becky's husband Tran emerged from a darkened corner of the O.R. "We only learned today she was sick," he said in the perfect English he used at his job at the American consulate. "We were in Hue visiting my family."

He picked up the body and started down the corridor, with Becky following behind weeping. I was glad the anesthesia students had all been given immunizations.

I followed the mourners to the parking lot, where rain fell in a steady torrent. When I offered them a ride, Becky climbed silently into a seat and put her arms out for her sister's body. Her husband transferred it gently to his wife's arms and got into the front seat to direct me to the home of Becky's mother.

We traveled a series of narrow streets that wound farther and farther out of Danang. When Tran motioned for me to stop on the muddy dirt road we traveled, it was in front of a tin and plywood shack where the silhouette of a woman could be seen in the light of a flickering candle. "Thank you," Tran said before getting out. "Americans are good to our country."

"Thank you," I replied, wishing I could have done more to deserve his generous praise. "I'm sorry about the child."

I waited while they carried the body inside. The woman's soulful wail could still be heard when I drove off into the rain, hoping I would find my way safely back to Danang. The gun I had brought with me rested on the seat, but I wondered if I could actually bring myself to use it.

"How's the child?" Jean called from her room when she heard me come up the stairs.

"She died." I went to stand in her doorway. "Ron thinks it might have been plague."

"Great Jesus," Jean said quietly. "Just what we need."

"I drove them home afterwards. Becky's mother lives in a crummy little shack way outside of town. It was spooky driving back alone."

"You're nuts, Mouse. That's Cong territory."

"There's no power at the hospital," I said before returning to my bed.

"What else is new?"

Becky was absent the following day, but the other students went about their work without having to be asked. When Dr. Brandt called for help with a resuscitation at his hospital, one of them responded immediately.

Dan came to Danang the Sunday before our R&R, acting worried and distracted. "What's wrong?" I said after he asked me to repeat something the second time.

"Just a couple of problems around Hoi An." He was changing out of wet and soiled combat attire into a set of civilian clothes he kept in a small bag in my room.

"What kind of problems?"

"Ambushes. My boss seems to think the culprits are hiding on my island." He sat down on my bed and pulled off his boots, dropping them heavily to the floor. "He wants me to check the place out."

"Dan, don't go out there," I said in a voice that betrayed my fear. "Let's go on our R&R tomorrow."

He laughed and held me tightly. "There's no one hiding there. I know every square inch of that island. The people will look out for me."

"Please, Dan. I'm afraid."

He raised my hand to his lips and kissed it. "Don't be. I wish I hadn't even mentioned it."

We laid back on the bed, fully clothed. "How much longer is your tour?" I asked after several minutes of listening quietly to the music on my tape player.

"Three months," he said. "What about you?"

"Ten." It sounded like a long time. "Unless I pay my own way home," I added.

"I'll help you pay it," he said. "I'm not leaving here without you."

"What about our R&R?"

"We'll have to postpone it a few of weeks."

He stayed only a few hours before returning to Hoi An. But he was back again the following weekend.

"I just stopped by to say hello," he said. "I have an important mission to complete before I can get out of these wet clothes." The words important mission were said with disgust. He was dressed in fatigues that were soaked through and covered with mud. He wore a helmet and had left an M16 leaning against the wall downstairs.

"Where have you been?" I asked.

"Squatted in a stinking rice paddy all night looking for Cong," he replied testily. "Now I have to take care of the high-priority stuff."

"What high-priority stuff?"

"I'll tell you later. If I talked about it now I might not have the stomach to do it."

He handed me a light weight, quilted, camouflage blanket designed for troops in the field. "I want you to have this," he said in a gentler tone. "It'll keep you warm if you have to sleep in the bunker." He stopped to look at me. "You have been sleeping in the compound, haven't you?"

"Sometimes," I said. "It's been quiet, Dan. We don't even have many casualties."

"Well, all that is going to change," he said. "Charlie's up to something."

He was gone most of the morning and when he returned his mood was even worse. "Fucking politicians," he said as he pulled off his muddy shoes and tossed them to one side of my room. "They're more concerned with their fucking tea parties than they are with the men fighting the fucking war." I said nothing. "I've just spent the whole morning tracking down some goddamned teacups for a reception my boss up here is throwing for some asshole Congressmen."

"What does that have to do with you?"

"The boss ordered teacups from Saigon and they got lost somewhere along the way. He made me come all the way up here after a night of patrol to find them, and I ended up having to get a medevac chopper to fly to Chou Lai to pick them up."

"You used a medevac chopper to transport teacups?" I knew from Tom that ambulances were having difficulty getting through the mud and medevac choppers were the only hope for our injured men.

"I had orders to get them no matter what it took," Dan almost shouted at me. "And that's what it took."

I was quiet until he finished pulling off his clothes, wet from the rain outside. "So why didn't you refuse to do it?" I asked when I couldn't keep quiet any longer.

"Because I don't want to spend the next twenty years in Leavenworth." He threw his wet clothes on the floor next to his boots. "I don't know why I got mixed up in this CIA shit anyway. I'm trained to be a Marine, not some fucking errand boy."

I talked him into a shower and laid out dry clothes. When he was dressed he lay down on my bed.

"Our trucks and tanks are mired down in the muck so bad we can't move," he said as he looked up at the ceiling. "And Charlie's shooting our asses off as he whistles past."

"How can they move if you can't?"

"Because they don't use heavy equipment. Everything is transported on bicycles or hauled on their backs."

"Why don't you do the same?"

"The brass in Washington insists the rain should slow the enemy down as much as it does us and they won't listen to anything different." I covered him with the field blanket he had given me. "I can't stay long," he said. "I promised my men I would be back for patrol tonight."

"The Vietnamese you're training?" I lay down beside him, and he spread part of the blanket over me.

"They're getting pretty good at reconnaissance," he said in a more optimistic voice. "I think they're actually beginning to think on their own."

His voice trailed off and he fell soundly asleep. I considered letting him sleep until dark, when it would be too late for him to drive back to Hoi An. It frightened me to know he was going out on patrols with only Vietnamese troops, even though he had no evidence of enemy infiltration on the island they had pacified.

When I woke him, I reminded him it was Thanksgiving the following week. "Tien's making a big feast, if we can find a turkey someplace."

"I'll try to make it," he said as he put on his uniform Tien had laundered and pressed. "But don't count on me."

I went to church alone the next day, then drove out to the orphanage. The cribs had been moved from the wet courtyard to crowded rooms that reverberated with noise from children unhappy about being confined inside four walls. Danny was happy to see me, but for the first time Sister Marie acted uncomfortable in my presence. When I asked if there was something wrong she seemed reluctant to answer.

"I'm sorry I haven't been out," I said. "I've been busy."

"You have done nothing," she said, touching one of my shoulders in a maternal fashion. "There has been a tragedy at one of our orphanages."

"Where?"

"The Delta. Many children and sisters were killed by Viet Cong." The nun had difficulty getting the words out.

"Fuzzy."

It was said more to myself, but Sister Marie knew immediately something was wrong. She offered me a chair while I told her about the article in the magazine.

"You do not know for certain that is where she was sent," she consoled. "And you do not know if she was harmed even if she were."

"But why would they attack an orphanage?" I asked in disbelief. "I thought even the Viet Cong valued the lives of children."

The mother superior hesitated for a moment, then spoke with the directness that was her custom. "They were killed because they are friends with Americans."

"You mean Americans like me?" Danny had come to where we sat and was trying to climb up onto my lap. I reached down automatically to lift him up.

"I am afraid so," Sister Marie said. "And the American soldiers who help us as well."

Danny put his head on my shoulder and I hugged him close to me. "I'll stop coming here," I said when I realized my actions could be putting him in danger. "I can get money to you through Sister Nicole and you can buy the things you need yourself."

The mother superior smiled at me. "We cannot buy love at the marketplace," she said. "The children need you to come." Danny was looking up at me with a bewildered expression.

"But what if the same thing happens to you?"

"We must trust God to protect us."

CHAPTER TWENTY-SEVEN

We learned from Otto that the visiting Congressmen Dan had to procure teacups for were also to make a stop at our hospital as part of their one-week fact finding mission. He came by the O.R.s to brief us on the visit and give us instructions on how he expected us to behave.

"I want all of you looking your best tomorrow," he said. "These people are the ones we need to impress to get continued cooperation from Washington." Our new chief was getting us regular shipments of supplies.

"Can we wear our boots?" I asked.

"Hell yes. You'll probably need them to wade through all the bullshit." He paused to flick ashes from his cigar. "And try to clean up your language," he added. "At least until the bastards are out of earshot."

The team was recovered enough from hepatitis for all of us to be at work the next morning, wearing clean uniforms for the benefit of the Congressional delegation. Our Vietnamese staff was spotlessly groomed and giggled in anticipation. Even Becky was there, dressed in white with a swatch of black cloth pinned to her sleeve to signify mourning the death of her sister.

Just before the delegation was to arrive, casualties were brought in. I put on my conical Vietnamese hat to keep rain off my head. Jean's pilot friend had given me a WAR IS HELL button I had pinned to the front of it. We unloaded the new casualties and had to put several in the corridor outside triage because it was full.

We were still working on them when several sleek black cars came through the hospital gates. "We'd better wash some of this blood off so we can shake hands," I said to Shelly.

"I'm just washing my right hand," she said. "I don't want them to get the idea that we don't do any work."

The caravan of cars, which had been flown in for the occasion, was guarded by jeeps of M.P.s carrying M-16s and machine guns mounted on the back of the front seat. The Congressmen got out of the cars wearing flak jackets and helmets.

"Look at that," Shelly said. "We can't get a helmet or flak jacket, and we have to live in this mule-shit pie."

The Congressmen went first to the Swiss Hospital next door, where they stayed for some time. Another ambulance of casualties arrived in the meantime; many of them napalm victims that needed immediate attention. The power was off, and I was crawling from one stretcher to the other in the screened corridor while Shelly worked in triage.

"I could get a job teaching Braille when I leave here," I called in to Shelly. "It's so dark out here I have to feel for the bullet holes."

"Just be careful what you're feeling," Shelly called back. "No fair getting your jollies from peasants."

I was crawling to the next stretcher when I found several pair of shiny black shoes in my path. I got to my feet just as Shelly reeled off an oath of obscenities we commonly referred to as Marine Mouth.

"I stuck myself with a fucking needle I've used on half a dozen patients," she said. "I just get over fucking Ho Chi Minh's revenge, and now I'll probably get fucking syphilis."

Otto ignored the tirade and introduced me to the dignitaries. I extended my hand, then quickly withdrew it when I saw that it was once more covered with blood. "I'm happy to meet you," I said, bowing slightly. They said nothing while they stared at the WAR IS HELL button.

"There's one good thing about working on these people," Shelly said, still unaware of the visitors' presence. "They're not fat like the lardass patients we get back home." Several of the Congressmen sucked in bellies that protruded beneath flak jackets.

I excused myself and went to the door of triage. "We have company," I said. Shelly poked her head out and quickly disappeared making the sign of the cross.

Otto took the cigar from his mouth and laughed. "These girls don't let things get them down," he said.

The Congressmen did not laugh with him. "Don't you find all of this terribly depressing?" one of them asked in a wavering voice.

I was concerned that our careless banter might have given the impression that we didn't care about the patients. But I didn't know how to explain that foul language and gallows humor were one of the few outlets for the frustrations we faced on a daily basis.

"I guess you must get used to all the blood and gore," the congressman concluded when I didn't respond.

"Not used to it, sir. Numb to it."

They took several photographs and went on to the O.R.s. It struck me that, unlike our medical team, visitors to our hospital always carried cameras. If we didn't have the necessary things to save our patients or relieve their pain, we did not wish to document their suffering by sticking an expensive camera in their faces.

When the delegation came back out of the surgery suite, they asked where we had gotten the Vietnamese anesthetists they observed doing cases. "They're our students," I replied. "We train them ourselves."

"You actually run a school?" one of them asked. He looked around at the surroundings as if that should have been impossible.

"Isn't that what Vietnamization is supposed to be all about?" I said. "Training the locals so they can take over when we leave?"

"Of course," he said. "Good job."

The convoy of cars and jeeps nearly ran down amputees hobbling around the shacks when they drove out of the hospital compound. But we were not finished with the visit.

A television camera crew came in shortly after their departure to take footage of us caring for casualties. The power was still out, but they carried their own battery packs to provide lights for their cameras. We did not object to their presence until they turned their bright lights on napalm patients and they screamed in anguish.

"The lights are hot on their burns," I told them. "You'll have to leave."

They took some additional shots and left triage, but stopped to film patients out in the corridor, where Shelly was starting I.V.s. While they were filming, our janitors came shuffling down the corridor carrying a stretcher containing a cadaver that looked as if it had been in the morgue for days.

"What the hell is that?" Shelly demanded.

Jean came out of the surgery suite and began berating the two opium-obtunded janitors. "I told you to get a fresh body from the wards," she said sharply. "Not one from the morgue." She chased the janitors and their prize back down the corridor while the camera crew continued to film. They seemed delighted with the footage and immediately packed up and left.

Shelly and I were baffled by the incident until Jean explained that a new AMA surgeon wanted to try cadaver grafts on napalm victims, who lost huge amounts of precious body fluids through their extensive burns. The technique was unprecedented and involved peeling the skin from a newly expired cadaver, then laying it over the burn areas to seal in tissue fluids until healing could begin. When granulation tissue began to form beneath the grafts, they were simply peeled away and discarded.

"I can't wait until they show that scene on T.V. back home," Shelly laughed. "That cadaver was so stiff the janitors didn't even need a stretcher."

Dan came for Thanksgiving, along with Bird-dog. Rick had been coming into town to see Jean once more, and he managed to bribe the mess cook at the air base out of a turkey. We helped Tien prepare whatever trimmings we could find and invited all of the doctors from our hospital. Tom got the afternoon off from Navy Hospital, and Margaret's boyfriend Keith was there from the consulate.

"Let's give thanks that our forefathers freed themselves from the insufferable British," Shelly said as she raised her glass in a toast. She looked first at Margaret, then around the table at the rest of the assembled group. "And special thanks for all the people at this table," she added in a serious tone. "May we all be home next Thanksgiving, safe and sound."

"Hear, hear," Bird-dog said as the rest of us clinked glasses.

We were finishing the meal when Dr. Fitch, who had declined our invitation, came to tell us we had casualties to do. Tom called Navy Hospital to get permission to help, and the others volunteered their services as well.

Tom operated on the orthopedic cases while the general surgeons did the others. Dan was anxious for us to leave before dark, but not until gunfire sounded nearby did we heed his warnings.

"Sew them up and get out," Otto ordered. "That's all we're doing tonight."

Dan insisted that we stay in the CIA compound and led the procession of vehicles through the darkened streets. "You have to get out of here," he said to me as we sat together in a bunker. "That place you work in is too damned insecure."

"I'll leave when you do," I said. "Not before."

He left for Hoi An early the next morning, and I returned with the others to finish up the cases we had left the night before. There was a letter from my mother in the afternoon mail telling me she had seen me on the evening news.

"Listen to this," I said waving the letter at the people gathered around the heater next to the mailboxes. “My mother claims she saw me working on patients while visiting congressmen looked on.”

“But the television crews came in after the politicians left,” Shelly said.

“That doesn’t matter,” Ruth said. “They take the footage and cut them in later. I’ve seen them do it many times.”

“No wonder this war is so screwed up,” I said, looking back over the letter to make sure I wasn’t mistaken. “If people back home are relying on shysters like that for information.”

The congressional visit proved to be a precursor for a host of people that increased each day it grew closer to Christmas. Bob Hope came to put on a show, which was held on an open-air platform built at the foot of a high hillside bordering the air base. We went for only a few minutes, but long enough to see thousands of nineteen year old troops scattered up the hillside as far as one could see. Patients from military hospitals, clad only in pajamas and bandages, were given places of honor down in front. Fortunately, it was not raining.

The jokes were about Ho Chi Minh and the men laughed heartily as Mr. Hope read them from large cue cards held up at the foot of the makeshift stage. But it was the bevy of beautiful girls he brought that the men came to see. They danced and sang until the roar of applause, whistles, and cheers grew so loud it sounded like a football stadium at a championship game.

Reporters looking for human interest stories began descending on our hospital, searching for an orphan who would have no Christmas, or an American nurse who missed her family.

With all the reporters wandering the corridors, we were especially upset when Gertie pulled another of her blunders. Shelly and I had left her with Becky while we went home for lunch, only to be called back in the middle of the meal. When we entered the O.R. where she was working, we found Becky and Ron trying to hold a seizuring patient on the table while Gertie attempted to intubate her.

“What happened?” Shelly asked as she grabbed the tube from Gertie and quickly inserted it in the woman’s trachea.

“God girl, I don’t know,” Gertie said. “I was waking her up and everything was going fine. Then all of a sudden she started having a fit.”

“She’s red hot,” I said when I touched the woman’s skin to restart the I.V. that had become dislodged during the seizure.

“I don’t know why,” Ron said. “She didn’t have a fever before we started.”

"Check the machine while I go through these," Shelly told me. She began checking the collection of used syringes Gertie had thrown on her anesthesia table to see if the wrong drug had been given by mistake.

"Where did you get this tank?" I asked Gertie. A huge rusted blue gas tank was attached to the anesthesia machine.

"The janitors got it for me," she said. "I asked them to get me some nitrous oxide in a blue tank from the storeroom and that's what they brought."

"Gertie, we don't have nitrous oxide in a container this size," I said. The tank towered above my head like a rocket.

We pulled it out of the system and hooked it to a canister of soda lime, used to remove carbon dioxide from the gases the patient exhaled while under anesthesia. When we opened the valve on the mysterious tank, the soda lime heated up so fast it boiled out of its container.

"I don't know what this is," Shelly said as she turned off the tank. "But we'd better cool that patient down fast."

We soaked towels in cold water and sponged the woman to lower her temperature. Ron found Lan and asked him to see if he could identify the tank so we would know what we were dealing with. The interpreter climbed onto a stool and scraped at the rusted surface of the tank for several minutes until he found writing.

"What mean A-C-E-T-Y-L-E-N-E?" he asked.

"Christ, she's been giving her acetylene," Ron said. He ran to open the windows, and switched off all electrical equipment in the room.

"But it's a blue tank," Gertie defended. "Nitrous oxide is always in a blue tank."

"For god's sake, Gertie, you can't rely on color coding in this place," Shelly said. "That tank's probably been sitting around the warehouse for twenty years."

Gertie removed her cap and mask with one swift motion. "I know what I'm doing!" she shouted at Shelly. "How else do you think I could keep a patient alive for an hour on acetylene!"

"I think I've been here too long," Shelly said when our elderly anesthetist stomped out of the room. "She's starting to make sense."

"What should we do with the patient?" Ron asked. She had stopped seizuring but was still fiery red.

"I guess we could set her out on the veranda and see if the rain cools her off," I suggested. "I'm not really an expert on acetylene anesthesia."

Becky apologized profusely for the incident, but Gertie had convinced her all blue tanks were nitrous oxide. She appeared flattered when we confided in her that we were using her and the other students to look after our colleague, rather than the other way around. The dedicated student promised to be more vigilant in the future.

Dan went with me to the orphanage the week before Christmas to help decorate a large sea pine. The nuns were as excited as the children and led them singing carols that were a mixture of French and Vietnamese, but still vaguely familiar. Sister Marie gratefully accepted the money we gave her to buy Christmas gifts, and Dan gave Danny a hat decorated with sergeant's stripes.

I told Sister Marie we would not be back for awhile since we planned to go to Hong Kong after Christmas. I had accumulated so many hours working overtime, for which we were not paid, Teresa had approved my second R&R without question.

"Thank you for helping us make celebration," Sister Marie said when we were ready to leave. "Say 'Merry Christmas,'" she instructed the children. They shouted something similar and burst into laughter.

"Kids are the same all over," Dan said as we drove away. I thought of Fuzzy and wondered what she would be doing for Christmas, or whether she was alive to celebrate.

"Danny's a pretty nice little guy," Dan said after driving silently for some time. "I've gotten kind of attached to him."

"He likes you too."

We were crossing the bridge over the Danang River when he asked if I would consider taking Danny home with us. "That is, if you agree to marry me." He turned to see my reaction. "Not many girls get a proposal with gunfire in the background." The sentries on the bridge had just unleashed a resounding volley of shots toward the water.

"Yes to both," I said excitedly. "I would like to take Danny home with us, and I would like to marry you." I started to move over in the jeep next to him but stopped when I bumped into the box of grenades sitting between us. Dan leaned over and kissed me.

"I wanted to be in Hong Kong when I proposed," he said. "But I couldn't wait."

"I'm glad you didn't." A perfect setting was not necessary. I was as happy as I could ever imagine being.

"The first thing we do when we take Danny home is buy him some new clothes," Dan said when we reached the other side of the bridge. "He spends half his time hitching up those britches that are always falling off him."

We had to go to the R&R center at the air base to make new arrangements for our trip. The dirt stretch of road was almost impassible from deep potholes filled with rainwater, but I didn't mind. Dan and I would be getting out of Vietnam for five glorious days, and in two months we would be on our way home to a lifetime together. This was the best Christmas of my life.

"I hate that place," Dan said when we passed the morgue.

We had orders cut for Hong Kong and got on the manifest for the January twentieth R&R flight. "Do you think there might be a Christmas truce?" I asked Dan while he gathered up his belongings in my room before returning to Hoi An. The newspapers from home had been filled with predictions for a cease-fire during the holidays, and everyone was hoping it would become a reality.

"There won't be any letup for me," Dan said. "My boss wants me to look for stockpiles in case Charlie is planning a surprise attack. That means patrols day and night."

"I wish we could go on R&R now."

"I'm already dreaming of a nice big bed," he said. "And maybe a fancy nightie." He teased me so about the flannel ones I ordered from Sears, I sometimes regretted not getting the silk parachute Shelly had gone after.

Bird-dog and Julia were already waiting when we got downstairs. "See you Christmas, me darlin's," Bird-dog called as they drove away.

Ron left early in the week to spend Christmas with his family in Hawaii. The enemy was getting in its last licks before the cease-fire that had finally been agreed upon, and we had only AMA surgeons to rely on in Ron's absence. We were also having to spend our nights in the CIA compound because of the stepped-up fighting. The only bright spot in our dismal routine was the packages arriving from home.

Two days before Christmas I received a large parcel that emitted a heavenly scent. "I hope it's not more fruitcake," Jean said. Everyone on the team seemed to have been sent one.

"It's not food." I tore open the box and inside a protective wooden frame I found a beautifully shaped miniature blue spruce. An attached note read: "The cardboard box this was originally mailed in arrived at our post office badly damaged. We took the liberty of repackaging it, knowing how much a tree would mean to someone so far away from home. Merry Christmas, the San Francisco Fleet Post Office."

The accompanying letter was from my sister, Kitty, who told how she had cut the tree on our family farm, where we had always cut our Christmas trees. Jean and Julia said nothing about the tears that ran down my face while I read.

The night before Christmas Eve was spent in the CIA compound, even though the truce appeared to be slowly taking effect. Everyone joined in singing Christmas carols, and I curled up in the blanket Dan had given me to feel closer to him.

The next day we went to the Swiss team's house for the lighting of their tree. They used real candles on a sparsely bowed evergreen and served us honey cakes sent from home.

One of the nurses held a tiny baby abandoned at their hospital. They had knitted a red sweater and bonnet that made the wrinkled premature infant look like a monkey. But she was surviving by always being with one of the nurses to keep her warm and fed.

Dan came to Danang early Christmas Eve with Bird-dog. There was a party at Teresa and Margaret's, but Dan and I went instead to midnight Mass at Navy Hospital.

Patients in blue pajamas and bandages filed into the small chapel. Staff pushed others in wheel chairs up to the front. Lastly, patients with bandaged heads were pushed in on stretchers, their only sign of life being the surgical masks they wore moving in and out with their breaths. I saw Dan staring at them with a strained expression.

The chaplain was the same one who had said the first Mass I attended in Vietnam. He was no longer gun shy, but he did give general absolution to the long line of men waiting to go to Confession. After the service he stood at the door wishing everyone a merry Christmas.

"I noticed you two in the congregation," he said to Dan and me. "You look so happy together."

"We're going to be married," I said.

"How wonderful. Did you meet over here?"

"Yes, sir," Dan said, taking my hand in his.

"It's good to see joy in such an unhappy place," the priest said. "God bless both of you."

I sat back in the seat of Dan's jeep and looked up at the sky on the drive home. "Without flares you can see the stars."

Dan looked up. "I'd forgotten what they looked like."

We drove on in the eerily peaceful night. "I finally understand that song,"

I said.

"What song?"

"Silent Night."

Back in my room Dan watched me wrap packages. "Where did you get all this stuff?" he asked. He was examining a statue of an old man that was carved of marble taken from Marble Mountain.

"Off the economy," I said. "At a ransom price."

Just before dawn we heard Tien slip up the stairs and place her gifts to us under the small tree we had decorated with popcorn and red ribbons. Then we heard her go into the kitchen to begin preparing dinner for all the guests we had invited.

"Our first Christmas together," Dan whispered.

CHAPTER TWENTY-EIGHT

Our Vietnamese staff was happy there would be a Tet truce as their lunar new year holiday on January thirtieth drew near. Tet was a time to clear up past debts and make preparations for the future, and nobody was doing that better than Becky. She would be going to Hue to spend the holiday with her husband's family.

"We have celebration," she told Shelly and me. "You come make Tet with us."

"I would like to," Shelly told her. "But I will be busy getting ready to go home." There was some truth to Shelly's statement, but her reluctance to go to Hue had more to do with a drastic change in her usual behavior.

Tom's tour was up in less than a month, and she had stopped taking unnecessary risks that might put her life in danger. She had even sold her motorbike and no longer made evening trips to Navy Hospital. It was known as short-timer's syndrome, when people became superstitious about being killed just before they were due to go home. Pilots had such a problem with jitters their last few weeks, they were found to be far more prone to make mistakes in the cockpit. To compensate, the military surprised them with a departure date earlier than the one on the short-timer calendars the men checked off daily their last month of service.

"You come Hue?" Becky said to me with an expectant look on her face that was difficult to refuse. "I show you old city."

"Leo took me up there when I was new in-country," Shelly told me. "You should see the place at least once." I was not opposed to visiting the former imperial city, but Tet fell only three days after Dan and I were to return from R&R in Hong Kong.

"I can't leave you alone with Gertie for a whole week then take off again so soon," I said to Shelly.

"Forget it, I'll be leaving in a little over three weeks. I can stand on my head for that long."

Becky was delighted when I said I would go. She and her husband had also invited Keith, Tran's boss at the American Consulate, and Margaret would be accompanying him. We would go to Hue on January twenty-ninth, the eve of Tet, and return the day following the holiday.

Dan was not happy when I told him of my plans. "There're rumors flying around of stepped-up activity," he said when he called to tell me he would not be to Danang until the Saturday we were to leave on R&R.

We received a few casualties the next day from battles in outlying areas. All was quiet around Danang.

"I'll be glad when we get on that R&R plane," I told Shelly.

I was working on a woman whose leg had been blown away at the hip. "I'm afraid to take out this packing," I said after inspecting the blood soaked rags packed into the wound. "She'll probably start bleeding like hell."

Shelly came to look. "She smells like buffalo shit," she said.

We decided to take the woman back to the O.R. to pull the packing out. Ron was there, ready to clamp bleeders if the wound began to hemorrhage.

"God girl, it is buffalo shit," Shelly said when we pulled the last of the packs from the gaping hole. Large quantities of manure had been stuffed into the wound to control the bleeding.

"It did the trick," Ron said. "But she'll probably die of infection."

He debrided the wound and irrigated it with large dosages of antibiotics, thanks to Otto. The woman had little chance of survival, even with the antibiotics we lavished on her, but we wanted to do everything we could to return her to the three small children who had been brought in with her.

The last case of the day was a man from the shacks who had developed severe pain under his leg cast. When Jean cut it off she found the leg crawling with maggots.

"I thought we might as well bring him in here," she said when I helped her carry the patient into the room where Ron and Shelly had finished the woman with the manure-packed wound. "It's the last case of the day and your room is already contaminated."

"Last case?" Shelly said. "My, how time flies when you're playing with shit and maggots."

There were casualties the morning of our R&R flight. I barely got home from the hospital and washed the blood off me before Dan arrived. I was throwing things into a suitcase when he came into my room in wet fatigues, helmet and flak jacket.

"You look exhausted," I said.

"Long night." He looked away from me, avoiding my eyes.

"Did Bird-dog come with you?"

He nodded as he pulled off his wet clothing and I saw his body begin to tremble. "You're cold," I said. "Put this around you." I made him sit down and wrapped my electric blanket around his shoulders.

"I have some news you aren't going to like," he said after sitting quietly several minutes watching me pack. "We're going to have to postpone our R&R again."

"No, Dan." The plane would be leaving that afternoon and I was determined to be on it.

"There's been an ambush in Hoi An," he said. "My boss is insisting the culprits are hiding on my island, even though we've done several recon patrols there and found nothing."

"Please don't cancel our trip."

"Pat, there's a fucking war being fought here. I can't go running off on vacation whenever I want to." He yanked the blanket from his shoulders and pushed it aside.

"But I don't want you to go back to that island looking for Viet Cong." I started to cry and he took me in his arms.

"I'm sorry to cancel out on the R&R, Patty," he said gently. "But I need to take my men back there and do a complete sweep."

"Will you take Bird-dog with you? He's always telling everyone how he can sniff Cong out anywhere."

"This is my responsibility, not Bird-dog's."

It was late when I told Dan a secret I had been planning to keep until we were in Hong Kong. "Dan, I think I might be pregnant."

He bolted upright so suddenly he almost fell off my narrow bed. "What?"

I gestured for him to be quiet so Jean wouldn't hear. "I know a nurse should be better prepared," I said quietly. "I was going to wait until I saw a doctor in Hong Kong, but with the R&R being cancelled ..."

"Don't apologize," he interrupted. He put both hands on my shoulders and looked at me intently in the light from flares outside my window. "I've felt nothing but hate for the past twenty-four hours, squatting in the rain in the jungle looking for enemy."

He didn't say if he had found any or what he had done with them.

"I wanted to kill every Vietnamese I saw. He kissed me on my forehead, then both cheeks. "You've changed that."

Dan lay back down and pulled me close to him. "You have to quit your job now," he said. "You work too hard at that dump and you're exposed to too many diseases."

I laughed at his sudden paternalism. "I don't think USAID gives maternity leave. Besides, I'm not really sure yet."

"O.K. It'll be our maybe baby."

"Can we still adopt Danny?"

"Sure, why not? You could get the paperwork started."

We made love and lay quietly together, listening to the rumbling in the background. "I hope it's a boy," he whispered and fell asleep.

Dan was allowed to stay in Danang the whole weekend. I woke him early Sunday morning to go with me to Mass at the Army chapel. The Ba was there to take us back across the river after the service, so we were at my quarters in time for breakfast with the others. "I'm not hungry," I told Jean when she put a plate of food in front of me.

Dan looked at me with concern. "Are you feeling O.K.?"

"I'm fine," I said as I sipped at a cup of tea. But I felt feverish and my head ached unmercifully.

"Maybe you shouldn't go to work tomorrow."

"I'll be all right," I said.

Julia and Bird-dog were not at the table, but Bird-dog was standing with Julia when I walked Dan to his jeep.

I had promised myself I wouldn't cry, but tears refused to be held back when Dan kissed me good-bye.

"Bird-dog, don't let him go to the island alone," I said impulsively.

"I know the people on my island," Dan told me. "They'll look out for me."

"You go with him, Bird-dog," I persisted. Bird-dog looked embarrassed.

"I told you, this is my responsibility, not Bird-dog's," Dan said in a voice that he reserved for conversations with other military. "If the Cong are there, I'll find them with my troops." He got into the jeep and turned to Julia. "Pat's not feeling well. Make her go see a doctor if she isn't better by tomorrow." Julia promised she would.

"I love you," I said to Dan after a kiss.

"I adore you." He gunned the jeep and backed out of the driveway. Bird-dog called his usual farewell as he waved his bush hat.

"I hate monsoon," I said as it began to rain. "It makes everything so much grimmer."

"Let's get you inside," Julia said in a concerned voice.

CHAPTER TWENTY-NINE

Dan had forgotten his shaving kit, and I put it on the table next to my bed so it would be near me while I slept. But when I closed my eyes I could not sleep.

I went to work Monday even though I felt feverish and weak. Becky came into triage midmorning to tell me Keith had arranged for all of us to travel to Hue by helicopter. When I told her I wasn't sure I could go because of the change in my R&R, she looked so disappointed I assured her I would do my best to attend.

She patted her stomach. "We tell Tran family we have baby."

"Congratulations!" I said as I hugged her. I wished I could tell her I might also be pregnant, but I didn't want word to get out and be sent home by USAID before Dan was due to leave next month.

Teresa called Shelly and me to her office later that afternoon. Another letter from Washington was lying in front of her on her desk.

"Now what?" I said. "Did somebody else report us for killing patients?"

Teresa glanced down at the letter. "Not exactly," she said. "The people responsible for this one were actually trying to compliment you."

She told us one of the members of the recent congressional delegation had included in his report a flattering statement about our anesthesia school, a copy of which was sent to USAID headquarters at the Department of State. But rather than simply accept the compliment, USAID had checked both Shelly and my files and discovered that neither of us had a degree in education.

"They say your school doesn't meet government regulations," Teresa told us. "They want it disbanded immediately."

"What the hell are we doing here if we aren't suppose to teach?" Shelly asked as she got up from her chair. "Do they expect us to just patch up the bullet holes and go home?"

"We're supposed to be advising," the nursing supervisor said. "I'm not sure what the distinction is between that and teaching, but apparently Washington sees one."

"Leo started the training program because he needed help," I told Teresa. "He took people off the backs of water buffalo and taught them how to give anesthesia with no help from the bureaucrats sitting in Washington making up rules."

"Your program sounds pretty much like monkey-see, monkey-do," Teresa said.

"So what? It works."

"We have students in the middle of training," Shelly said. "We can't just drop them."

"How long is the course?" Teresa asked.

"However long it takes," Shelly replied. "Some learn in a year; others need more time."

The nursing supervisor put the letter back into its envelope. "Work with the ones you have until you're satisfied, but don't take anymore," she said. "And keep your mouths shut around visiting firemen."

The latest reprimand was quickly forgotten when I returned to triage. Ron was so lonesome for his family after his Christmas visit, he was engaged in an all-out assault on the shacks to keep himself busy. There was nothing like a series of gangrenous legs to make one forget the stench of a letter from Washington.

The woman with the manure-packed wound had died during the day, leaving her children huddled against her body on the veranda. Sister Nicole was able to coax them into my car and I drove them out to the orphanage.

"Why are you not in Honk Kong?" Sister Marie asked.

"Dan was too busy to go now," I said.

I told her we had decided to adopt Danny, and she suggested we wait to tell him until closer to our date of departure. But the little boy wearing the sergeant's hat Dan had given him seemed to sense something special was going on and stayed close by while I talked to the mother superior. And when I said good-bye to him, he waved the hat.

My temperature was soaring and my head and muscles ached when I arrived home. I went directly to bed and shivered with chills. Tien fussed over me with rice gruel I had difficulty swallowing. When it grew dark, she helped me out onto the balcony, wrapped in Dan's blanket, to watch children dance through the streets in pre-Tet celebrations. A giant dragon breathed real flames, produced by the boy under the head section rinsing his mouth with a liquid, then exhaling over a lighted torch. Tien showed us how to tie sweets to the end of long strings to dangle in front of the children.

It was after ten when our telephone rang. I answered it, and the military operator asked if Dr. Walsh was available to speak to someone about a patient in Hoi An.

"What patient?" I was afraid to hear Dan's name as I fingered the small gold cross around my neck.

"Are you Doctor Walsh?" the operator asked.

"This is Pat Walsh."

"Go ahead," he said, and Dan came on the line.

"Doctor Walsh, we have a patient of yours who's suffering chest pain," he said in a professional tone. "We need to know what medication he's on." There was a discernable click as the military operator hung up. "I had to make it sound official," Dan said. "The phone lines are secured for business-only after eight."

"Are you all right?" My heart was still racing from my initial fright.

"Except for this pain in my chest," he said. "I could use a good nurse." His laugh was nervous.

"Why are you calling? Did you cancel the patrol to the island?" I waited for him to say yes.

"No, I go out tomorrow." He paused for a moment and I thought the line had gone dead. "I just wanted to hear your voice," he said suddenly.

"I'm glad to hear yours."

"Why aren't you over at the compound? I called there first looking for you."

"It's quiet here, Dan. There're children dancing in the streets getting ready for Tet."

"I still don't like you staying there. How are you feeling?"

"Fine," I lied.

"I wrote to my mother," he said.

I had made him promise to write to her at least once a week. "I'm glad," I said. "Will you call me when you get back from the patrol?"

"As soon as I can."

"Don't forget."

"I won't." There was loud static on the line. "Has anything changed?" he asked when it cleared.

"What? Oh, no, nothing to report."

"I hope it's a boy."

"You forgot your shaving kit here."

"I know. I'll have a big bushy beard to tickle you with when I get there." He paused a moment. "Maybe schedule our R&R for a week from Sunday to make real sure I'm free."

I was disappointed but didn't want to argue. I started to tell him I would go to Hue to visit Becky's in-laws, but I knew he would ask me not to. "I'll be waiting for your call tomorrow," I said.

"I love you, Patty." His voice was faint on the other end of the line.

"I'm having trouble hearing you."

"I miss you," he said above the static. "I can't wait to get to Hong Kong."

"I love you."

"Have to go. Keep thinking of Hong Kong."

I went to bed but lay awake thinking. Dan seemed genuinely happy about the possibility of a child, but I worried that his feelings would change when we went home. I wondered, too, if his family would accept me. Or whether they would be upset that he got so involved while on the other side of the world.

When I finally fell asleep, I dreamed I was sitting on a row of sandbags outside an operating hut at Navy Hospital. Dan had lost a leg in a land mine explosion on his island and Tom was operating on him. I was waiting for him to be brought out of surgery so I could tell him I still loved him and wanted to marry him. That's where the dream ended, with me sitting on the row of sandbags in the rain.

I woke feeling even worse. Julia wanted to take me to Navy Hospital. But I felt I could not miss work because I would be taking time off to go to Hue, followed by a week of R&R.

The night had been quiet and there were few casualties in triage. I was comforted to know the fighting had slackened, but the ache in my head and muscles had now moved to my chest. I told Shelly I would cover for lunch but asked if she would come back early so I could go home and go to bed.

"I think I might have pleurisy," I said. "My chest is killing me."

"Maybe you should go out to Navy and see someone," she suggested.

But I was as resistant as Julia had been. I didn't want to miss Becky's celebration in Hue, and not even pneumonia would keep me from going on R&R with Dan.

When Shelly hadn't returned by two, I decided to walk home. I found her sitting in my living room with Julia, Jean and Margaret having a drink, an unheard of activity during working hours. Especially for those who had given up alcohol after having hepatitis.

"What's going on?" I asked Shelly. "Why didn't you come back to work?"

"I'm sorry," she said. "We got talking and forgot the time."

"Are there casualties?" Jean asked.

"No, everything's quiet."

"How about a Scotch?" Shelly said. She went to the cupboard to pour one for me before I had time to answer. "We're celebrating my liberation," she said over her shoulder. "In exactly fifteen days I lift out of this mule-shit pie."

I took a sip of the drink she handed me and coughed. "This is straight Scotch."

"Guess I've lost my touch at bartending."

"Are you still going to Hue?" Margaret asked. "Keith needs to know how many people will be on the chopper he's arranging."

"I plan to," I said. "If you promise I can get back before Dan catches me. He doesn't like me running around where I might get shot."

"You'll be back," Margaret assured. I was surprised she didn't make a remark about Dan's concern for my safety.

Shelly began telling us about the trip she and Tom planned to take through the orient on their way home. I sipped at my drink, happy to be distracted from the dream that had stayed with me all day. Tien came in while Shelly was talking and said she had a phone call from Tom in her quarters next door.

"I wish Dan would call," I said as she hurried out.

"He will," Jean said, glancing at her watch. "It's early."

I was still waiting for Dan's call nearly an hour later when I heard the downstairs door open. Shelly came up the stairs, followed by the Catholic chaplain from Navy Hospital and Dan's boss. The pain in my chest intensified with each step they took toward me.

"No," I heard my voice say.

Julia put an arm around my shoulders and Shelly stood facing me. "I'm sorry, Mouse," she said. "They did everything they could to save him."

The pain in my chest exploded. Water was flooding in around me, collecting in the back of my throat and choking off my breath.

I was transported across the room as if there was no weight to my body.

Hands touched me; voices murmured, but no one tried to stop the water pouring in.

"Mouse, are you all right?" I was in a chair. Shelly was stooped in front of me.

"He can't be dead." It was difficult to form words through the water. "I knew he would be wounded, but he can't be dead."

"They've been working on him at Navy Hospital for over an hour," Shelly said. "We didn't want to tell you until we knew something."

Jean and Julia were crying on the other side of the room. "I'm going out there." I got up from the chair despite Shelly's attempts to hold me down.

I was at the staircase when the chaplain stepped in front of me. "Dan is already with God," he said. "You must rely on your faith to get you through this terrible time." I was surprised at the tears in his eyes after all the young men he had seen die.

"God let him die while I was saving the lives of total strangers!" I shouted.

The chaplain spoke, but I was slipping beneath the water, with no Dan to save me. Jean helped me to the sofa, where she insisted I lie down. Tom arrived from Navy Hospital.

"I worked on him when they brought him into Receiving," he told me. "The bullet perforated his iliac artery."

"Are you sure it was Dan?" I sat up on the sofa and Tom sat down next to me. "There could have been a mistake."

"I didn't recognize him at first," Tom said gently. "We were already working on him when Shelly called to tell me he was wounded and on his way in."

"Did he say anything? Was he in pain?"

"He was unconscious when he arrived. He never regained consciousness." His manner was professional, but his fingers moved nervously over a syringe in his shirt pocket.

"Bird-dog called us. He said he was conscious when they picked him up," Julia told me. "He asked for you."

"The chopper pilots said he was joking with them about getting a million dollar wound and a ticket home," Tom added. "He told them he had his own private-duty nurse waiting for him in Danang."

"He didn't know how badly he was hurt?" I held onto Tom's forearm, not wanting him to leave until I heard every detail.

"They said he went into shock from blood loss and just slipped away.

One minute he was laughing and the next he was unconscious." He glanced down at my hand gripping his arm, and I let go. "It's better than the way a lot of guys go," he said quietly.

"Why didn't the medic try to resuscitate him?"

"He wasn't on a medevac chopper."

"Why not?" My voice was loud in the quiet room.

"I don't know, you'll have to ask the guys in Hoi An."

I held my chest that felt like it had received a blast of dynamite. "I can't believe I'll never see him again."

"We're going to give you a sedative now." Tom handed the syringe he had brought with him to Shelly. The chaplain turned to leave, but Dan's boss came over to me.

"We had a chopper there as soon as the ambush started," he said. "They just couldn't get him out of the water soon enough."

"Water?" I said. "Where was he shot?"

"On the island." He seemed reluctant to say more.

"On Dan's island?"

He smoothed a hand over his silver hair and cleared his throat. "They were ambushed," he said. "They were leaving, but the engine on Dan's boat wouldn't start. He was working on it when he was hit."

"But why didn't he get into one of the other boats?"

He cleared his throat again. "It seems they had already departed."

"His men left him?" I sat for a moment trying to comprehend what he had said. "Were there any other casualties? Any of the Vietnamese troops he trained?"

"No." He made a motion to leave, then said, "There's already an investigation underway."

"Investigation! Why did you order him to go there alone!"

"He had his troops."

A needle jabbed into my arm and the room began to swirl, then went black.

"I've trained myself not to look at the faces," I heard Tom say from the living room. I was in my bed, with Dan's blanket spread over me. "I didn't even know it was him until Shelly called."

"It wouldn't have mattered," Julia said. "You did everything you could."

All through the night I could hear their subdued voices in the outer room, and their soft footsteps as they slipped in and out of my room to check on me. I thanked God for their friendship and prayed that I was carrying Dan's child so I wouldn't feel so alone.

"I hope it's a boy," I heard him whisper whenever I closed my eyes.

CHAPTER THIRTY

Towards dawn my mind cleared enough to recognize Julia sitting next to my bed. My head was thick from the sedative, and my mind a jumble of events that raced at equal speed to nowhere. Each breath was an agonizing chore. "I have a terrible pain in my chest," I told her.

"Probably from that rotten fever," she said. "You've been burning up all night." She reached a hand to my forehead. "We need to take you out to Navy Hospital so someone can have a look at you."

Jean brought me in a cup of tea and the two discussed who should drive me to the hospital. "I'll take her so you can go to work," Jean told Julia. "Mr. Hai can run the O.R.s for a change."

"I don't want to go," I said when Jean went to my wardrobe to get me a dress. "I don't want to go out there where he died."

"I know," she said. "But it's the only place you can be properly evaluated to see what's causing your fever and chest pain."

I kept my eyes closed on the drive - while we crossed the bridge where Dan had proposed, past the lane leading to the orphanage where Danny waited, and beyond the turn-off for the beach. When chopper blades sounded overhead, I looked up at a medevac coming into Navy Hospital. Jean tried to turn the car away from the landing pad, but the helicopter swooped down in front of us. Men dressed in blue pajamas ran to unload it.

"Don't look," Jean said. "I can drive on in a minute."

I didn't want to watch, yet I could not look away. Limp bodies were being pulled from the craft and laid to the side of the pad, to be worked on later or pronounced dead. Screaming young men, who had been medevaced under fire, were pulled from the tangled pile trying to wipe blood from their eyes, unsure if it was theirs or their buddies.

"Is that how Dan came in?" I was too nauseous to speak above a whisper.

"No," Jean said firmly. "Tom told you how it was."

When the cries became unbearable, I got out of the jeep and ran until they were only echoes. I vomited the tea I had for breakfast and collapsed on a row of sandbags outside one of the operating huts. It was raining and I lifted my face into its coolness.

"Are you all right?" I opened my eyes and saw the Catholic chaplain standing over me.

"I'm just waiting," I said. "Dan is in surgery."

The chaplain looked disturbed. "I have to give the Sacrament to the men just brought in," he said. "When I finish we can go up to my office and talk about Dan."

A grey mist rose up from the ground, enveloping the chaplain as he hurried away. He wanted to talk about Dan. I wasn't waiting for him to be brought out of surgery because he had lost a leg. Dan was dead.

"Let's go to the lab and have some blood drawn." Jean was standing in front of me, offering a hand to help me up from the sandbags. "Tom will see you afterwards."

"This will hurt but don't pull away," the corpsman said before inserting the needle to take blood. My chest felt as if it was being spread open with the rusted rib cutter at our hospital. How could a needle stick possibly hurt?

Tom examined me in one of the receiving areas. I hoped it was not the one where Dan died. "You should return to the States," he said after listening to my chest. "There's no point in staying here now."

"I can't," I said. "I feel like I would be leaving Dan behind."

"Then at least take an R&R to Hawaii where you can think things over in peace."

"What about the pain?" I asked. "Do I have pneumonia?" I didn't care, but I didn't want to talk about taking an R&R.

"Your chest doesn't sound bad, but I don't like that fever." He was writing out a prescription. "I'll give you a broad spectrum antibiotic and hope it works." He turned his attention to Jean. "She really should go to Hawaii," he said. "She could be treated at Tripler Hospital where they have the time and facilities to make a decent diagnosis." He handed her the prescription and a bottle of pills. "Give her one of these at bedtime," he said. "They'll help her sleep."

I thanked Tom and walked with Jean to the chaplain's office, located up a sandy hill near the chapel where Dan and I had attended Mass on Christmas

Eve. The chaplain got to his feet when I entered his office.

"Please, sit down," he said, indicating a chair next to his desk.

"I wanted to know if you gave Dan the Last Rites," I said.

"I must tell you that I don't recall actually seeing your young man," he said. "But I'm sure I gave him the Sacrament."

He picked up a notebook with "1968" scrawled across the cover. It was only the end of January and already he had to turn several pages. "Sergeant Daniel Cowan," he read. "One fifteen p.m."

He handed me the notebook so I could see for myself. The date, the time, K.I.A. after the name; all of it was in order. Precise, to the point, but with no trace of the person who went with the brief entry. No mention of who he was before he came to this terrible place, who loved him, or what dreams he had left behind. Killed in action; enough said.

"I wish I could say something to comfort you," the priest said when he saw tears dropping on the opened page. "I haven't had to deal with the grief of loved ones over here and you are a painful reminder of all the suffering people back home." He rubbed a hand over his eyes and looked away from me. His profile was changed from the young man who had said Mass when I first arrived in Danang. His shoulders drooped and his head stayed in a somewhat bowed position.

"Will you notify his family?" I asked when I handed the notebook back to him.

"They have already been notified."

"But will you tell them he had the Sacrament?"

"Ordinarily I would. But I think it would be better if you could manage to write them."

"But I don't even know them. Dan and I were going to call his parents when we were on R&R in Hong Kong in a week."

"I'm so sorry," the chaplain said and paused. "Most people have terrible visions of how their loved ones died. I'm sure any comfort you can give them would be most appreciated."

"I can't give them comfort, Father. Dan shouldn't have died on that island where he worked so hard. And he shouldn't have bled to death after all the lives I've struggled to save." I could hear the bitterness in my voice but didn't care.

"The anger will pass," the priest said. "God does not give us burdens too difficult to bear." I got up to leave. "I will say Mass for your Dan tonight."

"What time?"

"You shouldn't drive out here. It will be after dark."

"I'll bring someone with me."

Julia offered to go, even though she was Lutheran. "I haven't been inside a church since I came over here," she said. "It won't hurt me."

The chapel was filled with pajama-clad patients. I envied them their survival, even though many were missing limbs. At least they were alive.

Tien was waiting with hot tea and sandwiches on our return. She had not cried in my presence, but her eyes were swollen and she wore a swatch of black cloth on the sleeve of her white blouse. I managed to drink the tea and swallow part of a sandwich under her watchful gaze. When I went to my room, I wrapped myself in the field blanket Dan had given me. Jean came in with the pills Tom gave her to help me sleep. A cherry bomb exploded outside and I jumped.

"They're celebrating Tet early," Jean said, as a series of fire crackers sounded. "I called the R&R center," she said. "They can get you on the R&R manifest for Hawaii Monday morning." She sat down on the side of my bed to give me the pill. "Both Teresa and Otto say you don't have to come back to work," she said. "You can go straight home from Hawaii."

"But I don't want to go home." Jean looked at me with concern. "I'll go to Hawaii," I said. "I have a cousin I can stay with."

"Don't forget to take that," Jean said, indicating the pill I still held. "And knock on the wall if you need anything during the night. We might as well sleep here with the Tet truce keeping things quiet." I was relieved I would not have to go to the compound, but startled every time a cherry bomb or firecracker exploded outside.

I didn't tell her that I couldn't take the sleeping pill because I might be pregnant. There was no need to worry her any more than she already was.

Margaret came into my room the next morning. "I told Keith we won't be going to Hue on Monday. He'll still go because of Tran."

"Why don't you go, too," I said.

"I don't feel much like celebrating." She left with the others for work.

When I couldn't stand to lie in bed thinking of Dan any longer, I went out to the living room. There was a pack of playing cards on the coffee table in front of the sofa and I laid out a game of solitaire. But my hands shook so badly I had trouble handling the cards. As I found spaces for discards, I slapped them down faster and faster. I went on to a second game, slapping the cards down so hard on the table it hurt my hand.

I continued the frantic games, every nerve inside me vibrating as if I was standing on a rail platform with hundreds of trains thundering by. Tien came and went from kitchen to dining table, saying nothing as she prepared lunch.

Finally, my friends came home. "I'm going back to work with you," I told them.

"Do you think that's wise?" Julia asked.

"I don't know. But I do know I can't stay here."

My hands shook too badly to start I.V.s, but I could pump blood, examine patients for multiple wounds and help transport stretchers. I worked even on Sunday, throwing a few items of clothing into a small bag for Hawaii the next day.

Julia drove me to the airbase and went with me to the R&R center. We found it empty, except for one airman behind a counter.

"What time's the flight for Hawaii?" Julia asked.

"Canceled, ma'am. Engine trouble."

I felt relieved. I wasn't looking forward to being with people who knew nothing of the war, other than what they read in the papers or saw on T.V.

"Back to work," I said to Julia.

"I'm sorry, Patty."

"Don't be. I'm in no hurry to leave."

The eve of Tet was in full swing while we ate dinner that night, with firecrackers going off everywhere. I was still awake just past midnight when several loud explosions set my windows rattling. "It's cherry bombs," Jean called to me through the wall separating our rooms.

The fireworks were growing louder and I got out of bed. Each explosion tore through my body like the bullet had torn through Dan's. I could see him falling, over and over; sinking into the depths of a stinking river with no one to help him.

When I heard someone pounding on the door downstairs, I went with Jean to answer it. "They used the cover of cherry bombs to attack. They're hitting everywhere," Shelly told us breathlessly. "We have to get out."

Still wrapped in Dan's blanket, I followed her and Jean to our van where Julia, Margaret and Teresa waited. We sped through darkened streets that were coming alive with tanks and trucks. The sky was orange with flares and gunfire sounded everywhere. The noise hurt my already aching head and made my body tremble. I wasn't afraid of dying, I just wanted the noise to stop.

The other members of our team arrived with clothing pulled hastily over pajamas. Dan's boss and his men hurried from one end of the compound to the other, shouting into field telephones and radios. Only this time it wasn't a red alert just for Danang. The enemy was hitting everywhere simultaneously. They had slipped into every surrounding city and village the CIA was able to contact, launching an all-out offensive under the guise of fireworks. And judging from the activity in the compound, our intelligence community knew nothing about the strike until it began.

There was no sleep with the pounding and explosions all around us. I found an unoccupied corner in one of the bunkers and pulled Dan's blanket up around my ears to drown out some of the noise. I thought of how he thought the Viet Cong were up to something and whether he told his boss. And whether CIA officials would believe a lowly Marine sergeant.

The fighting was still going at daybreak, but I returned to my quarters with Jean to get into a uniform and try going to the hospital. When I opened my wardrobe, my eyes fell on the small bag of clean clothes Dan kept in my room. I picked it up and clutched it to me as I went to sit on my bed. His shaving kit was on my bedside table.

As I picked it up, I remembered him telling me he would have a bushy beard when he came to Danang. Was that why the chaplain had not recognized him, or had he trained himself not to look at the faces the same as Tom? I wondered if Dan's family would be allowed to see him, and whether he would be shaved and fixed up. I had never been to a Marine's funeral; I had only seen dead Marines.

I opened the shaving kit and lifted the articles from it one by one - his comb, his bar of soap covered with dried bubbles from his last shower. I touched them to feel something that had been close to him and they crumbled beneath my fingers. His mother would want these things, to take out and hold like I had seen my own mother do when her baby brother's belongings had been sent home from France. I remembered her reading his letters, with portions blackened out by the censors, and thought of the letter I had urged Dan to write his mother just before he died. I prayed it had reached her before the family was notified of his death; before it became a voice from the grave.

I wrapped the shaving kit so I could mail it, then wrote the letter the chaplain suggested. It was easy to tell Dan's family about the good things;

our Christmas together, and how much he was looking forward to coming home. I wrote only briefly about his death, telling them that he had not suffered. I concluded by telling them he believed in the work he was doing in Vietnam, leaving out the part about the people who he had worked so hard to help harboring the Viet Cong who had killed him. And the troops he had trained setting him up for the ambush.

Tien came in to indicate she had fixed me breakfast. I told her I wasn't hungry. She moved silently about my room, straightening a mirror, picking up a loose shoe. Then she came to stand squarely in front of me. "Co Pat, you eat," she said in the first English I had ever heard her use.

The others had already left for work, but they were home at noon for a hasty lunch. "You might not be able to get out even next Monday," Jean told me. "The air base is heavily damaged and closed to all nonessential traffic."

"Is it that bad?"

"They've hit everywhere in I Corps. Khe Sanh, Quang Tri, Hue, Phu Bai. It's the biggest offensive of the war."

I thought automatically of Hoi An, then remembered that Dan was already gone. There was no more worrying, just remembering and hurting. Johnny was propped in a chair in the living room, and I went to hold him while the others ate. They had worked hard all morning and I did not want to make them feel guilty for their appetites.

"I'll go back to work with you," I said when they were finished.

"I don't think you should," Shelly said.

"I can't just sit around," I said. "Let me help in triage."

My hands still shook so badly I had to stick the patients two and three times for an I.V., when I had never missed one on the first try before. The moaning and pleading was the same as it had always been, but it bothered me more. Blood looked redder and felt warm and sticky on my hands. And it smelled both sweet and nauseating.

The hurt remained in my chest, and I felt pain in my back and limbs from lifting heavy stretchers. We quit at six so we would have time to get to the compound before dark. There were cold C-rations for dinner, in small army-green tins the men in the field carried in their packs as their only source of food. I still was not hungry. Talk of the Tet Offensive was constant, as was the unrelenting noise of battle. I could no longer distinguish between incoming and outgoing; it all sounded equally loud and threatening. People were dying out there; Dan was being hit again and again.

I was awake at midnight when I heard CIA men talking into phones.

The enemy had hit Saigon and everywhere else in the southern half of the country.

Five days passed before an R&R plane was given clearance to come into Danang. "Go to Tripler Hospital as soon as you get to Hawaii," Jean told me while she helped me pack a bag. "You've lost so much weight you look awful."

"I'm just tired," I said. "I'll be all right."

Two heavily armed M.P.s drove me to the air base, after first dressing me in a flak jacket and helmet. My head had recently begun shaking as much as my hands. I felt I must look like one of the bobble-head dolls that people put in the rear windows of their cars. I sat in the passenger side of the jeep, beneath the barrel of a machine gun mounted over my head. It was just after dawn and rain fell in grey sheets that limited our visibility. I was grateful I could not see the morgue when we passed by.

A group of fighters were screaming in from a mission up north as we crossed the end of the airfield and the driver stopped to let them come in low over the road. When they landed, parachutes popped out behind them to slow their speed. We proceeded to the R&R terminal, arriving just as rockets thundered onto the runway.

I was half-carried by the M.P.s into a bunker, where we were met by dozens of sweaty bodies already crammed into its dark interior. When the attack ended, I returned with the other passengers to the waiting area. The plane, which was hours late, was just about to set down when a burst of mortar fire hit the runway. Clouds of dust flew up to meet it as it put on full power and climbed back into the sky. The mortar fire continued, but I stood watching the departing plane. Someone took my arm and pulled me toward the bunker. Just inside its dark confines, a pair of combat boots crashed into my back and sent me sprawling.

"I'm sorry, ma'am," a young soldier said as he helped me up. "I didn't see you ahead of me when I swung in."

"I'm fine," I said. But a searing pain ran through my entire lower back and down my left leg.

When two hours had passed and the plane had not reappeared, we were told the flight was cancelled. I caught a ride in the back of a troop truck to the hospital, where my extra pair of hands was welcomed.

Two days later Rick stopped by to see if Jean was all right, their first meeting since the beginning of the offensive. He told me the runways were open again and an R&R flight would be taking off for Hawaii sometime before dark. "They're trying to get men out who're on emergency leave," he said. "If you show up, they'll probably let you on." He offered to drop me at the R&R terminal on his way back to his squadron.

"Go," Jean told me. "No arguments."

Shelly caught me at the door. "I'll say good-bye now in case you decide not to come back." She hugged me, and I winced from the pain it caused in my back. "What's wrong?" she asked.

"I hurt my back getting into a bunker."

"All the more reason to get out of here. Have it looked at in Hawaii."

Rick was silent as he drove along the road where he had accidentally hit the child. Jean had told him about Dan, and he told me how sorry he was as we pulled through the gates of the air base. "You two had something special," he said. "I just wish it could have lasted."

"Thank you. I hope it works out better for you and Jean."

"I'm afraid not," he said. "I was separated when I came over here and planning to get a divorce. But I have three young boys." He stopped next to the R&R terminal and took my bag out of the rear seat. "I've done some hard thinking since the accident," he said. "It made me reconsider a lot of things in my life."

"You're not going to get a divorce?"

"No, at least not now. I'm going to get out of the Marine Corps and raise my kids."

"When will you tell Jean?"

"Tomorrow night. If I get into town."

I didn't have long to wait before the Pan Am jet arrived. "SCRAMBLE!" someone ordered over a microphone, and a herd of men in combat attire thundered toward the plane. We were still buckling our seat belts when it began rolling down the runway and lifted into the air above puffs of smoke.

The passengers sat quietly until we landed in Guam to refuel. Then an air of jubilation broke out as they realized they were safely on their way to visit the families and girlfriends whose pictures they passed around. Even those on emergency leave seemed happy to be on their way home.

When we took off for Hawaii, I took a rosary Sister Marie had given me from my pocket so I would not have to talk to the men on either side of me. It was made of small pebbles from the South China Sea, strung together with fishing line salvaged from the surf. I was the only woman on board, and the male passengers looked at me curiously. But the questions remained only in their eyes.

CHAPTER THIRTY-ONE

When we reached Hawaii, I had to be helped off the plane. Not only was my back hurting, my left leg was cramping with spasms.

An R&R official assisted me with a taxi to my cousin's, where I spent the next two days in bed. My back improved, but there was no rest for my mind. It raced on in disjointed bursts, refusing to let me sleep or to concentrate. I couldn't stop thinking, yet I understood nothing. And the sudden quiet was as unnerving as the sounds of battle.

On the third day I called my family. They were relieved to know I was safe, and I felt badly that I had not let them know sooner. As I expected, they begged me not to return to Vietnam.

"I'll call you again," I told my mother. "When I've decided what to do."

"But the war is over," she said. "The television says they've overrun the American embassy and all the Americans are being killed." I handed the telephone to my cousin and hurried to the television set, praying that my mother was wrong.

Walter Cronkite was reporting the news in a somber voice like I had heard on old broadcasts of the attack on Pearl Harbor. Footage was shown of the American embassy in Saigon, with the bodies of enemy soldiers lying about while American Marines fought to defend it. The coverage switched to the streets, where an American civilian hung out a hotel window brandishing a pistol.

I stood in front of the set, unable to believe what I was seeing. If Saigon and the American embassy were lost, what hope did my friends in Danang have?

"You shouldn't watch that," my cousin said behind me. She was in her forties, with grown children, and had fussed over me ever since my arrival.

"It's too depressing, and you're here now," she said. "You need to forget all that and take care of yourself."

I sat down in the chair she offered, but I would not allow her to turn off the set. I had left Vietnam only three days earlier. How could the American forces have been defeated as quickly as Mr. Cronkite was reporting?

The scene at the embassy was shown again, and only then did I realize the footage was several days old. The events I was watching had happened while I was still in Vietnam.

"They keep showing it over and over," my cousin said when I inquired. "They took the embassy in the beginning."

"There're only a few Viet Cong bodies lying there," I said. "They just keep showing the same ones from different angles."

As I watched the coverage, it became apparent most of the reporters had been caught in Saigon when the Tet Offensive hit. And since travel on helicopters was now severely restricted, there was little they could do but cover what was happening in the capital. A few suicide sappers had been hoisted over the walls of the American embassy, where they were killed by Marine guards. But because of the hordes of journalists looking for a story, the extensive coverage made it look as if the embassy had been invaded by a battalion. There was some fierce fighting at the race track, located outside the city, and a brutal clip of a Vietnamese official blowing out the brain of a V.C. involved in an attack that killed his family members. But Saigon looked no more under siege than Danang did any night at the bewitching hour.

I was about to turn off the set when a special report interrupted the regular broadcast. "Fighting in Hue had escalated to house-to-house and man-to-man combat, with American Marines and North Vietnamese engaged in full-scale battle." I didn't know where Tran's parents lived, but I tried to catch a glimpse of a familiar face in the crowds fleeing in boats on the Perfume River that ran through the city.

"You can't go back there," my cousin said. "The war is over and we lost."

"I'm not so sure of that."

"Walter Cronkite seems to think so."

"Walter Cronkite is a journalist looking for a story."

Protesters were shown celebrating in the streets of New York and San Francisco, but I didn't share in their jubilation. The dirty faces of battle-weary Marines fighting to retake Hue were the people with whom I identified.

My cousin was in the kitchen doing a crossword puzzle went I went in search of aspirin the next morning. Sleep had continued to elude me and my head ached as much as my chest and back.

"Would you like to go shopping?" one of my cousin's daughters asked when I joined them at the table. "We have the world's largest shopping center." My back was stiff with pain and my legs felt as if I had just stepped off a carnival ride that left them tingling with vibrations. But it was difficult to say no to a smiling eighteen year old anxious to help, and I did not want to spend the day listening to her mother trying to convince me not to return to Vietnam.

"I guess I could use a few things," I said after some hesitation.

Chrissy had an MG, which she drove at eighteen year old speed. The radio blared Bob Dylan while I held onto the dashboard and kept both feet braced against the floor. "We don't drive very fast in Vietnam," I said.

"Why not?" the young girl asked. "No fast cars?"

"Bad roads."

We were approaching an A&W root beer stand. "Want one?" she asked, and swung into the parking lot before I could answer. The menu posted on a plastic board had so many selections I was still reading them when Chrissy pressed the button to order.

"May I help you please," a voice scratched over the speaker. It was all familiar, yet somehow alien. Had there been a time when I rode in fast cars and ordered hamburgers from a box?

"Hamburger?" Chrissy asked when she turned to me.

"Sure. Hamburger would be fine."

"Anything to drink?" the box asked.

"Anything to drink?" my companion repeated. She wore sun glasses that covered most of her face and her hair covered the rest.

"Do they have ice?"

She laughed and removed her dark glasses to look at me. "You're kidding, aren't you?"

"A drink would be fine."

The cold root beers were served almost immediately by a young girl in an orange and brown uniform with matching hat and apron. I took the heavy, frosted mug in both hands, turning it slowly to marvel at how cold it was. Much colder than I remembered.

By the time the hamburgers were served, I found I could not eat. A war was raging only hours away, yet all around me I saw people eating, laughing and listening to music as if it was just another warm afternoon.

"I guess I'm not hungry," I said after several minutes of staring at the sandwich. Chrissy put it back on the tray without comment.

The shopping mall was as large as she had predicted. Agreeing to meet later, Chrissy looked through a record shop while I went to a clothing store and made a few purchases. When the salesclerk handed me the packages, I was hit with such a wave of back pain my legs began to wobble.

"You'd better see a doctor," she said when I explained that I had recently hurt my back. "There are lots of good ones right over there." She indicated a tall office building within the shopping center.

The directory of physicians and lawyers was long, but I managed to find the name of a specialist in orthopedics. While I waited for an elevator, I watched people bustling around me to get to places I could only imagine. For almost a year I had not gone to a bank, a dry cleaners, the grocery store or paid rent. My life had been reduced to doing my job and staying alive, and it startled me to realize I preferred it that way.

The doctor's waiting room was air-conditioned to a frigid degree and had carpet so thick I had to lift my feet painfully in order to get across it. Patients sat in overstuffed chairs instead of squatting in a screened porch with scraps of paper in their hands.

"Do you have an appointment?" the receptionist asked when I inquired about seeing the doctor.

"No, but I hurt my back and need to see someone."

"If it's an emergency you need to go to an emergency room." Her hair was teased into a mountain of curls on top of her head, and she surveyed my faded cotton dress and broken sandals with nothing less than dismay.

"I just need a muscle relaxant and something for pain," I said. "It wouldn't take much time."

"You also need an appointment and a referral from your family physician."

"I don't have a family physician," I said. "I'm here on R&R from Vietnam." Several heads bobbed up from where they were submerged in magazines.

"Then you need to go to the military hospital," the receptionist said. "It's called Tripler."

I knew that I would be admitted if I went to the military hospital, and the prospect of lying in bed with nothing to do but watch news reports was more than I could bear. The spasms in my back and left leg intensified as I stood contemplating my options, and I dropped the packages I was carrying to the floor. The receptionist watched as I struggled to retrieve them.

"Please, I'm in terrible pain," I said when I abandoned the packages and sank into a nearby chair. "Just ask the doctor if he will see me."

"If you're that bad, you should be admitted to a hospital."

"My R&R flight leaves for Vietnam in two days." Not until I said it did I realize that's where I wanted to be, back with my friends and the patients who needed me.

She stood and smoothed the wrinkles from her mini-skirt. "All right," she said. "But I don't know why anyone would want to go back to all that killing."

She returned with a nurse who led me to an examining room and gave me a gown that hung like a tent on my thin body.

"What can I do for you, young lady?" the doctor asked when he came in minutes later. He looked in his fifties and had the brisk, confident manner of a successful physician.

I told him about being kicked in the back while getting into a bunker, then briefly described the events leading up to the accident. He listened with concern.

"Your back is all bruised," he said when he looked at it. "I'll have to take a couple of pictures to see what's going on."

"I can't have x-rays," I said. "I might be pregnant."

"Might be?" He sat down in a chair facing the examining table. "Don't you think you'd better find out?"

"I guess I should."

He called the nurse back into the room, and she took me to an office next door. I was examined by an obstetrician after first giving blood and urine samples.

"You really should have that back of yours looked after," he said when he was finished with the exam.

"But what about the baby?"

"The lab results won't be back for awhile," he said slowly. "But I'm fairly certain you are not pregnant. You're probably off schedule from something else - that fever you told me you had, or some other problem you've picked up in that god forsaken country."

I started to cry and he handed me a box of tissues. "It sounds to me like you have enough to cope with right now without a pregnancy," he said kindly. "Why don't you be good to yourself and go home where you can rest and get better."

"I think I would be better off working," I said. "Especially now." The only reservation I had had about returning to Danang was concern for the baby.

"Suit yourself," he said. "But you have to start eating or you'll be suffering from malnutrition on top of everything else. Your weight is eighty pounds." He held up the notes the nurse had made while checking me in.

"I have a pain in my chest that won't go away."

He poked at the spot I indicated. "When did it start?"

I tried to remember but everything seemed a blur. "In Vietnam," I said. "I guess around the time my Marine was killed." I remembered then that it actually started the night before, when I dreamed Dan was injured by a land mine.

The doctor continued to poke for awhile. "Have it looked at if it doesn't go away," he said when he finished. "But it's quite common to have chest pain following the death of a loved one. That's what is known, my dear, as a broken heart."

The orthopedist took x-rays of my back which were inconclusive. "You need a better work-up," he said. "And you should be on bed rest."

"Could I just get something for the spasms and pain?" I asked. "I promise I'll get worked-up if I don't get better."

He handed me two prescriptions, along with instructions to sleep on a firm surface. That would be easy enough in the bunkers, but his warning not to lift anything heavy would be impossible with the stretchers I carried. I thanked him for seeing me and he wished me well. When I asked the receptionist how much I owed, she told me both doctors had said there was no charge.

My last night in Hawaii was as sleepless as the others and I was packed and ready to go before the sun came up. Chrissy drove me to the airport, which was already crowded with passengers and relatives. The sweet perfume of flowers was everywhere from colorful leis being placed around the necks of arriving and departing visitors to the island.

R&R flights used the regular terminal, but the passengers were kept to one side in a roped-off section. Wives, girlfriends and assorted family members sat next to their men with faces that reflected the pain they were feeling at being separated again. Children seemed to sense the gloom and fretted at their parents.

When the flight to Danang was called, I was the only woman, as well as the only civilian, to get in line. "Who's that, the company hooker?" a female voice said. I turned to see two women in long hair and flowing skirts standing just outside the roped-off section. They held signs telling the American military to get out of Vietnam.

"It don't mean nothin'," a young G.I. standing next to me said.

I was glad to be leaving, to be going back to people who knew and understood me. I didn't sleep on the long flight. When we landed in Danang, the signs of battle were everywhere, and the cold rain so unlike the bright sunshine I had left in Hawaii. No one seemed surprised when I arrived at the hospital carrying my suitcase.

We worked until sundown, then went home for a quick dinner before going to the compound. It was good to be back at the table with my colleagues, although I knew Rick had talked to Jean by her sadness.

"We've been living like moles," Shelly told me. "We're in the hospital all day and the bunkers every night."

"It doesn't look like you got much sun," Julia said. "I thought you would come back with a tan."

"I didn't go out much," I said. "But I did do some shopping."

I got up from the table and went to my room, feeling almost happy as I gathered up the gifts I had bought for my friends. But when I reached into one of the bags, I pulled out a filmy nightgown that floated to the floor as my hand released it. Somewhere in the back of my mind I could remember telling a sales clerk that I needed a special nightgown for a trip to Hong Kong.

I sat down on the floor next to where it had fallen, fingering the silky fabric. I hadn't come back to Vietnam to be with my friends, or to take care of patients. I had come back to be with Dan.

"Perhaps you should have gone to the funeral," Margaret said from the doorway. "It might have put things in perspective."

I couldn't answer her. A sharp ache thundered through my chest and my body felt hollow without Dan's child.

"It's time to go to the compound." Her voice was gentler than I remembered.

"I think I'll stay here," I said.

"Hoping you'll be killed?" She came into the room. "You're not the only one who lost someone, you know."

I looked up at her from where I sat on the floor.

"Becky's husband was killed."

"Tran?"

"Becky's all right," she added. "He managed to hide her at his parents' home when they heard the North Vietnamese coming."

"He was killed in Hue?"

"His entire family was shot to death." Her voice wavered. "Keith was captured and is listed as missing."

"Oh, Margaret, I'm so sorry."

"Be sorry for his wife and kids," she said as she headed for the doorway. "Tarts don't count."

I pulled my blanket from Dan off the bed and wrapped it around me. Dan's death had kept me from going to Hue, where Margaret and I would surely have been captured or killed. I wondered if Becky and Margaret felt as cheated as I did that our lives had been spared.

Becky hadn't returned to work, but stories of her harrowing experience circulated among the Vietnamese staff. There had been little warning before the city was overrun, but Tran had managed to lift Becky to the rafter's of his parents' home, where she witnessed the slaughter of her loved ones below while silently protecting her unborn child. She swam down the Perfume River breathing through a reed to escape Hue.

Her maternal courage reminded me that even though I was not carrying Dan's child I still had Danny.

I left triage to Shelly and drove out to the orphanage. "I am so happy you have returned," Sister Marie said when she saw me. "You were fortunate to be in Hong Kong when the trouble came."

"I didn't go to Hong Kong," I said. I wanted her to know about Dan's death before Danny discovered my presence. "Dan was killed," I said. "I would have told you sooner, but I have been away."

"Oh, dear god!" She put a hand to her mouth, then took hold of both my hands. "He loved you so."

There was a squeal of delight as Danny came catapulting towards me. I stooped down and he threw his arms around me, but he pulled away when he felt my tears on his cheek. Sister Marie called one of the nuns to take him away.

"I still want to take him home," I said when he was gone and I had painfully righted myself. "Will you let me?"

"Of course. I am trying to get as many children out as possible."

"Has something else happened?" I thought immediately of the orphanage in the Delta.

"Nothing. But we are worried the Americans will leave." It was the first time I had heard her express any doubt about our commitment to her country. She had watched the French occupiers suffer their defeat at Dien Bien Phu, when nobody would have believed they could be chased out by a band of ragged peasants. America was apparently no different in her eyes.

"Will you and the sisters leave if we pull out?"

"Never. This is our home and there will always be children who need us."

"What should I tell Danny about Dan?"

"I will talk to him," she said. "These children understand such things."

No one objected when I brought Danny home with me for lunch and even Tien made an effort to show him special attention. When it came time to take him back, he would not be parted with Dan's blanket, which I had wrapped him in because of the chill in our unheated house. I let him keep it as a symbol of the life we would soon share together.

On Sunday morning I went to church at the Army compound across the river. The Ba turned away when she saw my face and took me across the river as quickly as possible.

It was cold and damp in the converted bar and the Mass seemed unusually long. When the priest came to the part in which he repeated Christ's words at the Last Supper I began shaking. "... This is the cup of my blood, the blood of the new and everlasting covenant. It will be shed for you and for all men so that sins may be forgiven. Do this in memory of me."

I wanted to shout at the priest that Dan had died for man's sins too. And how many people would remember him? Why should I show adoration for the sacrifice of one being when lives were being sacrificed all around me? Surely, young men spilling their blood in stinking jungles on the other side of the world from their loved ones was comparable to hanging on a cross. And what about children with their flesh burned away by napalm? Wasn't that worth a little remembrance?

I made my way outside and leaned against the building to steady myself. "Can I do anything for you?" A young lieutenant stood waiting for a reply. "I saw you leave and thought you might be sick."

"It was just hot in there," I said.

"Hot? You're shaking from the cold."

"I guess I'm not feeling well." I wanted him to go away.

"Why don't you let me drive you to your quarters?"

I looked toward the river and saw that the Ba was not waiting for me. The lieutenant drove me home and waited until I was safely inside.

“Maybe you shouldn’t go again if it bothers you so much,” Jean said when I told her about my reaction to church. There were casualties to do and she was getting ready for work.

“But the only consolation I have is that I will be with Dan again someday,” I told her.

“You’ll work it out,” she said. “But you’d better do it over here. Don’t expect people back home to understand, or even to care.”

“I don’t know how to work it out.”

Jean sighed. “Rick is going back to his wife and kids, so you’re not alone.”

“I’m sorry, Jean.”

The casualties were from Hue and were badly infected from having to wait so long to be evacuated. The Marines had retaken the city, but many people had died in the interim while helicopters were unable to land.

As I huddled in the bunker that night, cold and lonely without Dan’s blanket, I thought about what Jean had said about working out Dan’s death before I went home. Becky would have a difficult time, but she was carrying Tran’s baby, and would be surrounded by people who had known him and known war. I would be going back to a family who had never met Dan, and to a country that had not experienced war and was hostile to those who served in Vietnam.

The culture shock Washington had warned us about during orientation had not taken place here. It would happen when we returned to our own country.

Julia came over to where I sat with a bottle of Scotch. “Have some,” she said. “It’ll help you sleep.”

She handed me the bottle and I took a long drink. When I turned to hand it back, she shook her head. She sat there with an arm around me while I drank until I finally passed out.

CHAPTER THIRTY-TWO

Dan's boss pointedly avoided me in the compound, so I learned nothing more of the details of his death. What I did learn from the talk among the men was that the Tet Offensive had proven a decisive psychological victory for the Viet Cong and North Vietnamese. Even though the American and South Vietnamese forces had won tactically, including the retaking of Hue. We had been caught so off-guard it appeared Goliath had truly been slain. In the propaganda emanating from the north, as well as in America's own media, the war was lost.

Our interpreter Lan took advantage of the situation to expound on the inevitability of an American pull-out, which frightened the Vietnamese because of their association with us. They knew they would be the target of reprisals by communist forces for their disloyalty to the powers in Hanoi.

Suspicions resumed between the American and Vietnamese teams and general morale plummeted. Otto was considering having Lan fired when he suddenly disappeared. Only Shelly was not surprised when he resurfaced as part of the enemy body count.

A sweep of a village outside Danang that was suspected of being a launching sight for the rockets that continued to hit the air base resulted in the capture or death of dozens of Viet Cong and their sympathizers. The bodies of those slain were taken to a chopper pad out near the bridge, where I had left on my first trip to Hoi An. The bodies were placed in full view of the public as a warning to anyone who dared to harbor the enemy. It was one of our O.R. nurses who discovered Lan among the dead.

"Did you check at USAID headquarters?" Shelly asked Jean. "They're probably still paying him."

Mr. Hai was terrified by the incident and instructed his O.R. staff not to believe any of the anti-American rhetoric Lan had been spreading before his death. He repeatedly told us he knew nothing of Lan's Viet Cong connections, and begged us not to report him to our military for being a sympathizer.

"I don't blame him for being scared," Shelly said. "Those bodies have been lying out in the rain so long you can smell them all over town."

They were still there when I drove her and Tom to the air base the day of their departure. It might have been difficult to say good-bye if I hadn't been so relieved to see them getting out. Both were exhausted from nonstop work since the beginning of Tet and were anxious to get on with the life they would soon share as man and wife.

"Promise me you'll leave soon," Shelly said before boarding the plane. It was one of the special transports the American government contracted to take people who were finished with their tours out of country, known by G.I.s as the Freedom Bird.

"I'll leave as soon as the casualties let up," I said. "I can't leave Gertie alone until Becky comes back. And we still have students."

"Screw work," Shelly said. "Get out of this mule-shit pie and let them manage as best they can. Old 'god girl' will probably sign up for another tour so she won't have to leave all her men."

The plane was running up its engines and the other passengers were already on board. "Dan isn't here anymore," Tom shouted above the engine noise when he leaned over to hug me good-bye. "That isn't going to change."

"Be sure to think about settling close to us back home," Shelly said after we held each other in a long embrace. "Unless you have other plans."

"No plans."

"God, Mouse, I'm sorry."

"It's O.K., I know what you meant."

Tom waved to his corpsman, who had come along to see them off, and stepped inside the plane. Shelly stood at the top of the stairs waving to me. Both of us were crying.

I watched until the plane was out of sight, then drove Tom's corpsman back to Navy Hospital. Fast Eddie was upset about Tom leaving, after nearly a year of assisting him in the O.R. on each of his cases, and depressed about his own impending departure. He now not only had an illegal Vietnamese wife, but also a son.

"I can't get papers to get them out," he told me while I drove him to Navy Hospital. "My C.O. is pissed that I got involved with one of the locals." The corpsman looked like a young boy, until I looked into his eyes.

"I wish I could help," I said. "But the only person I knew at the American

Consulate was captured in Hue." There was still no trace of Keith, but Margaret refused to believe he would not be found alive.

"Don't worry about it, ma'am," Fast Eddie said as I pulled through the gates of the hospital. "I always find a way to get around the rules." He jumped out of the jeep when I stopped next to his barracks. "If I don't see you again before I leave, good luck."

"Thanks, same to you," I said. "And thanks again for saving me from drowning."

"It was nothing."

As I watched him walk away, hands in pockets, I realized I would probably never see him again. And I didn't even know his real name.

There was one other stop I wanted to make. I had not been able to make myself attend Mass again, and I wanted to talk to someone who could still believe in Christ's mercy after seeing so many young men die. But when I asked for the chaplain who had talked with me about Dan, I was told he was no longer there.

"I didn't realize his tour was up," I said to his replacement.

"It wasn't," the new chaplain replied. "He requested a change of duty station for emotional reasons."

"To where?"

"The States." He was a middle-aged man, but from his appearance I knew he was new to war. "Could I help you with anything?"

"No, nothing."

I didn't want to hear anyone else tell me that God didn't give burdens too difficult to bear. When I drove out the gates of Navy Hospital, I knew it was for the last time. The doctors had not been able to save Dan's life, and there was no one there who could save my soul.

Sister Nicole saw me drive down the lane to the orphanage, but she disappeared inside the building without even a greeting. Sister Marie met me in the courtyard.

"I am afraid I have unhappy news for you," the mother superior told me. She looked so distraught I was certain something terrible had happened.

"Where's Danny?" I asked, looking around for him.

"He is no longer here. His father came two days ago and took him away."

"His father? I thought Danny was an orphan?"

"We thought so as well. But the man lost a leg in the war and came looking for his son. He chose him from a group of boys the age his son would be."

"But how can you be sure? Did he have proof Danny was his child?"

"We can never be sure." The nun's eyes told me the decision to let Danny go had not been easy. "Danny seemed happy to have a father and the man lost all of his family. We thought it best to let him take him. It is important in this country to have a son."

"But Danny was all I had left."

"That is not true," the mother superior said firmly. "You have a family waiting for you in your country."

The normally boisterous children who had gathered around us watched with solemn curiosity. I automatically looked for Danny's sergeant's hat among them, and felt the dull ache return to my chest when I saw that he was not there. He would be raised in his own country by a man who had earned the right to a son, even if not by birth. Still, I felt betrayed. The nuns were supposed to be my friends, yet they had let him go without even notifying me. I tried not to show my anger as Sister Marie walked with me to my car.

Her hands were held tightly together and her face was more distressed than I had ever seen it. "God will give you someone else to love," she said.

"Please don't talk about God." I turned away from the hurt in her eyes and drove down the lane without looking back.

I had not wanted to be alone since Dan's death, but now I was grateful to find the house deserted. I lay down on my bed to rest my back and to try to calm the trembling that made me feel like a palsied old woman. But a ghastly dream began the moment I closed my eyes. It was the same one that alternated with the dream in which I was sitting on the sandbags outside surgery, waiting for Dan.

The second one, which had begun after my return from Hawaii, involved triage. Bloody patients missing whole parts of their bodies, and napalm victims charred beyond recognition, pleaded with me not to set them aside. One of them was Dan.

I woke trembling so badly I had difficulty lighting a cigarette. When I reached for the ashtray next to my bed, I saw the gun Dan had given me lying there. I picked it up almost lovingly, remembering the day he taught me how to use it. I turned it over in my hands, trying to imagine how I would go on without him.

How could I go back to working in a clean, modern hospital with the nightmares of triage that plagued me during the night and spilled over into my waking hours. There was nothing for me to look forward to without Dan, and I knew I could never feel about anyone the way I felt about him. He was everything in the world to me, and in the space of time it took one bullet to travel across a remote patch of jungle, it was over.

The metal was cold in my right hand, colder on my temple.

It was the first time in weeks my hand didn't shake. My mind was clear and focused. Even the pain in my chest was gone.

Then suddenly I heard my father's voice the day I left for Vietnam, "Pat, come back to us."

The gun dropped to the floor with the safety still on.

"Isn't it a little early for that?" Margaret asked when I poured my second Scotch while they ate lunch.

"It's been a long day."

"It isn't half over."

"A lot happened in the first half."

I told my friends about Danny. Tien listened quietly with Johnny held tightly to her.

"Mouse, don't you think it's time to give up and go home?" Julia said. "First you lost Fuzzy, now Danny. Maybe you just weren't meant to take a child home with you."

They knew nothing about the disappointing news I had received in Hawaii and I did not tell them now. They had stood by me and helped me; it was time to give them a rest from my grief.

"I can't leave yet. I have to be sure our students can give anesthesia safely on their own."

"Gertie is doing fine with the students," Jean said. "And Becky will be back eventually."

"I'm still running triage."

CHAPTER THIRTY-THREE

There were two letters in my mailbox, one from Jack and the other from Dan's mother. I opened the one from my brother first, afraid of the other.

He was on his way back to the States, but he had heard about Dan from our mother. "I'm usually so glad to be heading home," he wrote. "But this time it's different, knowing that I'm leaving you behind. I'm usually at the bow looking stateside. Now I'm in the stern worrying about you.

I was afraid for you when you told me about your guy. I hope you can accept what's happened and go on with your life." He ended by telling me to leave Vietnam, and that he would try to make things easier for me at home by telling the family not to ask too many questions. I put the letter in my pocket, remembering our R&R together in Taiwan. Life had been so good then. I was in love with Dan and sure of his love for me. Only Jack had foreseen the tragedy awaiting us.

The letter from Dan's mother was neatly typewritten, with her signature scrawled across the bottom in a shaky script. She thanked me for the letter I had written them and said she was glad Dan had a nice Christmas with me. "I knew he was gone when I saw the officer walk up to the house," she wrote. "Someone told me they send an enlisted man if they're wounded and an officer if they're dead."

I wondered if she had been alone when she received the news. Dan would not have wanted it that way. "A letter arrived from my Danny the next day," she went on. "Our mailman was always so happy when he could deliver a letter from him because he knew how I looked forward to them. I went home for lunch every day to check my mail.

He didn't know what had happened so things were difficult for awhile. I read the letter once, but I can't bear to look at it again. It's so full of his plans to call us from Hong Kong while you were there, and his excitement about coming home. I can't believe he never will."

She told me about the funeral and asked me to visit when I returned to the States so she could take me to his grave. "I had him buried close to home so I can go there often," she wrote. "I can barely bring myself to go, then can't tear myself away. There's such an emptiness in my life."

CHAPTER THIRTY-FOUR

People back home thought the Tet Offensive lasted only a few days. But the heavy fighting continued week after week. My painful back and leg would spasm if I barely turned the wrong way. I was grateful for the saw horses in triage that let me work on the patients without stooping. I was back to starting I.V.s and putting in spinals with the accuracy I had before Dan's death. But the sickening smell of blood and burned flesh followed me home at night and to the table, where I drank Scotch while the others ate.

"You need to eat something," Julia told me, as she did each night.

"I can't." I took a swallow of my drink.

"I wish I'd never given you that bottle of Scotch to help you sleep."

"Well, now it helps me live."

The others had been eating silently. Jean put down her fork and looked at me like a mother. "You're going to end up like Captain Miles."

Her remark got through the cloud surrounding my brain. I pushed the drink aside and reached for the bowl of steamed rice. It didn't smell like anything. Not even triage.

Tien saw me eating and smiled. From then on she cooked me rice three times a day.

I wish I could say I gave up the Scotch. But it had become a nightly ritual, even on nights we didn't spend in the bunker.

Our students were doing so well, I took Mr. Shat into triage with me to teach him how to get patients ready for the O.R.

Becky returned with a swatch of black fabric sewn to the sleeve of her white uniform. She was now four months pregnant. I caught her slowly rubbing her stomach with tears running down her face more than once.

She had moved her mother from the shack where she lived outside of town to the small house she had shared with Tran in Danang.

When I received a box from home, I took her into our locked lounge.

"For you," I said, indicating the cardboard box on the table.

She sat down on the sofa and slowly tore off the tape. "Choi oih," she said with surprise when she looked inside.

The first thing she pulled out was a stuffed Winnie the Pooh.

"Winnie the Pooh," I said to her.

She worked her lips before getting out, "Funny Pooh."

I laughed and she laughed with me. It was the first I had laughed since Dan's death. And the first I had heard Becky laugh since her return to work.

"Funny Pooh," I repeated. "That's a good name."

It took some time to empty the box of baby clothing and blankets. The sister I had sent money to with the request to go shopping had done an excellent job.

Becky let out a sigh of pleasure with each article she removed. "Too much," she told me when she finished.

"Not too much," I said and hugged her.

She hugged me, then pulled back abruptly, feeling my arms and back. "Co Pat, you must eat!"

"I am," I said. The rice was just keeping me alive.

"You eat," I said and patted her belly.

She smiled down at her ever expanding stomach. Then she took my hand. "Tran chet roi," she said sadly. "Sergeant Dan chet roi."

"Yes. Both dead."

We sat there quietly for several minutes. Then I began putting all of the baby items back in the box.

"Com on, Co Pat," Becky said.

"You're welcome," I replied.

Both of us looked toward the window when we heard a military ambulance come through the gates.

"Patients," I said as we both got up.

CHAPTER THIRTY-FIVE

The days went by like words to an unending song. Casualties, back pain, grief and orphaned children; all washed down with a generous portion of alcohol.

I was pouring my first Scotch of the evening when Jean came out of her room. "You need to go home," she told me.

"I still have students."

"The students are doing fine and you know Gertie is."

She was right. Gertie had stepped up after Shelly's departure, starting I.V.s and putting in spinals with only one stick. I had begun to let her run a room alone, but I wasn't sure Mr. Shat was ready to take over triage.

"I don't want to leave Leo and Shelly's anesthesia program until I'm sure it can function without me."

Julia came up the stairs for dinner. She sat down with Jean and me in the living room area. "Are you leaving?" she asked me.

I looked from one to the other. "Did the two of you make a plan to talk me into going home?"

"Dan's death has been hard on us, too," Julia replied.

Until that moment I had not once considered their feelings. I had been so consumed by my own grief, it had not even occurred to me they were feeling their own loss of a friend.

"I'm sorry. My head is just so mixed up."

"That's why you need to leave," Jean said. "You've done over a year, that's more than the troops do."

"Besides the emotional problems, your limp is getting worse," Julia said without her usual smile.

She had talked to Bird-dog on the phone only once. He had sent his sympathy to me and promised he would be up to Danang soon. But he had not kept his promise.

"Have you heard anything from Bird-dog?" I asked. She shook her head and went to the kitchen, returning with a can of Coke.

I slept that night with the usual dream of Dan losing a leg. I woke when a thunderous explosion rattled my windows.

Jean knocked on the wall. "Time to go to the bunker," she called.

The rest of the night passed with me lying on the cold floor of the bunker because my back could not stand the cots that had been set up for us. I did not have Dan's blanket to warm or comfort me. But somewhere it was doing so for Danny.

When I arrived at work the next morning I saw Mr. Shat hurrying into the Swiss hospital with one of their nurses. I followed them into the hospital to see what was happening and found Mr. Shat working over a small child.

The Swiss doctor was compressing the patient's chest while Mr. Shat expertly inserted an endotracheal tube. He hooked it up to a breathing bag, which he attached to a small tank of oxygen. I stood watching as the resuscitation continued until the child began moving her arms and legs and trying to cry.

Mr. Shat looked up and saw me. "Numbah one?" he said.

"Number one!"

CHAPTER THIRTY-SIX

It had been almost three months since Dan had died. An ambulance pulled up to the entrance with a load of moaning casualties. I started toward it, then turned and walked away.

I did not stop until I was behind the shacks, safe from the view of my colleagues. Before Dan's death, I had not cried. I worked, I ate, I slept, but I did not cry. Now the tears would not stop. I cried for Dan, I cried for my patients, I cried for every young man I had seen lying torn and broken in military hospitals, or lined up in body bags in front of the morgue.

A woman hobbled over to me and held out a scrawny infant, imploring me to take it. I looked at the child, first with sympathy, then with rage. I wanted to take the whimpering bundle and throw it to the ground. I was sick to death of starving children and helpless mothers. A year had passed, and the shacks were even fuller than when I arrived. The fighting continued, the casualties continued and I was becoming a pathetic spectacle that could not sleep without a bottle of Scotch in my hand.

In the end, I gave the woman all the money I had in my pocket. I went to Otto's office and told him I would be leaving as soon as I could get on a plane. He informed me that a new directive from Washington was allowing any nurse in I Corps to leave without having to pay her own way home. "They've decided it's too insecure for women this far north," he said. "A representative from Saigon is coming up tomorrow to give us the details."

The official from our Saigon office was the first I had seen in my year of duty in Danang. She called a meeting and asked how many of us would like to leave. Several new nurses raised their hands. When I raised mine, she reminded me that I was an anesthetist and the directive only mentioned nurses.

"But Saigon refers to me as nursing personnel," I corrected.

"That's only for paperwork," the official said.

"Isn't this paperwork?"

"I'm sorry, I'll have to get clarification from Washington."

"That could take months," Julia, who had not raised her hand, said behind me. "Buy your own ticket and get out of here."

"I'm sorry, Pat," Teresa said after the meeting. "I don't know why Saigon's suddenly become so precise about terminology." She suggested I wait for the clarification if I didn't want to spend the six hundred dollars to get home. We were in Otto's office and he listened to our conversation.

"You might as well pay the six hundred bucks and get the hell out of here," he said. "I'll try to get the bastards in Washington to reimburse you."

"Thanks, Otto. But don't get in trouble because of me."

He took the cigar from his mouth and laughed. "Honey, when you get to be my age, there's no such thing as getting into trouble."

CHAPTER THIRTY-SEVEN

Preparations for leaving were simpler than expected. I was given a physical examination at Navy Hospital, which I failed because of my back. Then I was given a packet of pills to flush from my intestines the parasites I had undoubtedly picked up. I thought it a pity they couldn't give me pills to flush my mind.

Jean and Julia hosted a small farewell party for me on the Saturday before I left. Everyone from the hospital came, including Dr. Fitch, who had to be reminded to leave his gun at the door. Ruth came for a few minutes.

Bird-dog had called to tell Julia he would be up to see us and I anxiously awaited his arrival. When he finally came up the stairs, I automatically looked for Dan behind him. Bird-dog noticed and lowered his head. "I'm sorry," he said.

"I'm sorry for you, too," I replied. "I know how you loved Dan."

"I've thought of so many things to say to you. Now that I'm here, I can't remember one of them."

He looked much older wearing a helmet rather than his bush hat. He was a tired old soldier waiting for his tour to end.

"Maybe we can talk later," I said.

I went to say good-bye to departing guests. "Take it easy on Gertie," I told Ron. "She's been doing a good job lately."

"Speak of the devil," Otto said.

Gertie rushed up the stairs in a red mini-skirt and matching heels. "God, girl, I forgot the time," she said. "I have a date waiting for me downstairs." Her hair was no longer grey, but a vivid henna.

"I'm glad you could stop by," I said. She handed me a box, which contained a lovely silver statue of the Blessed Virgin. Otto coughed behind me. "It's beautiful, Gertie," I said.

"I'll bet you never dreamed I was Catholic," she cackled. Several others laughed with her. "God, girl, I have to run," she said when a horn sounded outside. She galloped down the stairs in her high-heels, nearly flying through the door at the bottom.

Dan's boss still seemed uncomfortable in my presence when I went with the others to the compound that night. But when I told him I would be leaving, he invited me into his office and shared what he knew about Dan's death. As I suspected, the men he had trained knowingly led him into the ambush. They were also responsible for sabotaging the engine on Dan's boat so he couldn't escape when the attack began.

His silver hair was not as well groomed as usual and his clothes looked as if he had slept in them. The Tet offensive had been hard on him, especially when intelligence was being blamed for not predicting it. "I'm sorry all this happened," he told me. "But you have the consolation of knowing that your young man was bravely serving his country when he died."

I was not consoled.

Bird-dog corroborated the story when he arrived at the compound, but with a different ending than the courage Dan had displayed while dying for his country. "It's a bloody waste," he said. "Dying for a lot of gooks on an island that doesn't mean a damn to anyone." He looked around him to make sure the men assigned to the compound weren't listening.

"Dan thought it did," I said.

"You mean the CIA did." He took my arm and guided me into a deserted bunker where we could talk alone. "Dan was a stand up straight Marine," he said when we were seated on sandbags. "But he bought that shit he was taught by the intelligence folk; thinking everyone was their friend instead of seeing them as the bloody enemy. Those islanders were taking everything Dan gave them or did for them while harboring the V.C. who killed him. And the troops he trained were all V.C."

"I didn't want him to go on that patrol," I said, "not with only his troops."

"I'm sorry I didn't go with him," he said with tears in his eyes.

"Don't be, Bird-dog. You'd probably be dead too."

"He would have been fine if he hadn't been trying to play Marine and pacifist at the same time," Bird-dog said. "He wasn't doing things the way he was trained."

"Is anybody?"

"No," he said finally. "We've been made a lot of fools playing games instead of soldiering." A man from the compound stuck his head in and quickly retreated. "These CIA jackasses didn't care if they put him in a dangerous situation," Bird-dog continued. "The young people they recruit to do their dirty work are expendable." I wished he was not so candid.

"What are your plans for the future?" I asked when he fell silent.

"What future?" he said, getting up to leave. "I've learned not to count on a future."

Julia came into the bunker shortly thereafter. This time we shared the bottle of Scotch.

The next morning we learned that mass graves had been found in Hue. Hundreds of people captured by the North Vietnamese during the seige of the city had been buried alive.

"Some of the poor bastards were standing with their hands held over their heads," Otto said. "Their mouths were full of dirt." I was glad Margaret was not there to hear. She still had not given up on Keith being found alive, and vowed to stay in Vietnam until he was.

My last errand in Danang was a trip to the orphanage. "I am so happy to see you," Sister Marie said. "I was worried after your last visit."

"I'm feeling better," I lied. "I'll be leaving for home tomorrow."

"It is best that you go."

The rain stopped long enough for us to have tea in the courtyard, as we had on my first visit. I leaned forward and the small cross my mother had given me slipped from beneath my collar. Sister Marie reached for it.

"You still believe," she said.

I looked down at the cross on her finger tips and then into her wise eyes. "I believe in people like you, Sister. Please don't ask for more."

The other nuns came to say their farewells, and to present me with a beautifully embroidered tablecloth made by their students. Sitting there under the sea pine, it was difficult to believe I would probably never see any of them again.

"We shall never forget your kindness," Sister Marie said when it was time for me to go. "I pray that God will grant you happiness."

"Thank you, sister." I handed her an envelope filled with Vietnamese currency. "I thought it best not to give you American money."

"You have been good to us," she said with tears in her eyes. "Americans have all been good to us."

I couldn't look back as I drove down the dusty lane for the last time.

It took less than an hour to pack my belongings. Most of my clothing I gave to Tien. I had lost so much weight none of it fit, and I wanted to take as few reminders home as possible. Julia offered to pack my other belongings with hers so I wouldn't have to pay shipping fees.

When all my chores were completed, I borrowed Margaret's bicycle and rode to the riverbank where Dan and I caught the boat to church. I knew he was no longer in Vietnam, but I felt closer to him in the places we had shared. The Ba was not on the river, and the Bamboo Hut was dark and shuttered. But Dan was there with me. No one could convince me he was in some strange cemetery on the other side of the world.

Darkness had fallen and flares lit the sky when I emerged from my thoughts and climbed up the river bank the final time. I spent the last night in my room, surrounded by Dan's presence. I could feel his excitement when I told him I might be pregnant.

On the plane the next morning, I sat next to a window waving to Tien and my friends standing on the tarmac below. As we lifted off I could see the landscape was scarred beyond recognition and China Beach awash in monsoon rain. I felt I was leaving Dan behind, and a very large part of me with him, as I watched Danang recede in the distance.

The plane was a troop transport that stopped midway to Saigon to let off a group of nervous looking Marines who had just arrived in country. The men they were relieving boarded in mud-caked combat attire, with bandoleers of ammunition crisscrossing their sagging shoulders. They reclined against the walls of the stripped-down aircraft with their legs splayed out before them, gaze fixed straight ahead in the thousand yard stare. I was glad when we landed in Saigon and I could escape the old soldiers' eyes in young men's faces.

The commercial jet I boarded in Saigon was spacious and clean compared to the troop transports and helicopters to which I had become accustomed. Men in business suits, with brightly colored shirts and matching ties replaced muddied Marines. Their eyes were curious rather than empty. When one of them sat down beside me, I found myself longing to be back on the transport with the troops.

I turned to the window as we lifted into the air, looking at a landscape that was no longer lush and green as it had been the day I first flew to Danang.

The jungles had been cruelly defoliated; stripped as naked as I felt. And there were bomb craters everywhere.

"Excuse me, honey," the man sitting next to me said. "How long have you been over here?"

"A year."

I could tell by his smile that he didn't smell the stench of burned flesh. Nor did he hear the moans.

"What was a little bit of a girl like you doing here for a whole year?" His smile was inviting; his face reflected nothing but his own pleasure.

The stewardesses were opening overhead compartments filled with casualties, trying to stuff jackets into the spaces crowded with patients who pleaded with me to save them.

"Working," I said, and turned to watch the rice paddies become smaller and more distant as we headed out over the South China Sea.

The End

CPSIA information can be obtained
at www.ICGtesting.com
Printed in the USA
BVHW081008270620
582374BV00001B/129

9 780982 298909